Readings in the ANC Tradition

Volume II

UNDERSTANDING THE ANC TODAY

General Editor: Professor Ben Turok

Volume 1: The Historical Roots of the ANC

Volume 2: The ANC and the Turn to Armed Struggle

Volume 3: Readings in the ANC Tradition, I

Volume 4: Readings in the ANC Tradition, II

Volume 5: Development in a Divided Country

Volume 6: The Controversy about Economic Growth

Readings in the ANC Tradition
Volume II

History and Ideology

Edited by Ben Turok

Grateful thanks are due to the following organisations for allowing us to reproduce material in which they hold copyright: the Kwame Nkrumah Pan-African Cultural Center (Dr Gamal Nkrumah) and Panaf Books for permission to quote from Class Struggle in Africa *and* Africa Must Unite *by Kwame Nkrumah; Monthly Review Foundation for 'The Development of Underdevelopment' by A.G. Frank (Monthly Review, 1966); the Mwalimu Nyerere Foundation for* Nyerere on Socialism *by Julius Nyerere; the Amilcar Cabral Foundation for 'Brief Analysis of the Situation in Guinea' and 'Tell No Lies, Claim No Easy Victories' by Amilcar Cabral; HarperCollins Publishers Ltd (UK) for an extract from chapter 3 of* The Wretched of the Earth *by Frantz Fanon. The author and publisher have made every effort to contact the copyright-holders of the material reproduced in this book. Should there be any omission or error, we shall be glad to rectify it in the next impression.*

First published by Jacana Media (Pty) Ltd in 2011

10 Orange Street
Sunnyside
Auckland Park 2092
South Africa
+2711 628 3200
www.jacana.co.za

© 2011 Ben Turok (this selection)

All rights reserved.

ISBN 978-1-77009-970-8

Set in Minion 9.5/12pt
Printed and bound by Ultra Litho (Pty) Limited, Johannesburg
Job No. 001413

See a complete list of Jacana titles at www.jacana.co.za

Contents

Preface to the Series vii
Introduction ix

Part One: Ideological Influences
Karl Marx, *Wage Labour and Capital* (1849) 3
Karl Marx and Friedrich Engels, *The Communist Manifesto* (1851) 28
Mao Tse-tung, *On the People's Democratic Dictatorship* (1949) 56

Part Two: Africa's Experience
W.E.B. DuBois, *The Birth of African Unity* (1947). 71
Frantz Fanon, 'The Pitfalls of National Consciousness' from
    The Wretched of the Earth (1961) 86
Kwame Nkrumah, *Africa Must Unite* (1963) 102
Amilcar Cabral, *Brief Analysis of the Situation in Guinea* (1964) 116
Amilcar Cabral, *Tell No Lies, Claim No Easy Victories* (1965). 132
A.G. Frank, *The Development of Underdevelopment* (1966) 135

Part Three: African Socialism
Julius Nyerere, 'Introduction' to *Nyerere on Socialism* (1969) 149
Kwame Nkrumah, *Class Struggle in Africa* (1970). 172
Claude Ake, 'The Class Struggle' from *Revolutionary Pressures*
    in Africa (1978). 192

Preface to the Series

As we go to press, the ANC is preparing to mark the centenary of its existence. This is a remarkable achievement for any political movement, with few precedents anywhere in the world. Even more remarkable is the fact that it has been the ruling party in South Africa for 16 years and remains the most powerful political force in the country, despite many shortcomings. The ANC may not rule forever, but it has made a huge impact on South Africa in every dimension of its existence, hence its history and present-day work merit special recognition.

This series 'Understanding the ANC Today' is an attempt to map in broad outlines the party's history, the external influences that shaped its policies and actions, the depth of the policy challenges it faced in the decades prior to its victory over apartheid, and the problems it is now confronting as a ruling party.

The scope of the whole series is vast. But the contributors are among the top thinkers in the ANC and they have not shirked exploring all these issues to the full. Since their writing deals with the realities facing all the people of the country, and shaping the future, the books should be of interest to the general public and not just members of the ANC and its allies.

It is our hope that the books will become standard texts in university courses and used in schools to broaden the understanding of our youth of where they come from and where the ANC would like to lead them. It is also our hope that the presentation of these books to the movement as a whole will encourage reading and study so that our cadres will be better prepared for the enormous but exciting tasks ahead as we plan for the new South Africa.

These books are not written in the spirit of propaganda. They are analytical and historical. They deal frankly and without reservation about the diverse influences on the ANC of many ideologies and historical experiences across the globe for over a century. At the same time the organic development of the movement as an indigenous force is also given its proper recognition.

Ben Turok

Introduction

Throughout its long history the ANC has striven to maintain a unique political profile reflecting the actual social relations in the country. It has resisted many attempts to characterise its role and policies in terms of other traditions and in the context of struggles in other countries. Critics and hostile commentators have tried to label the ANC as communist, African socialist, social democratic or other denominations, without hitting the mark. It would seem that the special character of the ANC arises from the unique configuration of social forces that make up its complex history.

This volume of readings contains documents and extracts that have been seminal in influencing the policies and praxis of the ANC and its allies in the liberation movement.

Part One, 'Ideological Influences', contains classic texts of Marxism by the founders of Communist thought and a major work by Mao Tse-tung, who was totally rooted in that tradition but presented a variation based on the impact of imperialism and colonialism. The fact that the Chinese Revolution was fought by a largely peasant force rather than urban workers changed the theories and strategies of many colonial movements. These texts will continue to play an important part as the liberation struggle evolves from a conventional model of democracy to some variation reflecting aspirations for a more equal social formation.

Part Two, 'Africa's Experience', contains extracts from the writings of the heroes of Africa's struggles for independence. The choice of essays reflects a need to go beyond rhetoric and uncover the underlying political, economic and social problems facing the continent over the last half a century. The essays show that the aspiration to African unity and political freedom was insufficient to build a better society once colonial rulers departed.

Nkrumah, Cabral and Fanon attempted to dig deeper into the structure of their societies in order to develop a more scientific understanding of the nature of the social forces at work, and many of their ideas have influenced ANC thinking. They may also be directly relevant to finding solutions to some of the political, economic and social problems facing South Africa now.

Part Three, 'African Socialism', includes several essays that reflect a desire by African leaders and thinkers to develop a political philosophy which includes influences from the classical works of Marxism but offer a different road to socialism. No doubt this attempt to beat a path for Africa different from that of Europe and Asia took account of the different character of Africa's social formations, but it also reflected a certain idealism and aspiration for a more egalitarian society in terms of pre-colonial traditional values, such as *ubuntu*, across the continent.

Unfortunately, the ideology of African socialism has not taken root, nor has it matured into a coherent political philosophy, but its ideas continue to influence political leaders.

Part One

Ideological Influences

Karl Marx
Wage Labour and Capital
(This pamphlet first appeared as a series of articles published in the *Neue Rheinische Zeitung*, April–May 1849)

Preliminary

From various quarters we have been reproached for neglecting to portray the economic conditions which form the material basis of the present struggles between classes and nations. With set purpose we have hitherto touched upon these conditions only when they forced themselves upon the surface of the political conflicts.

It was necessary, beyond everything else, to follow the development of the class struggle in the history of our own day, and to prove empirically, by the actual and daily newly created historical material, that with the subjugation of the working class, accomplished in the days of February and March, 1848, the opponents of that class – the bourgeois republicans in France, and the bourgeois and peasant classes who were fighting feudal absolutism throughout the whole continent of Europe – were simultaneously conquered; that the victory of the 'moderate republic' in France sounded at the same time the fall of the nations which had responded to the February revolution with heroic wars of independence; and finally that, by the victory over the revolutionary workingmen, Europe fell back into its old double slavery, into the English–Russian slavery. The June conflict in Paris, the fall of Vienna, the tragi-comedy in Berlin in November 1848, the desperate efforts of Poland, Italy, and Hungary, the starvation of Ireland into submission – these were the chief events in which the European class struggle between the bourgeoisie and the working class was summed up, and from which we proved that every revolutionary uprising, however remote from the class struggle its object might appear, must of necessity fail until the revolutionary working class shall have conquered; that every social reform must remain a Utopia until the proletarian revolution and the feudalistic counter-revolution have been pitted against each other in a world-wide war. In our presentation, as in reality, Belgium and Switzerland were tragicomic caricaturish genre pictures in the great historic tableau; the one the model State of the bourgeois monarchy, the other the model State of the bourgeois republic; both of them, States that flatter themselves to be just as free from the class struggle as from the European revolution.

But now, after our readers have seen the class struggle of the year 1848 develop into colossal political proportions, it is time to examine more closely the economic conditions themselves upon which is founded the existence of the capitalist class and its class rule, as well as the slavery of the workers.

We shall present the subject in three great divisions:

> The Relation of Wage-Labour to Capital, the Slavery of the Worker, the Rule of the Capitalist.
> The Inevitable Ruin of the Middle Classes [petty-bourgeois] and the so-called Commons [peasants] under the present system.
> The Commercial Subjugation and Exploitation of the Bourgeois classes of the various European nations by the Despot of the World Market – England.

We shall seek to portray this as simply and popularly as possible, and shall not presuppose a knowledge of even the most elementary notions of political economy. We wish to be understood by the workers. And, moreover, there prevails in Germany the most remarkable ignorance and confusion of ideas in regard to the simplest economic relations, from the patented defenders of existing conditions, down to the socialist wonder-workers and the unrecognized political geniuses, in which divided Germany is even richer than in duodecimo princelings. We therefore proceed to the consideration of the first problem.

What Are Wages? How Are They Determined?
If several workmen were to be asked: 'How much wages do you get?', one would reply, 'I get two shillings a day,' and so on. According to the different branches of industry in which they are employed, they would mention different sums of money that they receive from their respective employers for the completion of a certain task; for example, for weaving a yard of linen, or for setting a page of type. Despite the variety of their statements, they would all agree upon one point: that wages are the amount of money which the capitalist pays for a certain period of work or for a certain amount of work.

Consequently, it appears that the capitalist buys their labour with money, and that for money they sell him their labour. But this is merely an illusion. What they actually sell to the capitalist for money is their labour-power. This labour-power the capitalist buys for a day, a week, a month, etc. And after he has bought it, he uses it up by letting the worker labour during the stipulated time. With the same amount of money with which the capitalist has bought their labour-power (for example, with two shillings) he could have bought a certain amount of sugar or of any other commodity. The two shillings with which he bought 20 pounds of sugar is the price of the 20 pounds of sugar. The two shillings with which he bought 12 hours' use of labour-power is the price of 12 hours' labour. Labour-power, then, is a commodity, no more, no less so than is the sugar. The first is measured by the clock, the other by the scales.

Their commodity, labour-power, the workers exchange for the commodity of the capitalist, for money, and, moreover, this exchange takes place at a certain ratio. So much money for so long a use of labour-power. For 12 hours' weaving, two shillings. And these two shillings, do they not represent all the other commodities which I can buy for two shillings? Therefore, actually, the worker has exchanged his commodity, labour-power, for commodities of all kinds, and, moreover, at a certain ratio. By giving him two shillings, the capitalist has given him so much meat, so much clothing, so much wood, light, etc., in exchange for his day's work. The two shillings therefore expresses the relation in which labour-power is exchanged for other commodities, the exchange value of labour-power.

The exchange value of a commodity estimated in money is called its price. Wages therefore are only a special name for the price of labour-power, and are usually called the price of labour; it is the special name for the price of this peculiar commodity, which has no other repository than human flesh and blood.

Let us take any worker; for example, a weaver. The capitalist supplies him with the loom and yarn. The weaver applies himself to work, and the yarn is turned into cloth. The capitalist takes possession of the cloth and sells it for 20 shillings, for example. Now are the wages of the weaver a share of the cloth, of the 20 shillings, of the product of his work? By no means. Long before the cloth is sold, perhaps long before it is fully woven, the weaver has received his wages. The capitalist, then, does not pay his wages out of the money which he will obtain from the cloth, but out of money already on hand. Just as little as loom and yarn are the product of the weaver to whom they are supplied by the employer, just so little are the commodities which he receives in exchange for his commodity – labour-power – his product. It is possible that the employer found no purchasers at all for the cloth. It is possible that he did not get even the amount of the wages by its sale. It is possible that he sells it very profitably in proportion to the weaver's wages. But all that does not concern the weaver. With a part of his existing wealth, of his capital, the capitalist buys the labour-power of the weaver in exactly the same manner as, with another part of his wealth, he has bought the raw material – the yarn – and the instrument of labour – the loom. After he has made these purchases, and among them belongs the labour-power necessary to the production of the cloth, he produces only with raw materials and instruments of labour belonging to him. For our good weaver, too, is one of the instruments of labour, and being in this respect on a par with the loom, he has no more share in the product (the cloth), or in the price of the product, than the loom itself has.

Wages, therefore, are not a share of the worker in the commodities produced by himself. Wages are that part of already existing commodities with which the capitalist buys a certain amount of productive labour-power.

Consequently, labour-power is a commodity which its possessor, the wage-worker, sells to the capitalist. Why does he sell it? It is in order to live.

But the putting of labour-power into action – i.e. the work – is the active expression of the labourer's own life. And this life activity he sells to another person in order to secure the necessary means of life. His life-activity, therefore, is but a means of securing his own existence. He works that he may keep alive. He does not count the labour itself as a part of his life; it is rather a sacrifice of his life. It is a commodity that he has auctioned off to another. The product of his activity, therefore, is not the aim of his activity. What he produces for himself is not the silk that he weaves, not the gold that he draws up the mining shaft, not the palace that he builds. What he produces for himself is wages; and the silk, the gold, and the palace are resolved for him into a certain quantity of necessaries of life, perhaps into a cotton jacket, into copper coins, and into a basement dwelling. And the labourer who for 12 hours long weaves, spins, bores, turns, builds, shovels, breaks stone, carries hods, and so on – is this 12 hours' weaving, spinning, boring, turning, building, shovelling, stone-breaking, regarded by him as a manifestation of life, as life? Quite the contrary. Life for him begins where this activity ceases, at the table, at the tavern, in bed. The 12 hours' work, on the other hand, has no meaning for him as weaving, spinning, boring and so on, but only as earnings, which enable him to sit down at a table, to take his seat in the tavern, and to lie down in a bed. If the silk-worm's object in spinning were to prolong its existence as caterpillar, it would be a perfect example of a wage-worker.

Labour-power was not always a commodity (merchandise). Labour was not always wage-labour, i.e. free labour. The slave did not sell his labour-power to the slave-owner, any more than the ox sells his labour to the farmer. The slave, together with his labour-power, was sold to his owner once for all. He is a commodity that can pass from the hand of one owner to that of another. He himself is a commodity, but his labour-power is not his commodity. The serf sells only a portion of his labour-power. It is not he who receives wages from the owner of the land; it is rather the owner of the land who receives a tribute from him. The serf belongs to the soil, and to the lord of the soil he brings its fruit. The free labourer, on the other hand, sells his very self, and that by fractions. He auctions off eight, 10, 12, 15 hours of his life, one day like the next, to the highest bidder, to the owner of raw materials, tools, and the means of life – i.e., to the capitalist. The labourer belongs neither to an owner nor to the soil, but 8, 10, 12, 15 hours of his daily life belong to whosoever buys them. The worker leaves the capitalist, to whom he has sold himself, as often as he chooses, and the capitalist discharges him as often as he sees fit, as soon as he no longer gets any use, or not the required use, out of him. But the worker, whose only source of income is the sale of his labour-power, cannot leave the whole class of buyers, i.e. the capitalist class, unless he gives up his own existence. He does not belong to this or that capitalist, but to the capitalist class; and it is for him to find his man – i.e. to find a buyer in this capitalist class.

Before entering more closely upon the relation of capital to wage-labour, we shall present briefly the most general conditions which come into consideration in the determination of wages.

Wages, as we have seen, are the price of a certain commodity, labour-power. Wages, therefore, are determined by the same laws that determine the price of every other commodity. The question then is, How is the price of a commodity determined?

By What Is the Price of a Commodity Determined?

By the competition between buyers and sellers, by the relation of the demand to the supply, of the call to the offer. The competition by which the price of a commodity is determined is threefold.

The same commodity is offered for sale by various sellers. Whoever sells commodities of the same quality most cheaply is sure to drive the other sellers from the field and to secure the greatest market for himself. The sellers therefore fight among themselves for the sales, for the market. Each one of them wishes to sell, and to sell as much as possible, and if possible to sell alone, to the exclusion of all other sellers. Each one sells cheaper than the other. Thus there takes place a competition among the sellers which forces down the price of the commodities offered by them.

But there is also a competition among the buyers; this upon its side causes the price of the proffered commodities to rise.

Finally, there is competition between the buyers and the sellers: these wish to purchase as cheaply as possible, those to sell as dearly as possible. The result of this competition between buyers and sellers will depend upon the relations between the two above-mentioned camps of competitors – i.e. upon whether the competition in the army of sellers is stronger. Industry leads two great armies into the field against each other, and each of these again is engaged in a battle among its own troops in its own ranks. The army among whose troops there is less fighting carries off the victory over the opposing host.

Let us suppose that there are 100 bales of cotton in the market and at the same time purchasers for 1,000 bales of cotton. In this case, the demand is 10 times greater than the supply. Competition among the buyers, then, will be very strong; each of them tries to get hold of one bale, if possible, of the whole 100 bales. This example is no arbitrary supposition. In the history of commerce we have experienced periods of scarcity of cotton, when some capitalists united together and sought to buy up not 100 bales, but the whole cotton supply of the world. In the given case, then, one buyer seeks to drive the others from the field by offering a relatively higher price for the bales of cotton. The cotton sellers, who perceive the troops of the enemy in the most violent contention among themselves, and who therefore are fully assured of the sale of their whole 100 bales, will beware of pulling one another's hair in order to force down the price of cotton at the very moment in which their opponents race with one another to screw it up high. So, all of a sudden, peace reigns in the army of sellers. They stand opposed to the buyers like one man, fold their arms in philosophic contentment and their claims would find no limit did not the offers of even the most importunate of buyers have a very definite limit.

If, then, the supply of a commodity is less than the demand for it, competition among the sellers is very slight, or there may be none at all among them. In the same proportion in which this competition decreases, the competition among the buyers increases. Result: a more or less considerable rise in the prices of commodities.

It is well known that the opposite case, with the opposite result, happens more frequently. Great excess of supply over demand; desperate competition among the sellers, and a lack of buyers; forced sales of commodities at ridiculously low prices.

But what is a rise, and what a fall of prices? What is a high and what a low price? A grain of sand is high when examined through a microscope, and a tower is low when compared with a mountain. And if the price is determined by the relation of supply and demand, by what is the relation of supply and demand determined?

Let us turn to the first worthy citizen we meet. He will not hesitate one moment, but, like Alexander the Great, will cut this metaphysical knot with his multiplication table. He will say to us: 'If the production of the commodities which I sell has cost me 100 pounds, and out of the sale of these goods I make 110 pounds – within the year, you understand – that's an honest, sound, reasonable profit. But if in the exchange I receive 120 or 130 pounds, that's a higher profit; and if I should get as much as 200 pounds, that would be an extraordinary, and enormous profit.' What is it, then, that serves this citizen as the standard of his profit? The cost of the production of his commodities. If in exchange for these goods he receives a quantity of other goods whose production has cost less, he has lost. If he receives in exchange for his goods a quantity of other goods whose production has cost more, he has gained. And he reckons the falling or rising of the profit according to the degree at which the exchange value of his goods stands, whether above or below his zero – the cost of production.

We have seen how the changing relation of supply and demand causes now a rise, now a fall of prices; now high, now low prices. If the price of a commodity rises considerably owing to a failing supply or a disproportionately growing demand, then the price of some other commodity must have fallen in proportion; for of course the price of a commodity only expresses in money the proportion in which other commodities will be given in exchange for it. If, for example, the price of a yard of silk rises from two to three shillings, the price of silver has fallen in relation to the silk, and in the same way the prices of all other commodities whose prices have remained stationary have fallen in relation to the price of silk. A large quantity of them must be given in exchange in order to obtain the same amount of silk. Now, what will be the consequence of a rise in the price of a particular commodity? A mass of capital will be thrown into the prosperous branch of industry, and this immigration of capital into the provinces of the favoured industry will continue until it yields no more than the customary profits, or, rather until the price of its products, owning to overproduction, sinks below the cost of production.

Conversely: if the price of a commodity falls below its cost of production, then capital will be withdrawn from the production of this commodity. Except in the case of a branch of industry which has become obsolete and is therefore doomed to disappear, the production of such a commodity (that is, its supply) will, owing to this flight of capital, continue to decrease until it corresponds to the demand, and the price of the commodity rises again to the level of its cost of production; or, rather, until the supply has fallen below the demand and its price has risen above its cost of production, for the current price of a commodity is always either above or below its cost of production.

We see how capital continually emigrates out of the province of one industry and immigrates into that of another. The high price produces an excessive immigration, and the low price an excessive emigration.

We could show, from another point of view, how not only the supply, but also the demand, is determined by the cost of production. But this would lead us too far away from our subject.

We have just seen how the fluctuation of supply and demand always brings the price of a commodity back to its cost of production. The actual price of a commodity, indeed, stands always above or below the cost of production; but the rise and fall reciprocally balance each other, so that, within a certain period of time, if the ebbs and flows of the industry are reckoned up together, the commodities will be exchanged for one another in accordance with their cost of production. Their price is thus determined by their cost of production.

The determination of price by the cost of production is not to be understood in the sense of the bourgeois economists. The economists say that the average price of commodities equals the cost of production: that is the law. The anarchic movement, in which the rise is compensated for by a fall and the fall by a rise, they regard as an accident. We might just as well consider the fluctuations as the law, and the determination of the price by cost of production as an accident – as is, in fact, done by certain other economists. But it is precisely these fluctuations which, viewed more closely, carry the most frightful devastation in their train, and, like an earthquake, cause bourgeois society to shake to its very foundations – it is precisely these fluctuations that force the price to conform to the cost of production. In the totality of this disorderly movement is to be found its order. In the total course of this industrial anarchy, in this circular movement, competition balances, as it were, the one extravagance by the other.

We thus see that the price of a commodity is indeed determined by its cost of production, but in such a manner that the periods in which the price of these commodities rises above the costs of production are balanced by the periods in which it sinks below the cost of production, and vice versa. Of course this does not hold good for a single given product of an industry, but only for that branch of industry. So also it does not hold good for an individual manufacturer, but only for the whole class of manufacturers.

The determination of price by cost of production is tantamount to the determination of price by the labour-time requisite to the production of a commodity, for the cost of production consists, first of raw materials and wear and tear of tools, etc., i.e. of industrial products whose production has cost a certain number of work-days, which therefore represent a certain amount of labour-time, and, secondly, of direct labour, which is also measured by its duration.

By What Are Wages Determined?

Now, the same general laws which regulate the price of commodities in general, naturally regulate wages, or the price of labour-power. Wages will now rise, now fall, according to the relation of supply and demand, according as competition shapes itself between the buyers of labour-power, the capitalists, and the sellers of labour-power, the workers. The fluctuations of wages correspond to the fluctuations in the price of commodities in general. But within the limits of these fluctuations the price of labour-power will be determined by the cost of production, by the labour-time necessary for production of this commodity: labour-power.

What, then, is the cost of production of labour-power?

It is the cost required for the maintenance of the labourer as a labourer, and for his education and training as a labourer.

Therefore, the shorter the time required for training up to a particular sort of work, the smaller is the cost of production of the worker, the lower is the price of his labour-power, his wages. In those branches of industry in which hardly any period of apprenticeship is necessary and the mere bodily existence of the worker is sufficient, the cost of his production is limited almost exclusively to the commodities necessary for keeping him in working condition. The price of his work will therefore be determined by the price of the necessary means of subsistence.

Here, however, there enters another consideration. The manufacturer who calculates his cost of production and, in accordance with it, the price of the product, takes into account the wear and tear of the instruments of labour. If a machine costs him, for example, 1,000 shillings, and this machine is used up in 10 years, he adds 100 shillings annually to the price of the commodities, in order to be able after 10 years to replace the worn-out machine with a new one. In the same manner, the cost of production of simple labour-power must include the cost of propagation, by means of which the race of workers is enabled to multiply itself, and to replace worn-out workers with new ones. The wear and tear of the worker, therefore, is calculated in the same manner as the wear and tear of the machine.

Thus, the cost of production of simple labour-power amounts to the cost of the existence and propagation of the worker. The price of this cost of existence and propagation constitutes wages. The wages thus determined are called the minimum of wages. This minimum wage, like the determination of the price of commodities in general by cost of production, does not hold good for the single individual, but only for the race. Individual workers, indeed, millions of workers, do not receive enough to be able to exist and to propagate themselves; but the wages of the whole working class adjust themselves, within the limits of their fluctuations, to this minimum.

Now that we have come to an understanding in regard to the most general laws which govern wages, as well as the price of every other commodity, we can examine our subject more particularly.

The Nature and Growth of Capital

Capital consists of raw materials, instruments of labour, and means of subsistence of all kinds, which are employed in producing new raw materials, new instruments and new means of subsistence. All these components of capital are created by labour, products of labour, accumulated labour. Accumulated labour that serves as a means to new production is capital. So say the economists.

What is a Negro slave? A man of the black race. The one explanation is worthy of the other. A Negro is a Negro. Only under certain conditions does he become a slave. A cotton-spinning machine is a machine for spinning cotton. Only under certain conditions does it become capital. Torn away from these conditions, it is as little capital as gold is itself money, or sugar is the price of sugar.

In the process of production, human beings work not only upon nature, but also upon one another. They produce only by working together in a specified manner and reciprocally exchanging their activities. In order to produce, they enter into definite connections and relations to one another, and only within these social connections and relations does their influence upon nature operate – i.e. does production take place.

These social relations between the producers, and the conditions under which they exchange their activities and share in the total act of production, will naturally vary according to the character of the means of production. With the discovery of a new instrument of warfare, the firearm, the whole internal organisation of the army was necessarily altered, the relations within which individuals compose an army and can work as an army were transformed, and the relation of different armies to another was likewise changed.

We thus see that the social relations within which individuals produce, the social relations of production, are altered, transformed, with the change and development of the material means of production, of the forces of production. The relations of production in their totality constitute what is called the social relations, society, and, moreover, a society at a definite stage of historical development, a society with peculiar, distinctive characteristics. Ancient society, feudal society, bourgeois (or capitalist) society, are such totalities of relations of production, each of which denotes a particular stage of development in the history of mankind.

Capital also is a social relation of production. It is a bourgeois relation of production, a relation of production of bourgeois society. The means of subsistence, the instruments of labour, the raw materials, of which capital consists – have they not been produced and accumulated under given social conditions, within definite special relations? Are they not employed for new production, under given special conditions, within definite social relations? And does not just the definite social character stamp the products which serve for new production as capital?

Capital consists not only of means of subsistence, instruments of labour, and raw materials, not only of material products; it consists just as much of exchange values. All products of which it consists are commodities. Capital, consequently, is not only a sum of material products, it is a sum of commodities, of exchange values, of social magnitudes. Capital remains the same whether we put cotton in the place of wool, rice in the place of wheat, steamships in the place of railroads, provided only that the cotton, the rice, the steamships – the body of capital – have the same exchange value, the same price, as the wool, the wheat, the railroads, in which it was previously embodied. The bodily form of capital may transform itself continually, while capital does not suffer the least alteration.

But though every capital is a sum of commodities – i.e. of exchange values – it does not follow that every sum of commodities, of exchange values, is capital.

Every sum of exchange values is an exchange value. Each particular exchange value is a sum of exchange values. For example: a house worth 1,000 pounds is an exchange value of 1,000 pounds: a piece of paper worth one penny is a sum of exchange values of 100 one-hundredths of a penny. Products which are exchangeable for others are commodities. The definite proportion in which they are exchangeable forms their exchange value, or, expressed in money, their price. The quantity of these products can have no effect on their character as commodities, as representing an exchange value, as having a certain price. Whether a tree be large or small, it remains a tree.

Whether we exchange iron in pennyweights or in hundredweights for other products, does this alter its character: its being a commodity, an exchange value? According to the quantity, it is a commodity of greater or of lesser value, of higher or of lower price.

How then does a sum of commodities, of exchange values, become capital?

Thereby, that as an independent social power – i.e. as the power of a part of society – it preserves itself and multiplies by exchange with direct, living labour-power.

The existence of a class which possesses nothing but the ability to work is a necessary presupposition of capital.

It is only the dominion of past, accumulated, materialized labour over immediate living labour that stamps the accumulated labour with the character of capital.

Capital does not consist in the fact that accumulated labour serves living labour as a means for new production. It consists in the fact that living labour serves accumulated labour as the means of preserving and multiplying its exchange value.

Relation of Wage-Labour to Capital

What is it that takes place in the exchange between capitalist and wage-labour?

The labourer receives means of subsistence in exchange for his labour-power; the capitalist receives, in exchange for his means of subsistence, labour, the productive activity of the labourer, the creative force by which the worker not only replaces what he consumes, but also gives to the accumulated labour a greater value than it previously possessed. The labourer gets from the capitalist a portion of the existing means of subsistence. For what purpose do these means of subsistence serve him? For immediate consumption. But as soon as I consume means of subsistence, they are irrevocably lost to me, unless I employ the time during which these means sustain my life in producing new means of subsistence, in creating by my labour new values in place of the values lost in consumption. But it is just this noble reproductive power that the labourer surrenders to the capitalist in exchange for means of subsistence received. Consequently, he has lost it for himself.

Let us take an example. For one shilling a labourer works all day long in the fields of a farmer, to whom he thus secures a return of two shillings. The farmer not only receives the replaced value which he has given to the day labourer, he has doubled it. Therefore, he has consumed the one shilling that he gave to the day labourer in a fruitful, productive manner. For the one shilling he has bought the labour-power of the day-labourer, which creates products of the soil of twice the value, and out of one shilling makes two. The day-labourer, on the contrary, receives in the place of his productive force, whose results he has just surrendered to the farmer, one shilling, which he exchanges for means of subsistence, which he consumes more or less quickly. The one shilling has therefore been consumed in a double manner – reproductively for the capitalist, for it has been exchanged for labour-power, which brought forth two shillings; unproductively for the worker, for it has been exchanged for means of subsistence which are lost forever, and whose value he can obtain again only by repeating the same exchange with the farmer. Capital therefore presupposes wage-labour; wage-labour presupposes capital. They condition each other; each brings the other into existence.

Does a worker in a cotton factory produce only cotton? No. He produces capital. He produces values which serve anew to command his work and to create by means of it new values.

Capital can multiply itself only by exchanging itself for labour-power, by calling wage-labour into life. The labour-power of the wage-labourer can exchange itself for capital only by increasing capital, by strengthening that very power whose slave it is. Increase of capital, therefore, is increase of the proletariat, i.e. of the working class.

And so, the bourgeoisie and its economists maintain that the interest of the capitalist and that of the labourer are the same. And in fact, so they are! The worker perishes if capital does not keep him busy. Capital perishes if it does not exploit labour-power, which, in order to exploit, it must buy. The more quickly the capital destined for production – the productive capital – increases, the more prosperous industry is, the more the bourgeoisie enriches itself, the better business gets, so many more workers does the capitalist need, so much the dearer does the worker sell himself. The fastest possible growth of productive capital is, therefore, the indispensable condition for a tolerable life to the labourer.

But what is growth of productive capital? Growth of the power of accumulated labour over living labour; growth of the rule of the bourgeoisie over the working class. When wage-labour produces the alien wealth dominating it, the power hostile to it, capital, there flow back to it its means of employment – i.e. its means of subsistence, under the condition that it again become a part of capital, that it become again the lever whereby capital is to be forced into an accelerated expansive movement.

To say that the interests of capital and the interests of the workers are identical signifies only this: that capital and wage-labour are two sides of one and the same relation. The one conditions the other in the same way that the usurer and the borrower condition each other.

As long as the wage-labourer remains a wage-labourer, his lot is dependent upon capital. That is what the boasted community of interests between worker and capitalists amounts to.

If capital grows, the mass of wage-labour grows, the number of wage-workers increases; in a word, the sway of capital extends over a greater mass of individuals.

Let us suppose the most favourable case: if productive capital grows, the demand for labour grows. It therefore increases the price of labour-power, wages.

A house may be large or small; as long as the neighbouring houses are likewise small, it satisfies all social requirement for a residence. But let there arise next to the little house a palace, and the little house shrinks to a hut. The little house now makes it clear that its inmate has no social position at all to maintain, or but a very insignificant one; and however high it may shoot up in the course of civilisation, if the neighbouring palace rises in equal or even in greater measure, the occupant of the relatively little house will always find himself more uncomfortable, more dissatisfied, more cramped within his four walls.

An appreciable rise in wages presupposes a rapid growth of productive capital. Rapid growth of productive capital calls forth just as rapid a growth of wealth, of luxury, of social needs and social pleasures. Therefore, although the pleasures of the labourer have increased, the social gratification which they afford has fallen in comparison with the increased pleasures of the capitalist, which are inaccessible to the worker, in comparison with the stage of development of society in general. Our wants and pleasures have their origin in society; we therefore measure them in relation to society; we do not measure them in relation to the objects which serve for their gratification. Since they are of a social nature, they are of a relative nature.

But wages are not at all determined merely by the sum of commodities for which they may be exchanged. Other factors enter into the problem. What the workers directly receive for their labour-power is a certain sum of money. Are wages determined merely by this money price?

In the 16th century, the gold and silver circulation in Europe increased in consequence of the discovery of richer and more easily worked mines in America. The value of gold and silver, therefore, fell in relation to other commodities. The workers received the same amount of coined silver for their labour-power as before. The money price of their work remained the same, and yet their wages had fallen, for in exchange for the same amount of silver they obtained a smaller amount of other commodities. This was one of the circumstances which furthered the growth of capital, the rise of the bourgeoisie, in the 18th century.

Let us take another case. In the winter of 1847, in consequence of bad harvests, the most indispensable means of subsistence – grains, meat, butter, cheese, etc. – rose greatly in price. Let us suppose that the workers still received the same sum of money for their labour-power as before. Did not their wages fall? To be sure. For the same money they received in exchange less bread, meat, etc. Their wages fell, not because the value of silver was less, but because the value of the means of subsistence had increased.

Finally, let us suppose that the money price of labour-power remained the same, while all agricultural and manufactured commodities had fallen in price because of the employment of new machines, of favourable seasons, etc. For the same money the workers could now buy more commodities of all kinds. Their wages have therefore risen, just because their money value has not changed.

The money price of labour-power, the nominal wages, do not therefore coincide with the actual or real wages – i.e. with the amount of commodities which are actually given in exchange for the wages. If then we speak of a rise or fall of wages, we have to keep in mind not only the money price of labour-power, the nominal wages, but also the real wages.

But neither the nominal wages – i.e. the amount of money for which the labourer sells himself to the capitalist – nor the real wages – i.e. the amount of commodities which he can buy for this money – exhausts the relations which are comprehended in the term wages.

Wages are determined above all by their relations to the gain, the profit, of the capitalist. In other words, wages are a proportionate, relative quantity.

Real wages express the price of labour-power in relation to the price of commodities; relative wages, on the other hand, express the share of immediate labour in the value newly created by it, in relation to the share of it which falls to accumulated labour, to capital.

The General Law That Determines the Rise and Fall of Wages and Profits
We have said: 'Wages are not a share of the worker in the commodities produced by him. Wages are that part of already existing commodities with which the capitalist buys a certain amount of productive labour-power.' But the capitalist must replace these wages out of the price for which he sells the product made by the worker; he must so replace it that, as a rule, there remains to him a surplus above the cost of production expended by him,

i.e. he must get a profit.

The selling price of the commodities produced by the worker is divided, from the point of view of the capitalist, into three parts: first, the replacement of the price of the raw materials advanced by him, in addition to the replacement of the wear and tear of the tools, machines, and other instruments of labour likewise advanced by him; second, the replacement of the wages advanced; and third, the surplus left over, i.e. the profit of the capitalist.

While the first part merely replaces previously existing values, it is evident that the replacement of the wages and the surplus (the profit of capital) are as a whole taken out of the new value, which is produced by the labour of the worker and added to the raw materials. And in this sense we can view wages as well as profit, for the purpose of comparing them with each other, as shares in the product of the worker.

Real wages may remain the same, they may even rise; nevertheless the relative wages may fall. Let us suppose, for instance, that all means of subsistence have fallen two-thirds in price, while the day's wages have fallen but one-third; for example, from 3 to 2 shillings. Although the worker can now get a greater amount of commodities with these 2 shillings that he formerly did with 3 shillings, yet his wages have decreased in proportion to the gain of the capitalist. The profit of the capitalist – the manufacturer's, for instance – has increased by 1 shilling, which means that for a smaller amount of exchange value, which he pays to the workers, the latter must produce a greater amount of exchange value than before. The share of capital in proportion to the share of labour has risen. The distribution of social wealth between capital and labour has become still more unequal. The capitalist commands a greater amount of labour with the same capital. The power of the capitalist class over the working class has grown, the social position of the worker has become worse, has been forced down still another degree below that of the capitalist.

What, then, is the general law that determines the rise and fall of wages and profit in their reciprocal relation? They stand in inverse proportion to each other. The share of capital (profit) increases in the same proportion in which the share of labour (wages) falls, and vice versa. Profit rises in the same degree in which wages fall; it falls in the same degree in which wages rise.

It might perhaps be argued that the capitalist can gain by an advantageous exchange of his products with other capitalists, by a rise in the demand for his commodities, whether in consequence of the opening up of new markets, or in consequence of temporarily increased demands in the old markets, and so on; that the profit of the capitalist, therefore, may be multiplied by taking advantage of other capitalists, independently of the rise and fall of wages, of the exchange value of labour-power; so that the profit of the capitalist may also rise through improvements in the instruments of labour, new applications of the forces of nature, and so on.

But in the first place it must be admitted that the result remains the same, although brought about in an opposite manner. Profit, indeed, has not risen because wages have fallen, but wages have fallen because profit has risen. With the same amount of another man's labour the capitalist has bought a larger amount of exchange values without having paid more for the labour on that account; i.e. the work is paid for less in proportion to the net gain which it yields to the capitalist.

In the second place, it must be borne in mind that, despite the fluctuations in the prices of commodities, the average price of every commodity, the proportion in which it exchanges for other commodities, is determined by its cost of production. The acts of overreaching and taking advantage of one another within the capitalist ranks necessarily equalise themselves. The improvements of machinery, the new applications of the forces of nature in the service of production, make it possible to produce in a given period of time, with the same amount of labour and capital, a larger amount of products, but in no wise a larger amount of exchange values. If by the use of the spinning-machine I can furnish twice as much yarn in an hour as before its invention – for instance, 100 pounds instead of 50 pounds – in the long run I receive back, in exchange for this 100 pounds, no more commodities than I did before for 50; because the cost of production has fallen by one-half, or because I can furnish double the product at the same cost.

Finally, in whatsoever proportion the capitalist class, whether of one country or of the entire world market, distribute the net revenue of production among themselves, the total amount of this net revenue always consists exclusively of the amount by which accumulated labour has been increased from the proceeds of direct labour. This whole amount, therefore, grows in the same proportion in which labour augments capital, i.e. in the same proportion in which profit rises as compared with wages.

The Interests of Capital and Wage-Labour Are Diametrically Opposed: Effect of Growth of Productive Capital on Wages

We thus see that, even if we keep ourselves within the relation of capital and wage-labour, the interests of capital and the interests of wage-labour are diametrically opposed to each other.

A rapid growth of capital is synonymous with a rapid growth of profits.

Profits can grow rapidly only when the price of labour – the relative wages – decrease just as rapidly. Relative wages may fall, although real wages rise simultaneously with nominal wages, with the money value of labour, provided only that the real wage does not rise in the same proportion as the profit. If, for instance, in good business years wages rise 5 per cent, while profits rise 30 per cent, the proportional, the relative wage has not increased, but decreased.

If, therefore, the income of the worker increases with the rapid growth of capital, there is at the same time a widening of the social chasm that divides the worker from the capitalist, an increase in the power of capital over labour, a greater dependence of labour upon capital.

To say that 'the worker has an interest in the rapid growth of capital' means only this: that the more speedily the worker augments the wealth of the capitalist, the larger will be the crumbs which fall to him, the greater will be the number of workers that can be called into existence, the more can the mass of slaves dependent upon capital be increased.

We have thus seen that even the most favourable situation for the working class, namely the most rapid growth of capital, however much it may improve the material life of the worker, does not abolish the antagonism between his interests and the interests of the capitalist. Profit and wages remain as before, in inverse proportion.

If capital grows rapidly, wages may rise, but the profit of capital rises disproportionately faster. The material position of the worker has improved, but at the cost of his social position. The social chasm that separates him from the capitalist has widened.

Finally, to say that 'the most favourable condition for wage-labour is the fastest possible growth of productive capital' is the same as to say: the quicker the working class multiplies and augments the power inimical to it – the wealth of another which lords over that class – the more favourable will be the conditions under which it will be permitted to toil anew at the multiplication of bourgeois wealth, at the enlargement of the power of capital, content thus to forge for itself the golden chains by which the bourgeoisie drags it in its train.

Growth of productive capital and rise of wages, are they really so indissolubly united as the bourgeois economists maintain? We must not believe their mere words. We dare not believe them even when they claim that the fatter capital is, the more will its slave be pampered. The bourgeoisie is too much enlightened, it keeps its accounts much too carefully, to share the prejudices of the feudal lord, who makes an ostentatious display of the magnificence of his retinue. The conditions of existence of the bourgeoisie compel it to attend carefully to its bookkeeping. We must therefore examine more closely the following question: In what manner does the growth of productive capital affect wages?

If, as a whole, the productive capital of bourgeois society grows, there takes place a more many-sided accumulation of labour. The individual capitals increase in number and in magnitude. The multiplication of individual capitals increases the competition among capitalists. The increasing magnitude of increasing capitals provides the means of leading more powerful armies of workers with more gigantic instruments of war upon the industrial battlefield.

The one capitalist can drive the other from the field and carry off his capital only by selling more cheaply. In order to sell more cheaply without ruining himself, he must produce more cheaply – i.e. increase the productive forces of labour as much as possible.

But the productive forces of labour are increased above all by a greater division of labour and by a more general introduction and constant improvement of machinery. The larger the army of workers among whom the labour is subdivided, the more gigantic the scale upon which machinery is introduced, the more in proportion does the cost of production decrease, the more fruitful is the labour. And so there arises among the capitalists a universal rivalry for the increase of the division of labour and of machinery and for their exploitation upon the greatest possible scale.

If, now, by a greater division of labour, by the application and improvement of new machines, by a more advantageous exploitation of the forces of nature on a larger scale, a capitalist has found the means of producing with the same amount of labour (whether it be direct or accumulated labour) a larger amount of products of commodities than his competitors – if, for instance, he can produce a whole yard of linen in the same labour-time in which his competitors weave half a yard – how will this capitalist act?

He could keep on selling half a yard of linen at the old market price; but this would not have the effect of driving his opponents from the field and enlarging his own market. But his need of a market has increased in the same measure in which his productive power has extended. The more powerful and costly means of production that he has called into existence enable him, it is true, to sell his wares more cheaply, but they compel him at the same time to sell more wares, to get control of a very much greater market for his commodities; consequently, this capitalist will sell his half-yard of linen more cheaply than his competitors.

But the capitalist will not sell the whole yard so cheaply as his competitors sell the half-yard, although the production of the whole yard costs him no more than does that of the half-yard to the others. Otherwise, he would make no extra profit, and would get back in exchange only the cost of production. He might obtain a greater income from having set in motion a larger capital, but not from having made a greater profit on his capital than the others. Moreover, he attains the object he is aiming at if he prices his goods only a small percentage lower than his competitors. He drives them off the field, he wrests from them at least part of their market, by underselling them.

And finally, let us remember that the current price always stands either above or below the cost of production, according as the sale of a commodity takes place in the favourable or unfavourable period of the industry. According as the market price of the yard of linen stands above or below its former cost of production, will the percentage vary at which the capitalist who has made use of the new and more faithful means of production sell above his real cost of production.

But the privilege of our capitalist is not of long duration. Other competing capitalists introduce the same machines, the same division of labour, and introduce them upon the same or even upon a greater scale. And finally this introduction becomes so universal that the price of the linen is lowered not only below its old but even below its new cost of production.

The capitalists therefore find themselves, in their mutual relations, in the same situation in which they were before the introduction of the new means of production; and if they are by these means enabled to offer double the product at the old price, they are now forced to furnish double the product for less than the old price. Having arrived at the new point, the new cost of production, the battle for supremacy in the market has to be fought out anew. Given more division of labour and more machinery, there results a greater scale upon which division of labour and machinery are exploited. And competition again brings the same reaction against this result.

Effect of Capitalist Competition on the Capitalist Class, the Middle Class and the Working Class

We thus see how the method of production and the means of production are constantly enlarged, revolutionised, how division of labour necessarily draws after it greater division of labour, the employment of machinery greater employment of machinery, work upon a large scale work upon a still greater scale. This is the law that continually throws capitalist production out of its old ruts and compels capital to strain ever more the productive forces of labour for the very reason that it has already strained them – the law that grants it no respite, and constantly shouts in its ear: March! march! This is no other law than that which, within the periodical fluctuations of commerce, necessarily adjusts the price of a commodity to its cost of production.

No matter how powerful the means of production which a capitalist may bring into the field, competition will make their adoption general; and from the moment that they have been generally adopted, the sole result of the greater productiveness of his capital will be that he must furnish at the same price 10, 20, 100 times as much as before. But since he must find a market for, perhaps, 1,000 times as much, in order to outweigh the lower selling price by the greater quantity of the sale; since now a more extensive sale is necessary not only to gain a greater profit, but also in order to replace the cost of production (the instrument of production itself grows always more costly, as we have seen), and since this more extensive sale has become a question of life and death not only for him, but also for his rivals, the old struggle must begin again, and it is all the more violent, the more powerful the means of production already invented are. The division of labour and the application of machinery will therefore take a fresh start, and upon an even greater scale.

Whatever be the power of the means of production which are employed, competition seeks to rob capital of the golden fruits of this power by reducing the price of commodities to the cost of production; in the same measure in which production is cheapened – i.e. in the same measure in which more can be produced with the same amount of labour – it compels by a law which is irresistible a still greater cheapening of production, the sale of ever greater masses of product for smaller prices. Thus the capitalist will have gained nothing more by his efforts than the obligation to furnish a greater product in the same labour-time; in a word, more difficult conditions for the profitable employment of his capital. While competition, therefore, constantly pursues him with its law of the cost of production and turns against himself every weapon that he forges against his rivals, the capitalist continually seeks to get the best of competition by restlessly introducing further subdivision of labour and new machines, which, though more expensive, enable him to produce more cheaply, instead of waiting until the new machines shall have been rendered obsolete by competition.

If we now conceive this feverish agitation as it operates in the market of the whole world, we shall be in a position to comprehend how the growth, accumulation and concentration of capital bring in their train an ever more detailed subdivision of labour, an ever greater improvement of old machines, and a constant application of new machines – a process which goes on uninterruptedly, with feverish haste, and upon an ever more gigantic scale.

But what effect do these conditions, which are inseparable from the growth of productive capital, have upon the determination of wages?

The greater division of labour enables one labourer to accomplish the work of 5, 10, or 20 labourers; it therefore increases competition among the labourers fivefold, tenfold, or twentyfold. The labourers compete not only by selling themselves one cheaper than the other, but also by one doing the work of 5, 10, or 20; and they are forced to compete in this manner by the division of labour, which is introduced and steadily improved by capital.

Furthermore, to the same degree in which the division of labour increases, is the labour simplified. The special skill of the labourer becomes worthless. He becomes transformed into a simple monotonous force of production, with neither physical nor mental elasticity. His work becomes accessible to all; therefore competitors press upon him from all sides. Moreover, it must be remembered that the more simple, the more easily learned the work is, so much the less is its cost to production, the expense of its acquisition, and so much the lower must the wages sink – for, like the price of any other commodity, they are determined by the cost of production. Therefore, in the same manner in which labour becomes more unsatisfactory, more repulsive, do competition increase and wages decrease.

The labourer seeks to maintain the total of his wages for a given time by performing more labour, either by working a great number of hours, or by accomplishing more in the same number of hours. Thus, urged on by want, he himself multiplies the disastrous effects of division of labour. The result is: the more he works, the less wages he receives. And for this simple reason: the more he works, the more he competes against his fellow workmen, the more he compels them to compete against him, and to offer themselves on the same wretched conditions as he does; so that, in the last analysis, he competes against himself as a member of the working class.

Machinery produces the same effects, but upon a much larger scale. It supplants skilled labourers by unskilled, men by women, adults by children; where newly introduced, it throws workers upon the streets in great masses; and as it becomes more highly developed and more productive it discards them in additional though smaller numbers.

We have hastily sketched in broad outlines the industrial war of capitalists among themselves. This war has the peculiarity that the battles in it are won less by recruiting than by discharging the army of workers. The generals (the capitalists) vie with one another as to who can discharge the greatest number of industrial soldiers.

The economists tell us, to be sure, that those labourers who have been rendered superfluous by machinery find new avenues of employment. They dare not assert directly that the same labourers that have been discharged find situations in new branches of labour. Facts cry out too loudly against this lie. Strictly speaking, they only maintain that new means of employment will be found for other sections of the working class; for example, for that portion of the young generation of labourers who were about to enter upon that branch of industry which had just been abolished. Of course, this is a great satisfaction to the disabled labourers. There will be no lack of fresh exploitable blood and muscle for the Messrs. Capitalists – the dead may bury their dead. This consolation seems to be intended more for the comfort of the capitalists themselves than their labourers. If the whole class of the wage-labourer were to be annihilated by machinery, how terrible that would be for capital, which, without wage-labour, ceases to be capital!

But even if we assume that all who are directly forced out of employment by machinery, as well as all of the rising generation who were waiting for a chance of employment in the same branch of industry, do actually find some new employment – are we to believe that this new employment will pay as high wages as did the one they have lost? If it did, it would be in contradiction to the laws of political economy. We have seen how modern industry always tends to the substitution of the simpler and more subordinate employments for the higher and more complex ones. How, then, could a mass of workers thrown out of one branch of industry by machinery find refuge in another branch, unless they were to be paid more poorly?

An exception to the law has been adduced, namely the workers who are employed in the manufacture of machinery itself. As soon as there is in industry a greater demand for and a greater consumption of machinery, it is said that the number of machines must necessarily increase; consequently, also, the manufacture of machines; consequently, also, the employment of workers in machine manufacture – and the workers employed in this branch of industry are skilled, even educated, workers.

Since the year 1840 this assertion, which even before that date was only half-true, has lost all semblance of truth; for the most diverse machines are now applied to the manufacture of the machines themselves on quite as extensive a scale as in the manufacture of cotton yarn, and the labourers employed in machine factories can but play the role of very stupid machines alongside of the highly ingenious machines.

But in place of the man who has been dismissed by the machine, the factory may employ, perhaps, three children and one woman! And must not the wages of the man have previously sufficed for the three children and one woman? Must not the minimum wages have sufficed for the preservation and propagation of the race? What, then, do these beloved bourgeois phrases prove? Nothing more than that now four times as many workers' lives are used up as there were previously, in order to obtain the livelihood of one working family.

To sum up: the more productive capital grows, the more it extends the division of labour and the application of machinery; the more the division of labour and the application of machinery extend, the more does competition extend among the workers, the more do their wages shrink together.

In addition, the working class is also recruited from the higher strata of society; a mass of small business men and of people living upon the interest of their capitals is precipitated into the ranks of the working class, and they will have nothing else to do than to stretch out their arms alongside the arms of the workers. Thus the forest of outstretched arms, begging for work, grows ever thicker, while the arms themselves grow every leaner.

It is evident that the small manufacturer cannot survive in a struggle in which the first condition of success is production upon an ever greater scale. It is evident that the small manufacturer cannot at the same time be a big manufacturer.

That the interest on capital decreases in the same ratio in which the mass and number of capitals increase, that it diminishes with the growth of capital, that therefore the small capitalist can no longer live on his interest, but must consequently throw himself upon industry by joining the ranks of the small manufacturers and thereby increasing the number of candidates for the proletariat – all this requires no further elucidation.

Finally, in the same measure in which the capitalists are compelled, by the movement described above, to exploit the already existing gigantic means of production on an ever-increasing scale, and for this purpose to set in motion all the mainsprings of credit, in the same measure do they increase the industrial earthquakes, in the midst of which the commercial world can preserve itself only by sacrificing a portion of its wealth, its products, and even its forces of production, to the gods of the lower world – in short, the crises increase. They become more frequent and more violent, if for no other reason than for this alone, that in the same measure in which the mass of products grows, and therefore the needs for extensive markets, in the same measure does the world market shrink ever more, and ever fewer markets remain to be exploited, since every previous crisis has subjected to the commerce of the world a hitherto unconquered or but superficially exploited market.

But capital not only lives upon labour. Like a master, at once distinguished and barbarous, it drags with it into its grave the corpses of its slaves, whole hecatombs of workers, who perish in the crises.

We thus see that if capital grows rapidly, competition among the workers grows with even greater rapidity – i.e. the means of employment and subsistence for the working class decrease in proportion even more rapidly; but, this notwithstanding, the rapid growth of capital is the most favourable condition for wage-labour.

Karl Marx and Friedrich Engels
The Communist Manifesto
(First published (in German) in London, 1848)

A spectre is haunting Europe – the spectre of communism. All the powers of old Europe have entered into a holy alliance to exorcise this spectre: Pope and Tsar, Metternich and Guizot, French Radicals and German police-spies.

Where is the party in opposition that has not been decried as Communistic by its opponents in power? Where is the opposition that has not hurled back the branding reproach of Communism, against the more advanced opposition parties, as well as against its reactionary adversaries?

Two things result from this fact:

I. Communism is already acknowledged by all European powers to be itself a power.
II. It is high time that Communists should openly, in the face of the whole world, publish their views, their aims, their tendencies, and meet this nursery tale of the Spectre of Communism with a manifesto of the party itself.

To this end, Communists of various nationalities have assembled in London and sketched the following manifesto, to be published in the English, French, German, Italian, Flemish and Danish languages.

I. BOURGEOIS AND PROLETARIANS

The history of all hitherto existing society is the history of class struggles. Freeman and slave, patrician and plebeian, lord and serf, guild-master and journeyman, in a word, oppressor and oppressed, stood in constant opposition to one another, carried on an uninterrupted, now hidden, now open fight, a fight that each time ended, either in a revolutionary reconstitution of society at large, or in the common ruin of the contending classes.

In the earlier epochs of history, we find almost everywhere a complicated arrangement of society into various orders, a manifold gradation of social rank. In ancient Rome we have patricians, knights, plebeians, slaves; in the Middle Ages, feudal lords, vassals, guild-masters, journeymen, apprentices, serfs; in almost all of these classes, again, subordinate gradations.

The modern bourgeois society that has sprouted from the ruins of feudal society has not done away with class antagonisms. It has but established new classes, new conditions of oppression, new forms of struggle in place of the old ones.

Our epoch, the epoch of the bourgeoisie, possesses, however, this distinctive feature: it has simplified class antagonisms. Society as a whole is more and more splitting up into two great hostile camps, into two great classes directly facing each other – Bourgeoisie and Proletariat.

From the serfs of the Middle Ages sprang the chartered burghers of the earliest towns. From these burgesses the first elements of the bourgeoisie were developed.

The discovery of America, the rounding of the Cape, opened up fresh ground for the rising bourgeoisie. The East Indian and Chinese markets, the colonisation of America, trade with the colonies, the increase in the means of exchange and in commodities generally, gave to commerce, to navigation, to industry, an impulse never before known, and thereby, to the revolutionary element in the tottering feudal society, a rapid development.

The feudal system of industry, in which industrial production was monopolised by closed guilds, now no longer sufficed for the growing wants of the new markets. The manufacturing system took its place. The guild-masters were pushed on one side by the manufacturing middle class; division of labour between the different corporate guilds vanished in the face of division of labour in each single workshop.

Meantime the markets kept ever growing, the demand ever rising. Even manufacture no longer sufficed. Thereupon, steam and machinery revolutionised industrial production. The place of manufacture was taken by the giant, Modern Industry; the place of the industrial middle class by industrial millionaires, the leaders of whole industrial armies, the modern bourgeois.

Modern industry has established the world market, for which the discovery of America paved the way. This market has given an immense development to commerce, to navigation, to communication by land. This development has, in its turn, reacted on the extension of industry; and as industry, commerce, navigation, railways extended, in the same proportion the bourgeoisie developed, increased its capital, and pushed into the background every class handed down from the Middle Ages.

We see, therefore, how the modern bourgeoisie is itself the product of a long course of development, of a series of revolutions in the modes of production and of exchange.

Each step in the development of the bourgeoisie was accompanied by a corresponding political advance of that class. An oppressed class under the sway of the feudal nobility, an armed and self-governing association in the medieval commune: here independent urban republic (as in Italy and Germany); there taxable 'third estate' of the monarchy (as in France); afterwards, in the period of manufacturing proper, serving either the semi-feudal or the absolute monarchy as a counterpoise against the nobility, and, in fact, cornerstone of the great monarchies in general – the bourgeoisie has at last, since the establishment of Modern Industry and of the world market, conquered for itself, in the modern representative State, exclusive political sway. The executive of the modern state is but a committee for managing the common affairs of the whole bourgeoisie.

The bourgeoisie, historically, has played a most revolutionary part.

The bourgeoisie, wherever it has got the upper hand, has put an end to all feudal, patriarchal, idyllic relations. It has pitilessly torn asunder the motley feudal ties that bound man to his 'natural superiors', and has left remaining no other nexus between man and man than naked self-interest, than callous 'cash payment'. It has drowned the most heavenly ecstasies of religious fervour, of chivalrous enthusiasm, of philistine sentimentalism, in the icy water of egotistical calculation. It has resolved personal worth into exchange value, and in place of the numberless indefeasible chartered freedoms, has set up that single, unconscionable freedom – Free Trade. In one word, for exploitation, veiled by religious and political illusions, it has substituted naked, shameless, direct, brutal exploitation.

The bourgeoisie has stripped of its halo every occupation hitherto honoured and looked up to with reverent awe. It has converted the physician, the lawyer, the priest, the poet, the man of science, into its paid wage-labourers.

The bourgeoisie has torn away from the family its sentimental veil, and has reduced the family relation to a mere money relation.

The bourgeoisie has disclosed how it came to pass that the brutal display of vigour in the Middle Ages, which reactionaries so much admire, found its fitting complement in the most slothful indolence. It has been the first to show what man's activity can bring about. It has accomplished wonders far surpassing Egyptian pyramids, Roman aqueducts, and Gothic cathedrals; it has conducted expeditions that put in the shade all former Exoduses of nations and crusades.

The bourgeoisie cannot exist without constantly revolutionising the instruments of production, and thereby the relations of production, and with them the whole relations of society. Conservation of the old modes of production in unaltered form was, on the contrary, the first condition of existence for all earlier industrial classes. Constant revolutionising of production, uninterrupted disturbance of all social conditions, everlasting uncertainty and agitation, distinguish the bourgeois epoch from all earlier ones. All fixed, fast-frozen relations, with their train of ancient and venerable prejudices and opinions, are swept away, all new-formed ones become antiquated before they can ossify. All that is solid melts into air, all that is holy is profaned, and man is at last compelled to face with sober senses his real conditions of life, and his relations with his kind.

The need of a constantly expanding market for its products chases the bourgeoisie over the entire surface of the globe. It must nestle everywhere, settle everywhere, establish connections everywhere.

The bourgeoisie has through its exploitation of the world market given a cosmopolitan character to production and consumption in every country. To the great chagrin of Reactionists, it has drawn from under the feet of industry the national ground on which it stood. All old-established national industries have been destroyed or are daily being destroyed. They are dislodged by new industries, whose introduction becomes a life and death question for all civilised nations, by industries that no longer work up indigenous raw material, but raw material drawn from the remotest zones; industries whose products are consumed, not only at home, but in every quarter of the globe. In place of the old wants, satisfied by the productions of the country, we find new wants, requiring for their satisfaction the products of distant lands and climes. In place of the old local and national seclusion and self-sufficiency, we have intercourse in every direction, universal interdependence of nations. And as in material, so also in intellectual production. The intellectual creations of individual nations become common property. National one-sidedness and narrow-mindedness become more and more impossible, and from the numerous national and local literatures, there arises a world literature.

The bourgeoisie, by the rapid improvement of all instruments of production, by the immensely facilitated means of communication, draws all, even the most barbarian, nations into civilisation. The cheap prices of commodities are the heavy artillery with which it batters down all Chinese walls, with which it forces the barbarians' intensely obstinate hatred of foreigners to capitulate. It compels all nations, on pain of extinction, to adopt the bourgeois mode of production; it compels them to introduce what it calls civilisation into their midst, i.e. to become bourgeois themselves. In one word, it creates a world after its own image.

The bourgeoisie has subjected the country to the rule of the towns. It has created enormous cities, has greatly increased the urban population as compared with the rural, and has thus rescued a considerable part of the population from the idiocy of rural life. Just as it has made the country dependent on the towns, so it has made barbarian and semi-barbarian countries dependent on the civilised ones, nations of peasants on nations of bourgeois, the East on the West.

The bourgeoisie keeps more and more doing away with the scattered state of the population, of the means of production, and of property. It has agglomerated population, centralised the means of production, and has concentrated property in a few hands. The necessary consequence of this was political centralisation. Independent or but loosely connected provinces, with separate interests, laws, governments and systems of taxation, became lumped together into one nation, with one government, one code of laws, one national class-interest, one frontier, and one customs-tariff.

The bourgeoisie, during its rule of scarce one hundred years, has created more massive and more colossal productive forces than have all preceding generations together. Subjection of Nature's forces to man, machinery, application of chemistry to industry and agriculture, steam navigation, railways, electric telegraphs, clearing of whole continents for cultivation, canalisation of rivers, whole populations conjured out of the ground – what earlier century had even a presentiment that such productive forces slumbered in the lap of social labour?

We see then: the means of production and of exchange, on whose foundation the bourgeoisie built itself up, were generated in feudal society. At a certain stage in the development of these means of production and of exchange, the conditions under which feudal society produced and exchanged, the feudal organisation of agriculture and manufacturing industry, in one word the feudal relations of property, became no longer compatible with the already developed productive forces; they became so many fetters. They had to be burst asunder; they were burst asunder.

Into their place stepped free competition, accompanied by a social and political constitution adapted to it, and the economic and political sway of the bourgeois class.

A similar movement is going on before our own eyes. Modern bourgeois society, with its relations of production, of exchange and of property, a society that has conjured up such gigantic means of production and of exchange, is like the sorcerer who is no longer able to control the powers of the nether world whom he has called up by his spells. For many a decade past the history of industry and commerce is but the history of the revolt of modern productive forces against modern conditions of production, against the property relations that are the conditions for the existence of the bourgeois and of its rule. It is enough to mention the commercial crises that by their periodical return put the existence of the entire bourgeois society on its trial, each time more threateningly. In these crises a great part not only of the existing products, but also of the previously created productive forces, are periodically destroyed. In these crises there breaks out an epidemic that, in all earlier epochs, would have seemed an absurdity – the epidemic of over-production. Society suddenly finds itself put back into a state of momentary barbarism; it appears as if a famine, a universal war of devastation, had cut off the supply of every means of subsistence; industry and commerce seem to be destroyed; and why? Because there is too much civilisation, too much means of subsistence, too much industry, too much commerce. The productive forces at the disposal of society no longer tend to further the development of the conditions of bourgeois property; on the contrary, they have become too powerful for these conditions, by which they are fettered, and so soon as they overcome these fetters, they bring disorder into the whole of bourgeois society, endanger the existence of bourgeois property. The conditions of bourgeois society are too narrow to comprise the wealth created by them. And how does the bourgeoisie get over these crises? On the one hand, by enforced destruction of a mass of productive forces; on the other, by the conquest of new markets, and by the more thorough exploitation of the old ones. That is to say, by paving the way for more extensive and more destructive crises, and by diminishing the means whereby crises are prevented.

The weapons with which the bourgeoisie felled feudalism to the ground are now turned against the bourgeoisie itself.

But not only has the bourgeoisie forged the weapons that bring death to itself; it has also called into existence the men who are to wield those weapons – the modern working class – the proletarians.

In proportion as the bourgeoisie, i.e. capital, is developed, in the same proportion is the proletariat, the modern working class, developed – a class of labourers, who live only so long as they find work, and who find work only so long as their labour increases capital. These labourers, who must sell themselves piecemeal, are a commodity, like every other article of commerce, and are consequently exposed to all the vicissitudes of competition, to all the fluctuations of the market.

Owing to the extensive use of machinery and to the division of labour, the work of the proletarians has lost all individual character, and, consequently, all charm for the workman. He becomes an appendage of the machine, and it is only the most simple, most monotonous and most easily acquired knack that is required of him. Hence, the cost of production of a workman is restricted, almost entirely, to the means of subsistence that he requires for maintenance, and for the propagation of his race. But the price of a commodity, and therefore also of labour, is equal to its cost of production. In proportion, therefore, as the repulsiveness of the work increases, the wage decreases. Nay more, in proportion as the use of machinery and division of labour increases, in the same proportion the burden of toil also increases, whether by prolongation of the working hours, by the increase of the work exacted in a given time or by increased speed of machinery, etc.

Modern Industry has converted the little workshop of the patriarchal master into the great factory of the industrial capitalist. Masses of labourers, crowded into the factory, are organised like soldiers. As privates of the industrial army they are placed under the command of a perfect hierarchy of officers and sergeants. Not only are they slaves of the bourgeois class, and of the bourgeois State; they are daily and hourly enslaved by the machine, by the overseer, and, above all, by the individual bourgeois manufacturer himself. The more openly this despotism proclaims gain to be its end and aim, the more petty, the more hateful and the more embittering it is.

The less the skill and exertion of strength implied in manual labour, in other words the more modern industry becomes developed, the more is the labour of men superseded by that of women. Differences of age and sex have no longer any distinctive social validity for the working class. All are instruments of labour, more or less expensive to use, according to their age and sex.

No sooner is the exploitation of the labourer by the manufacturer, so far, at an end, that he receives his wages in cash, than he is set upon by the other portions of the bourgeoisie, the landlord, the shopkeeper, the pawnbroker, etc.

The lower strata of the middle class – the small tradespeople, shopkeepers, and retired tradesmen generally, the handicraftsmen and peasants – all these sink gradually into the proletariat, partly because their diminutive capital does not suffice for the scale on which Modern Industry is carried on, and is swamped in the competition with the large capitalists, partly because their specialised skill is rendered worthless by new methods of production. Thus the proletariat is recruited from all classes of the population.

The proletariat goes through various stages of development. With its birth begins its struggle with the bourgeoisie. At first the contest is carried on by individual labourers, then by the workpeople of a factory, then by the operatives of one trade, in one locality, against the individual bourgeois who directly exploits them. They direct their attacks not against the bourgeois conditions of production, but against the instruments of production themselves; they destroy imported wares that compete with their labour, they smash to pieces machinery, they set factories ablaze, they seek to restore by force the vanished status of the workman of the Middle Ages.

At this stage the labourers still form an incoherent mass scattered over the whole country, and broken up by their mutual competition. If anywhere they unite to form more compact bodies, this is not yet the consequence of their own active union, but of the union of the bourgeoisie, which class, in order to attain its own political ends, is compelled to set the whole proletariat in motion, and is moreover yet, for a time, able to do so. At this stage, therefore, the proletarians do not fight their enemies, but the enemies of their enemies, the remnants of absolute monarchy, the landowners, the non-industrial bourgeois, the petty bourgeois. Thus, the whole historical movement is concentrated in the hands of the bourgeoisie; every victory so obtained is a victory for the bourgeoisie.

But with the development of industry, the proletariat not only increases in number; it becomes concentrated in greater masses, its strength grows, and it feels that strength more. The various interests and conditions of life within the ranks of the proletariat are more and more equalised, in proportion as machinery obliterates all distinctions of labour, and nearly everywhere reduces wages to the same low level. The growing competition among the bourgeois, and the resulting commercial crises, make the wages of the workers ever more fluctuating. The unceasing improvement of machinery, ever more rapidly developing, makes their livelihood more and more precarious; the collisions between individual workmen and individual bourgeois take more and more the character of collisions between two classes. Thereupon the workers begin to form combinations (Trades' Unions) against the bourgeois; they club together in order to keep up the rate of wages; they found permanent associations in order to make provision beforehand for these occasional revolts. Here and there, the contest breaks out into riots.

Now and then the workers are victorious, but only for a time. The real fruit of their battles lies, not in the immediate result, but in the ever expanding union of the workers. This union is helped on by the improved means of communication that are created by modern industry, and that place the workers of different localities in contact with one another. It was just this contact that was needed to centralise the numerous local struggles, all of the same character, into one national struggle between classes. But every class struggle is a political struggle. And that union, to attain which the burghers of the Middle Ages, with their miserable highways, required centuries, the modern proletarians, thanks to railways, achieve in a few years.

This organisation of the proletarians into a class, and, consequently into a political party, is continually being upset again by the competition between the workers themselves. But it ever rises up again, stronger, firmer, mightier. It compels legislative recognition of particular interests of the workers, by taking advantage of the divisions among the bourgeoisie itself. Thus, the ten-hours' bill in England was carried.

Altogether collisions between the classes of the old society further, in many ways, the course of development of the proletariat. The bourgeoisie finds itself involved in a constant battle at first with the aristocracy; later on, with those portions of the bourgeoisie itself whose interests have become antagonistic to the progress of industry; at all time with the bourgeoisie of foreign countries. In all these battles, it sees itself compelled to appeal to the proletariat, to ask for help, and thus, to drag it into the political arena. The bourgeoisie itself, therefore, supplies the proletariat with its own elements of political and general education; in other words, it furnishes the proletariat with weapons for fighting the bourgeoisie.

Further, as we have already seen, entire sections of the ruling class are, by the advance of industry, precipitated into the proletariat, or are at least threatened in their conditions of existence. These also supply the proletariat with fresh elements of enlightenment and progress.

Finally, in times when the class struggle nears the decisive hour, the process of dissolution going on within the ruling class, in fact within the whole range of old society, assumes such a violent, glaring character, that a small section of the ruling class cuts itself adrift, and joins the revolutionary class, the class that holds the future in its hands. Just as, therefore, at an earlier period, a section of the nobility went over to the bourgeoisie, so now a portion of the bourgeoisie goes over to the proletariat, and in particular, a portion of the bourgeois ideologists, who have raised themselves to the level of comprehending theoretically the historical movement as a whole.

Of all the classes that stand face to face with the bourgeoisie today, the proletariat alone is a really revolutionary class. The other classes decay and finally disappear in the face of Modern Industry; the proletariat is its special and essential product.

The lower middle class, the small manufacturer, the shopkeeper, the artisan, the peasant, all these fight against the bourgeoisie, to save from extinction their existence as fractions of the middle class. They are therefore not revolutionary, but conservative. Nay more, they are reactionary, for they try to roll back the wheel of history. If by chance they are revolutionary, they are only so in view of their impending transfer into the proletariat; they thus defend not their present, but their future interests; they desert their own standpoint to place themselves at that of the proletariat.

The 'dangerous class', the social scum, that passively rotting mass thrown off by the lowest layers of the old society, may, here and there, be swept into the movement by a proletarian revolution; its conditions of life, however, prepare it far more for the part of a bribed tool of reactionary intrigue.

In the conditions of the proletariat, those of old society at large are already virtually swamped. The proletarian is without property; his relation to his wife and children no longer has anything in common with the bourgeois family relations; modern industrial labour, modern subjection to capital, the same in England as in France, in America as in Germany, has stripped him of every trace of national character. Law, morality, religion are to him so many bourgeois prejudices, behind which lurk in ambush just as many bourgeois interests.

All the preceding classes that got the upper hand sought to fortify their already acquired status by subjecting society at large to their conditions of appropriation. The proletarians cannot become masters of the productive forces of society, except by abolishing their own previous mode of appropriation, and thereby also every other previous mode of appropriation. They have nothing of their own to secure and to fortify; their mission is to destroy all previous securities for, and insurances of, individual property.

All previous historical movements were movements of minorities, or in the interest of minorities. The proletarian movement is the self-conscious, independent movement of the immense majority, in the interest of the immense majority. The proletariat, the lowest stratum of our present society, cannot stir, cannot raise itself up, without the whole superincumbent strata of official society being sprung into the air.

Though not in substance, yet in form, the struggle of the proletariat with the bourgeoisie is at first a national struggle. The proletariat of each country must, of course, first of all settle matters with its own bourgeoisie.

In depicting the most general phases of the development of the proletariat, we traced the more or less veiled civil war, raging within existing society, up to the point where that war breaks out into open revolution, and where the violent overthrow of the bourgeoisie lays the foundation for the sway of the proletariat.

Hitherto, every form of society has been based, as we have already seen, on the antagonism of oppressing and oppressed classes. But in order to oppress a class, certain conditions must be assured to it under which it can, at least, continue its slavish existence. The serf, in the period of serfdom, raised himself to membership in the commune, just as the petty bourgeois, under the yoke of the feudal absolutism, managed to develop into a bourgeois. The modern labourer, on the contrary, instead of rising with the progress of industry, sinks deeper and deeper below the conditions of existence of his own class. He becomes a pauper, and pauperism develops more rapidly than population and wealth. And here it becomes evident that the bourgeoisie is unfit any longer to be the ruling class in society, and to impose its conditions of existence upon society as an over-riding law. It is unfit to rule because it is incompetent to assure an existence to its slave within his slavery, because it cannot help letting him sink into such a state, that it has to feed him, instead of being fed by him. Society can no longer live under this bourgeoisie; in other words, its existence is no longer compatible with society.

The essential condition for the existence and for the sway of the bourgeois class is the formation and augmentation of capital; the condition for capital is wage-labour. Wage-labour rests exclusively on competition between the labourers. The advance of industry, whose involuntary promoter is the bourgeoisie, replaces the isolation of the labourers, due to competition, by their revolutionary combination, due to association. The development of Modern Industry, therefore, cuts from under its feet the very foundation on which the bourgeoisie produces and appropriates products. What the bourgeoisie therefore produces, above all, is its own grave-diggers. Its fall and the victory of the proletariat are equally inevitable.

II. PROLETARIANS AND COMMUNISTS

In what relation do the Communists stand to the proletarians as a whole?

The Communists do not form a separate party opposed to the other working-class parties. They have no interests separate and apart from those of the proletariat as a whole. They do not set up any sectarian principles of their own, by which to shape and mould the proletarian movement.

The Communists are distinguished from the other working-class parties by this only:

1. In the national struggles of the proletarians of the different countries,

they point out and bring to the front the common interests of the entire proletariat, independently of all nationality.
2. In the various stages of development which the struggle of the working class against the bourgeoisie has to pass through, they always and everywhere represent the interests of the movement as a whole.

The Communists, therefore, are on the one hand, practically, the most advanced and resolute section of the working-class parties of every country, that section which pushes forward all others; on the other hand, theoretically, they have over the great mass of the proletariat the advantage of clearly understanding the line of march, the conditions, and the ultimate general results of the proletarian movement.

The immediate aim of the Communists is the same as that of all other proletarian parties: formation of the proletariat into a class, overthrow of the bourgeois supremacy, conquest of political power by the proletariat.

The theoretical conclusions of the Communists are in no way based on ideas or principles that have been invented, or discovered, by this or that would-be universal reformer. They merely express, in general terms, actual relations springing from an existing class struggle, from a historical movement going on under our very eyes. The abolition of existing property relations is not at all a distinctive feature of Communism.

All property relations in the past have continually been subject to historical change consequent upon the change in historical conditions. The French Revolution, for example, abolished feudal property in favour of bourgeois property.

The distinguishing feature of Communism is not the abolition of property generally, but the abolition of bourgeois property. But modern bourgeois private property is the final and most complete expression of the system of producing and appropriating products, that is based on class antagonisms, on the exploitation of the many by the few.

In this sense, the theory of the Communists may be summed up in the single sentence: Abolition of private property.

We Communists have been reproached with the desire of abolishing the right of personally acquiring property as the fruit of a man's own labour, which property is alleged to be the groundwork of all personal freedom, activity and independence.

Hard-won, self-acquired, self-earned property! Do you mean the property of the petty artisan and of the small peasant, a form of property that preceded the bourgeois form? There is no need to abolish that; the development of industry has to a great extent already destroyed it, and is still destroying it daily. Or do you mean the modern bourgeois private property?

But does wage-labour create any property for the labourer? Not a bit. It creates capital, i.e. that kind of property which exploits wage-labour, and which cannot increase except upon condition of begetting a new supply of wage-labour for fresh exploitation. Property, in its present form, is based on the antagonism of capital and wage-labour. Let us examine both sides of this antagonism.

To be a capitalist is to have not only a purely personal, but a social status in production. Capital is a collective product, and only by the united action of many members, nay, in the last resort, only by the united action of all members of society, can it be set in motion. Capital is therefore not only personal; it is a social power.

When, therefore, capital is converted into common property, into the property of all members of society, personal property is not thereby transformed into social property. It is only the social character of the property that is changed. It loses its class character.

Let us now take wage-labour.

The average price of wage-labour is the minimum wage, i.e. that quantum of the means of subsistence which is absolutely requisite to keep the labourer in bare existence as a labourer. What, therefore, the wage-labourer appropriates by means of his labour, merely suffices to prolong and reproduce a bare existence. We by no means intend to abolish this personal appropriation of the products of labour, an appropriation that is made for the maintenance and reproduction of human life, and that leaves no surplus wherewith to command the labour of others. All that we want to do away with is the miserable character of this appropriation, under which the labourer lives merely to increase capital, and is allowed to live only in so far as the interest of the ruling class requires it.

In bourgeois society, living labour is but a means to increase accumulated labour. In Communist society, accumulated labour is but a means to widen, to enrich, to promote the existence of the labourer.

In bourgeois society, therefore, the past dominates the present; in Communist society, the present dominates the past. In bourgeois society capital is independent and has individuality, while the living person is dependent and has no individuality.

And the abolition of this state of things is called by the bourgeois abolition of individuality and freedom! And rightly so. The abolition of bourgeois individuality, bourgeois independence and bourgeois freedom is undoubtedly aimed at.

By freedom is meant, under the present bourgeois conditions of production, free trade, free selling and buying. But if selling and buying disappears, free selling and buying disappears also. This talk about free selling and buying, and all the other 'brave words' of our bourgeois about freedom in general, have a meaning, if any, only in contrast with restricted selling and buying, with the fettered traders of the Middle Ages, but have no meaning when opposed to the Communistic abolition of buying and selling, of the bourgeois conditions of production, and of the bourgeoisie itself.

You are horrified at our intending to do away with private property. But in your existing society, private property is already done away with for nine-tenths of the population; its existence for the few is solely due to its non-existence in the hands of those nine-tenths. You reproach us, therefore, with intending to do away with a form of property, the necessary condition for whose existence is the non-existence of any property for the immense majority of society. In one word, you reproach us with intending to do away with your property. Precisely so; that is just what we intend.

From the moment when labour can no longer be converted into capital, money or rent, into a social power capable of being monopolised, i.e. from the moment when individual property can no longer be transformed into bourgeois property, into capital, from that moment, you say, individuality vanishes.

You must, therefore, confess that by 'individual' you mean no other person than the bourgeois, than the middle-class owner of property. This person must, indeed, be swept out of the way, and made impossible.

Communism deprives no man of the power to appropriate the products of society; all that it does is to deprive him of the power to subjugate the labour of others by means of such appropriations.

It has been objected that upon the abolition of private property, all work will cease, and universal laziness will overtake us. According to this, bourgeois society ought long ago to have gone to the dogs through sheer idleness; for those of its members who work acquire nothing, and those who acquire anything do not work. The whole of this objection is but another expression of the tautology: that there can no longer be any wage-labour when there is no longer any capital.

All objections urged against the Communistic mode of producing and appropriating material products have, in the same way, been urged against the Communistic mode of producing and appropriating intellectual products. Just as, to the bourgeois, the disappearance of class property is the disappearance of production itself, so the disappearance of class culture is to him identical with the disappearance of all culture.

That culture, the loss of which he laments, is, for the enormous majority, a mere training to act as a machine.

But don't wrangle with us so long as you apply, to our intended abolition of bourgeois property, the standard of your bourgeois notions of freedom, culture, law, etc. Your very ideas are but the outgrowth of the conditions of your bourgeois production and bourgeois property, just as your jurisprudence is but the will of your class made into a law for all, a will whose essential character and direction are determined by the economic conditions of existence of your class.

The selfish misconception that induces you to transform into eternal laws of nature and of reason the social forms springing from your present mode of production and form of property – historical relations that rise and disappear in the progress of production – this misconception you share with every ruling class that has preceded you. What you see clearly in the case of ancient property, what you admit in the case of feudal property, you are of course forbidden to admit in the case of your own bourgeois form of property.

Abolition of the family! Even the most radical flare up at this infamous proposal of the Communists. On what foundation is the present family, the bourgeois family, based? On capital, on private gain. In its completely developed form, this family exists only among the bourgeoisie. But this state of things finds its complement in the practical absence of the family among the proletarians, and in public prostitution.

The bourgeois family will vanish as a matter of course when its complement vanishes, and both will vanish with the vanishing of capital.

Do you charge us with wanting to stop the exploitation of children by their parents? To this crime we plead guilty.

But, you say, we destroy the most hallowed of relations, when we replace home education by social.

And your education! Is not that also social, and determined by the social conditions under which you educate, by the intervention direct or indirect of society, by means of schools, etc.? The Communists have not invented the intervention of society in education; they do but seek to alter the character of that intervention, and to rescue education from the influence of the ruling class.

The bourgeois clap-trap about the family and education, about the hallowed co-relation of parent and child, becomes all the more disgusting, the more, by the action of Modern Industry, all family ties among the proletarians are torn asunder, and their children transformed into simple articles of commerce and instruments of labour.

But you Communists would introduce community of women, screams the bourgeoisie in chorus.

The bourgeois sees in his wife a mere instrument of production. He hears that the instruments of production are to be exploited in common, and, naturally, can come to no other conclusion than that the lot of being common to all will likewise fall to the women. He has not even a suspicion that the real point aimed at is to do away with the status of women as mere instruments of production.

For the rest, nothing is more ridiculous than the virtuous indignation of our bourgeois at the community of women which, they pretend, is to be openly and officially established by the Communists. The Communists have no need to introduce community of women; it has existed almost from time immemorial.

Our bourgeois, not content with having wives and daughters of their proletarians at their disposal, not to speak of common prostitutes, take the greatest pleasure in seducing each other's wives.

Bourgeois marriage is, in reality, a system of wives in common and thus, at the most, what the Communists might possibly be reproached with is that they desire to introduce, in substitution for a hypocritically concealed, an openly legalised community of women. For the rest, it is self-evident that the abolition of the present system of production must bring with it the abolition of the community of women springing from that system, i.e. of prostitution both public and private.

The Communists are further reproached with desiring to abolish countries and nationality.

The working men have no country. We cannot take from them what they have not got. Since the proletariat must first of all acquire political supremacy, must rise to be the leading class of the nation, must constitute itself *the* nation, it is, so far, itself national, though not in the bourgeois sense of the word.

National differences and antagonism between peoples are daily more and more vanishing, owing to the development of the bourgeoisie, to freedom of commerce, to the world market, to uniformity in the mode of production and in the conditions of life corresponding thereto.

The supremacy of the proletariat will cause them to vanish still faster. United action, of the leading civilised countries at least, is one of the first conditions for the emancipation of the proletariat.

In proportion as the exploitation of one individual by another will also be put an end to, the exploitation of one nation by another will also be put an end to. In proportion as the antagonism between classes within the nation vanishes, the hostility of one nation to another will come to an end.

The charges against Communism made from a religious, a philosophical and, generally, from an ideological standpoint are not deserving of serious examination.

Does it require deep intuition to comprehend that man's ideas, views, and conceptions – in one word, man's consciousness – change with every change in the conditions of his material existence, in his social relations and in his social life?

What else does the history of ideas prove than that intellectual production changes its character in proportion as material production is changed? The ruling ideas of each age have ever been the ideas of its ruling class.

When people speak of the ideas that revolutionise society, they do but express the fact that within the old society the elements of a new one have been created, and that the dissolution of the old ideas keeps even pace with the dissolution of the old conditions of existence.

When the ancient world was in its last throes, the ancient religions were overcome by Christianity. When Christian ideas succumbed in the 18th century to rationalist ideas, feudal society fought its death battle with the then revolutionary bourgeoisie. The ideas of religious liberty and freedom of conscience merely gave expression to the sway of free competition within the domain of knowledge.

'Undoubtedly,' it will be said, 'religious, moral, philosophical and juridical ideas have been modified in the course of historical development. But religion, morality, philosophy, political science and law constantly survived this change.

'There are, besides, eternal truths, such as Freedom, Justice, etc., that are common to all states of society. But Communism abolishes eternal truths, it abolishes all religion, and all morality, instead of constituting them on a new basis; it therefore acts in contradiction to all past historical experience.'

What does this accusation reduce itself to? The history of all past society has consisted in the development of class antagonisms, antagonisms that assumed different forms at different epochs.

But whatever form they may have taken, one fact is common to all past ages, namely the exploitation of one part of society by the other. No wonder, then, that the social consciousness of past ages, despite all the multiplicity and variety it displays, moves within certain common forms, or general ideas, which cannot completely vanish except with the total disappearance of class antagonisms.

The Communist revolution is the most radical rupture with traditional property relations; no wonder that its development involves the most radical rupture with traditional ideas.

But let us have done with the bourgeois objections to Communism.

We have seen above that the first step in the revolution by the working class is to raise the proletariat to the position of ruling class to win the battle of democracy. The proletariat will use its political supremacy to wrest, by degrees, all capital from the bourgeoisie, to centralise all instruments of production in the hands of the State, i.e. of the proletariat organised as the ruling class, and to increase the total productive forces as rapidly as possible.

Of course, in the beginning, this cannot be effected except by means of despotic inroads on the rights of property, and on the conditions of bourgeois production; by means of measures, therefore, which appear economically insufficient and untenable, but which, in the course of the movement, outstrip themselves, necessitate further inroads upon the old social order, and are unavoidable as a means of entirely revolutionising the mode of production.

These measures will, of course, be different in different countries. Nevertheless, in the most advanced countries, the following will be pretty generally applicable.

1. Abolition of property in land and application of all rents of land to public purposes.

2. A heavy progressive or graduated income tax.

3. Abolition of all rights of inheritance.

4. Confiscation of the property of all emigrants and rebels.

5. Centralisation of credit in the hands of the State, by means of a national bank with State capital and an exclusive monopoly.

6. Centralisation of the means of communication and transport in the hands of the State.

7. Extension of factories and instruments of production owned by the State; the bringing into cultivation of waste-lands, and the improvement of the soil generally in accordance with a common plan.

8. Equal liability of all to work. Establishment of industrial armies, especially for agriculture.

9. Combination of agriculture with manufacturing industries; gradual abolition of the distinction between town and country by a more equable distribution of the population over the country.

10. Free education for all children in public schools. Abolition of children's factory labour in its present form. Combination of education with industrial production, etc., etc.

When, in the course of development, class distinctions have disappeared, and all production has been concentrated in the hands of a vast association of the whole nation, the public power will lose its political character. Political power, properly so called, is merely the organised power of one class for oppressing another. If the proletariat during its contest with the bourgeoisie is compelled, by the force of circumstances, to organise itself as a class, if, by means of a revolution, it makes itself the ruling class and, as such, sweeps away by force the old conditions of production, then it will, along with these conditions, have swept away the conditions for the existence of class antagonisms and of classes generally, and will thereby have abolished its own supremacy as a class.

In place of the old bourgeois society, with its classes and class antagonisms, we shall have an association, in which the free development of each is the condition for the free development of all.

III. SOCIALIST AND COMMUNIST LITERATURE

1. Reactionary Socialism

A. *Feudal Socialism*

Owing to their historical position, it became the vocation of the aristocracies of France and England to write pamphlets against modern bourgeois society. In the French Revolution of July 1830, and in the English reform agitation, these aristocracies again succumbed to the hateful upstart. Thenceforth, a serious political struggle was altogether out of the question. A literary battle alone remained possible. But even in the domain of literature the old cries of the restoration period had become impossible.

In order to arouse sympathy, the aristocracy was obliged to lose sight, apparently, of its own interests, and to formulate their indictment against the bourgeoisie in the interest of the exploited working class alone. Thus the aristocracy took their revenge by singing lampoons on their new master and whispering in his ears sinister prophecies of coming catastrophe.

In this way arose feudal Socialism: half lamentation, half lampoon; half echo of the past, half menace of the future; at times, by its bitter, witty and incisive criticism, striking the bourgeoisie to the very heart's core; but always ludicrous in its effect, through total incapacity to comprehend the march of modern history.

The aristocracy, in order to rally the people to them, waved the proletarian alms-bag in front for a banner. But the people, so often as it joined them, saw on their hindquarters the old feudal coats of arms, and deserted with loud and irreverent laughter.

One section of the French Legitimists and 'Young England' exhibited this spectacle.

In pointing out that their mode of exploitation was different from that of the bourgeoisie, the feudalists forget that they exploited under circumstances and conditions that were quite different and that are now antiquated. In showing that, under their rule, the modern proletariat never existed, they forget that the modern bourgeoisie is the necessary offspring of their own form of society.

For the rest, so little do they conceal the reactionary character of their criticism that their chief accusation against the bourgeois amounts to this, that under the bourgeois regime a class is being developed which is destined to cut up root and branch the old order of society.

What they upbraid the bourgeoisie with is not so much that it creates a proletariat, as that it creates a *revolutionary* proletariat.

In political practice, therefore, they join in all coercive measures against the working class; and in ordinary life, despite their high-falutin' phrases, they stoop to pick up the golden apples dropped from the tree of industry, and to barter truth, love and honour for traffic in wool, beetroot-sugar and potato spirits.

As the parson has ever gone hand in hand with the landlord, so has Clerical Socialism with Feudal Socialism.

Nothing is easier than to give Christian asceticism a Socialist tinge. Has not Christianity declaimed against private property, against marriage, against the State? Has it not preached, in the place of these, charity and poverty, celibacy and mortification of the flesh, monastic life and Mother Church? Christian Socialism is but the holy water with which the priest consecrates the heart-burnings of the aristocrat.

B. Petty-Bourgeois Socialism

The feudal aristocracy was not the only class that was ruined by the bourgeoisie, not the only class whose conditions of existence pined and perished in the atmosphere of modern bourgeois society. The medieval burgesses and the small peasant proprietors were the precursors of the modern bourgeoisie. In those countries which are but little developed, industrially and commercially, these two classes still vegetate side by side with the rising bourgeoisie.

In countries where modern civilisation has become fully developed, a new class of petty bourgeois has been formed, fluctuating between proletariat and bourgeoisie, and ever renewing itself as a supplementary part of bourgeois society. The individual members of this class, however, are being constantly hurled down into the proletariat by the action of competition, and, as modern industry develops, they even see the moment approaching when they will completely disappear as an independent section of modern society, to be replaced, in manufactures, agriculture and commerce, by overseers, bailiffs and shopmen.

In countries like France, where the peasants constitute far more than half of the population, it was natural that writers who sided with the proletariat against the bourgeoisie should use, in their criticism of the bourgeois regime, the standard of the peasant and petty bourgeois, and from the standpoint of these intermediate classes, should take up the cudgels for the working class. Thus arose petty-bourgeois Socialism. Sismondi was the head of this school, not only in France but also in England.

This school of Socialism dissected with great acuteness the contradictions in the conditions of modern production. It laid bare the hypocritical apologies of economists. It proved, incontrovertibly, the disastrous effects of machinery and division of labour; the concentration of capital and land in a few hands; overproduction and crises; it pointed out the inevitable ruin of the petty bourgeois and peasant, the misery of the proletariat, the anarchy in production, the crying inequalities in the distribution of wealth, the industrial war of extermination between nations, the dissolution of old moral bonds, of the old family relations, of the old nationalities.

In its positive aims, however, this form of Socialism aspires either to restoring the old means of production and of exchange, and with them the old property relations, and the old society, or to cramping the modern means of production and of exchange within the framework of the old property relations that have been, and were bound to be, exploded by those means. In either case, it is both reactionary and Utopian.

Its last words are: corporate guilds for manufacture; patriarchal relations in agriculture.

Ultimately, when stubborn historical facts had dispersed all intoxicating effects of self-deception, this form of Socialism ended in a miserable hangover.

C. German or 'True' Socialism

The Socialist and Communist literature of France, a literature that originated under the pressure of a bourgeoisie in power, and that was the expression of the struggle against this power, was introduced into Germany at a time when the bourgeoisie, in that country, had just begun its contest with feudal absolutism.

German philosophers, would-be philosophers, and *beaux esprits* eagerly seized on this literature, only forgetting that when these writings immigrated from France into Germany, French social conditions had not immigrated along with them. In contact with German social conditions, this French literature lost all its immediate practical significance and assumed a purely literary aspect. Thus, to the German philosophers of the eighteenth century, the demands of the first French Revolution were nothing more than the demands of 'Practical Reason' in general, and the utterance of the will of the revolutionary French bourgeoisie signified, in their eyes, the laws of pure Will, of Will as it was bound to be, of true human Will generally.

The work of the German *literati* consisted solely in bringing the new French ideas into harmony with their ancient philosophical conscience, or rather, in annexing the French ideas without deserting their own philosophic point of view.

This annexation took place in the same way in which a foreign language is appropriated, namely by translation.

It is well known how the monks wrote silly lives of Catholic Saints *over* the manuscripts on which the classical works of ancient heathendom had been written. The German *literati* reversed this process with the profane French literature. They wrote their philosophical nonsense beneath the French original. For instance, beneath the French criticism of the economic functions of money, they wrote 'Alienation of Humanity', and beneath the French criticism of the bourgeois state they wrote 'Dethronement of the Category of the General', and so forth.

The introduction of these philosophical phrases at the back of the French historical criticisms, they dubbed 'Philosophy of Action', 'True Socialism', 'German Science of Socialism', 'Philosophical Foundation of Socialism', and so on.

The French Socialist and Communist literature was thus completely emasculated. And, since it ceased in the hands of the German to express the struggle of one class with the other, he felt conscious of having overcome 'French one-sidedness' and of representing, not true requirements, but the requirements of Truth; not the interests of the proletariat, but the interests of Human Nature, of Man in general, who belongs to no class, has no reality, who exists only in the misty realm of philosophical fantasy.

This German Socialism, which took its schoolboy task so seriously and solemnly, and extolled its poor stock-in-trade in such a mountebank fashion, meanwhile gradually lost its pedantic innocence.

The fight of the German, and, especially, of the Prussian bourgeoisie, against feudal aristocracy and absolute monarchy, in other words the liberal movement, became more earnest.

By this, the long-wished-for opportunity was offered to 'True' Socialism of confronting the political movement with the Socialist demands, of hurling the traditional anathemas against liberalism, against representative government, against bourgeois competition, bourgeois freedom of the press, bourgeois legislation, bourgeois liberty and equality, and of preaching to the masses that they had nothing to gain, and everything to lose, by this bourgeois movement. German Socialism forgot, in the nick of time, that the French criticism, whose silly echo it was, presupposed the existence of modern bourgeois society, with its corresponding economic conditions of existence, and the political constitution adapted thereto, the very things whose attainment was the object of the pending struggle in Germany.

To the absolute governments, with their following of parsons, professors, country squires and officials, it served as a welcome scarecrow against the threatening bourgeoisie.

It was a sweet finish, after the bitter pills of flogging and bullets, with which these same governments, just at that time, dosed the German working-class risings.

While this 'True' Socialism thus served the government as a weapon for fighting the German bourgeoisie, it, at the same time, directly represented a reactionary interest, the interest of the German Philistines. In Germany, the petty-bourgeois class, a relic of the sixteenth century, and since then constantly cropping up again under the various forms, is the real social basis of the existing state of things.

To preserve this class is to preserve the existing state of things in Germany. The industrial and political supremacy of the bourgeoisie threatens it with certain destruction – on the one hand, from the concentration of capital; on the other, from the rise of a revolutionary proletariat. 'True' Socialism appeared to kill these two birds with one stone. It spread like an epidemic.

The robe of speculative cobwebs, embroidered with flowers of rhetoric, steeped in the dew of sickly sentiment, this transcendental robe in which the German Socialists wrapped their sorry 'eternal truths', all skin and bone, served to wonderfully increase the sale of their goods amongst such a public.

And on its part German Socialism recognised, more and more, its own calling as the bombastic representative of the petty-bourgeois Philistine.

It proclaimed the German nation to be the model nation, and the German petty Philistine to be the typical man. To every villainous meanness of this model man, it gave a hidden, higher, Socialistic interpretation, the exact contrary of its real character. It went to the extreme length of directly opposing the 'brutally destructive' tendency of Communism, and of proclaiming its supreme and impartial contempt of all class struggles. With very few exceptions, all the so-called Socialist and Communist publications that now circulate in Germany belong to the domain of this foul and enervating literature.

2. Conservative or Bourgeois Socialism

A part of the bourgeoisie is desirous of redressing social grievances in order to secure the continued existence of bourgeois society.

To this section belong economists, philanthropists, humanitarians, improvers of the condition of the working class, organisers of charity, members of societies for the prevention of cruelty to animals, temperance fanatics, hole-and-corner reformers of every imaginable kind. This form of Socialism has, moreover, been worked out into complete systems.

We may cite Proudhon's *Philosophie de la misère* as an example of this form.

The Socialistic bourgeois want all the advantages of modern social conditions without the struggles and dangers necessarily resulting therefrom. They desire the existing state of society, minus its revolutionary and disintegrating elements. They wish for a bourgeoisie without a proletariat. The bourgeoisie naturally conceives the world in which it is supreme to be the best; and bourgeois Socialism develops this comfortable conception into various more or less complete systems. In requiring the proletariat to carry out such a system, and thereby to march straightaway into the social New Jerusalem, it requires in reality that the proletariat should remain within the bounds of existing society, but should cast away all its hateful ideas concerning the bourgeoisie.

A second, and more practical, but less systematic, form of this Socialism sought to depreciate every revolutionary movement in the eyes of the working class by showing that no mere political reform, but only a change in the material conditions of existence, in economic relations, could be of any advantage to them. By changes in the material conditions of existence, this form of Socialism, however, by no means understands abolition of the bourgeois relations of production, an abolition that can be affected only by a revolution, but administrative reforms, based on the continued existence of these relations; reforms, therefore, that in no respect affect the relations between capital and labour, but, at the best, lessen the cost, and simplify the administrative work, of bourgeois government.

Bourgeois Socialism attains adequate expression when, and only when, it becomes a mere figure of speech.

Free trade: for the benefit of the working class. Protective duties: for the benefit of the working class. Prison reform: for the benefit of the working class. This is the last word and the only seriously meant word of bourgeois Socialism.

It is summed up in the phrase: the bourgeois is a bourgeois – for the benefit of the working class.

3. Critical-Utopian Socialism and Communism

We do not here refer to that literature which, in every great modern revolution, has always given voice to the demands of the proletariat, such as the writings of Babeuf and others.

The first direct attempts of the proletariat to attain its own ends, made in times of universal excitement, when feudal society was being overthrown, necessarily failed, owing to the then undeveloped state of the proletariat, as well as to the absence of the economic conditions for its emancipation, conditions that had yet to be produced, and could be produced by the impending bourgeois epoch alone. The revolutionary literature that accompanied these first movements of the proletariat had necessarily a reactionary character. It inculcated universal asceticism and social levelling in its crudest form.

The Socialist and Communist systems, properly so called, those of Saint-Simon, Fourier, Owen, and others, spring into existence in the early undeveloped period, described above, of the struggle between proletariat and bourgeoisie.

The founders of these systems see, indeed, the class antagonisms, as well as the action of the decomposing elements in the prevailing form of society. But the proletariat, as yet in its infancy, offers to them the spectacle of a class without any historical initiative or any independent political movement.

Since the development of class antagonism keeps even pace with the development of industry, the economic situation, as they find it, does not as yet offer to them the material conditions for the emancipation of the proletariat. They therefore search after a new social science, after new social laws, that are to create these conditions.

Historical action is to yield to their personal inventive action; historically created conditions of emancipation to fantastic ones; and the gradual, spontaneous class organisation of the proletariat to an organisation of society specially contrived by these inventors. Future history resolves itself, in their eyes, into the propaganda and the practical carrying out of their social plans.

In the formation of their plans, they are conscious of caring chiefly for the interests of the working class, as being the most suffering class. Only from the point of view of being the most suffering class does the proletariat exist for them.

The undeveloped state of the class struggle, as well as their own surroundings, causes Socialists of this kind to consider themselves far superior to all class antagonisms. They want to improve the condition of every member of society, even that of the most favoured. Hence, they habitually appeal to society at large, without distinction of class; nay, by preference, to the ruling class. For how can people, when once they understand their system, fail to see in it the best possible plan of the best possible state of society?

Hence, they reject all political and especially all revolutionary action; they wish to attain their ends by peaceful means, necessarily doomed to failure and, by the force of example, to pave the way for the new social Gospel.

Such fantastic pictures of future society, painted at a time when the proletariat is still in a very undeveloped state and has but a fantastic conception of its own position, correspond with the first instinctive yearnings of that class for a general reconstruction of society.

But these Socialist and Communist publications contain also a critical element. They attack every principle of existing society. Hence, they are full of the most valuable materials for the enlightenment of the working class. The practical measures proposed in them – such as the abolition of the distinction between town and country, of the family, of the carrying on of industries for the account of private individuals, and of the wage system, the proclamation of social harmony, the conversion of the function of the State into a more superintendence of production – all these proposals point solely to the disappearance of class antagonisms which were, at that time, only just cropping up, and which, in these publications, are recognised in their earliest indistinct and undefined forms only. These proposals, therefore, are of a purely Utopian character.

The significance of Critical-Utopian Socialism and Communism bears an inverse relation to historical development. In proportion as the modern class struggle develops and takes definite shape, this fantastic standing apart from the contest, these fantastic attacks on it, lose all practical value and all theoretical justification. Therefore, although the originators of these systems were, in many respects, revolutionary, their disciples have, in every case, formed mere reactionary sects. They hold fast by the original views of their masters, in opposition to the progressive historical development of the proletariat. They, therefore, endeavour, and that consistently, to deaden the class struggle and to reconcile the class antagonisms. They still dream of experimental realisation of their social Utopias, of founding isolated 'phalanstères', of establishing 'Home Colonies', or setting up a 'Little Icaria' – duodecimo editions of the New Jerusalem – and to realise all these castles in the air, they are compelled to appeal to the feelings and purses of the bourgeois. By degrees, they sink into the category of the reactionary or conservative Socialists depicted above, differing from these only by more systematic pedantry, and by their fanatical and superstitious belief in the miraculous effects of their social science.

They, therefore, violently oppose all political action on the part of the working class; such action, according to them, can only result from blind unbelief in the new Gospel.

The Owenites in England, and the Fourierists in France, respectively, oppose the Chartists and the *Réformistes*.

IV. POSITION OF THE COMMUNISTS IN RELATION TO VARIOUS EXISTING OPPOSITION PARTIES

Section II has made clear the relations of the Communists to the existing working-class parties, such as the Chartists in England and the Agrarian Reformers in America.

The Communists fight for the attainment of the immediate aims, for the enforcement of the momentary interests of the working class; but in the movement of the present, they also represent and take care of the future of that movement. In France, the Communists ally with the Social Democrats against the conservative and radical bourgeoisie, reserving, however, the right to take up a critical position in regard to phrases and illusions traditionally handed down from the great Revolution.

In Switzerland, they support the Radicals, without losing sight of the fact that this party consists of antagonistic elements, partly of Democratic Socialists, in the French sense, partly of radical bourgeois.

In Poland, they support the party that insists on an agrarian revolution as the prime condition for national emancipation, that party which fomented the insurrection of Cracow in 1846.

In Germany, they fight with the bourgeoisie whenever it acts in a revolutionary way, against the absolute monarchy, the feudal squirearchy, and the petty bourgeoisie.

But they never cease, for a single instant, to instil into the working class the clearest possible recognition of the hostile antagonism between bourgeoisie and proletariat, in order that the German workers may straightway use, as so many weapons against the bourgeoisie, the social and political conditions that the bourgeoisie must necessarily introduce along with its supremacy, and in order that, after the fall of the reactionary classes in Germany, the fight against the bourgeoisie itself may immediately begin.

The Communists turn their attention chiefly to Germany, because that country is on the eve of a bourgeois revolution that is bound to be carried out under more advanced conditions of European civilisation and with a much more developed proletariat than that of England in the seventeenth, and France in the eighteenth century, and because the bourgeois revolution in Germany will be but the prelude to an immediately following proletarian revolution.

In short, the Communists everywhere support every revolutionary movement against the existing social and political order of things.

In all these movements, they bring to the front, as the leading question in each, the property question, no matter what its degree of development at the time.

Finally, they labour everywhere for the union and agreement of the democratic parties of all countries.

The Communists disdain to conceal their views and aims. They openly declare that their ends can be attained only by the forcible overthrow of all existing social conditions. Let the ruling classes tremble at a Communistic revolution. The proletarians have nothing to lose but their chains. They have a world to win.

Working Men of All Countries, Unite!

Mao Tse-tung
On the People's Democratic Dictatorship
(On the twenty-eighth anniversary of the Chinese Communist Party, 1949)

The first of July 1949 marks the fact that the Communist Party of China has already lived through twenty-eight years. Like a man, a political party has its childhood, youth, manhood and old age. The Communist Party of China is no longer a child or a lad in his teens but has become an adult. When a man reaches old age, he will die; the same is true of a party. When classes disappear, all instruments of class struggle – parties and the state machinery – will lose their function, cease to be necessary, therefore gradually wither away and end their historical mission; and human society will move to a higher stage. We are the opposite of the political parties of the bourgeoisie. They are afraid to speak of the extinction of classes, state power and parties. We, on the contrary, declare openly that we are striving hard to create the very conditions which will bring about their extinction. The leadership of the Communist Party and the state power of the people's dictatorship are such conditions. Anyone who does not recognize this truth is no communist. Young comrades who have not studied Marxism-Leninism and have only recently joined the Party may not yet understand this truth. They must understand it – only then can they have a correct world outlook. They must understand that the road to the abolition of classes, to the abolition of state power and to the abolition of parties is the road all mankind must take; it is only a question of time and conditions. Communists the world over are wiser than the bourgeoisie, they understand the laws governing the existence and development of things, they understand dialectics and they can see farther. The bourgeoisie does not welcome this truth because it does not want to be overthrown. To be overthrown is painful and is unbearable to contemplate for those overthrown, for example, for the Kuomintang reactionaries whom we are now overthrowing and for Japanese imperialism which we together with other peoples overthrew some time ago. But for the working class, the labouring people and the Communist Party the question is not one of being overthrown, but of working hard to create the conditions in which classes, state power and political parties will die out very naturally and mankind will enter the realm of Great Harmony. We have mentioned in passing the long-range perspective of human progress in order to explain clearly the problems we are about to discuss.

As everyone knows, our Party passed through these twenty-eight years not in peace but amid hardships, for we had to fight enemies, both foreign and domestic, both inside and outside the Party. We thank Marx, Engels, Lenin and Stalin for giving us a weapon. This weapon is not a machine-gun, but Marxism-Leninism.

In his book *'Left-Wing' Communism, an Infantile Disorder* written in 1920, Lenin described the quest of the Russians for revolutionary theory. Only after several decades of hardship and suffering did the Russians find Marxism. Many things in China were the same as, or similar to, those in Russia before the October Revolution. There was the same feudal oppression. There was similar economic and cultural backwardness. Both countries were backward, China even more so. In both countries alike, for the sake of national regeneration progressives braved hard and bitter struggles in their quest for revolutionary truth.

From the time of China's defeat in the Opium War of 1840, Chinese progressives went through untold hardships in their quest for truth from the Western countries. Hung Hsiu-chuan, Kang Yu-wei, Yen Fu and Sun Yat-sen were representative of those who had looked to the West for truth before the Communist Party of China was born. Chinese who then sought progress would read any book containing the new knowledge from the West. The number of students sent to Japan, Britain, the United States, France and Germany was amazing. At home, the imperial examinations were abolished and modern schools sprang up like bamboo shoots after a spring rain; every effort was made to learn from the West. In my youth, I too engaged in such studies. They represented the culture of Western bourgeois democracy, including the social theories and natural sciences of that period, and they were called 'the new learning' in contrast to Chinese feudal culture, which was called 'the old learning'. For quite a long time, those who had acquired the new learning felt confident that it would save China, and very few of them had any doubts on this score, as the adherents of the old learning had. Only modernization could save China, only learning from foreign countries could modernize China. Among the foreign countries, only the Western capitalist countries were then progressive, as they had successfully built modern bourgeois states. The Japanese had been successful in learning from the West, and the Chinese also wished to learn from the Japanese. The Chinese in those days regarded Russia as backward, and few wanted to learn from her. That was how the Chinese tried to learn from foreign countries in the period from the 1840s to the beginning of the 20th century.

Imperialist aggression shattered the fond dreams of the Chinese about learning from the West. It was very odd – why were the teachers always committing aggression against their pupil? The Chinese learned a good deal from the West, but they could not make it work and were never able to realize their ideals. Their repeated struggles, including such a country-wide movement as the Revolution of 1911, all ended in failure. Day by day, conditions in the country got worse, and life was made impossible. Doubts arose, increased and deepened. World War I shook the whole globe. The Russians made the October Revolution and created the world's first socialist state. Under the leadership of Lenin and Stalin, the revolutionary energy of the great proletariat and labouring people of Russia, hitherto latent and unseen by foreigners, suddenly erupted like a volcano, and the Chinese and all mankind began to see the Russians in a new light. Then, and only then, did the Chinese enter an entirely new era in their thinking and their life. They found Marxism-Leninism, the universally applicable truth, and the face of China began to change.

It was through the Russians that the Chinese found Marxism. Before the October Revolution, the Chinese were not only ignorant of Lenin and Stalin, they did not even know of Marx and Engels. The salvoes of the October Revolution brought us Marxism-Leninism. The October Revolution helped progressives in China, as throughout the world, to adopt the proletarian world outlook as the instrument for studying a nation's destiny and considering anew their own problems. Follow the path of the Russians – that was their conclusion. In 1919, the May 4th Movement took place in China. In 1921, the Communist Party of China was founded. Sun Yat-sen, in the depths of despair, came across the October Revolution and the Communist Party of China. He welcomed the October Revolution, welcomed Russian help to the Chinese and welcomed co-operation of the Communist Party of China. Then Sun Yat-sen died and Chiang Kai-shek rose to power. Over a long period of twenty-two years, Chiang Kai-shek dragged China into ever more hopeless straits. In this period, during the anti-fascist Second World War in which the Soviet Union was the main force, three big imperialist powers were knocked out, while two others were weakened. In the whole world only one big imperialist power, the United States of America, remained uninjured. But the United States faced a grave domestic crisis. It wanted to enslave the whole world; it supplied arms to help Chiang Kai-shek slaughter several million Chinese. Under the leadership of the Communist Party of China, the Chinese people, after driving out Japanese imperialism, waged the People's War of Liberation for three years and have basically won victory.

Thus Western bourgeois civilization, bourgeois democracy and the plan for a bourgeois republic have all gone bankrupt in the eyes of the Chinese people. Bourgeois democracy has given way to people's democracy under the leadership of the working class and the bourgeois republic to the people's republic. This has made it possible to achieve socialism and communism through the people's republic, to abolish classes and enter a world of Great Harmony. Kang Yu-wei wrote *Ta Tung Shu*, or the *Book of Great Harmony*, but he did not and could not find the way to achieve Great Harmony. There are bourgeois republics in foreign lands, but China cannot have a bourgeois republic because she is a country suffering under imperialist oppression. The only way is through a people's republic led by the working class.

All other ways have been tried and failed. Of the people who hankered after those ways, some have fallen, some have awakened and some are changing their ideas. Events are developing so swiftly that many feel the abruptness of the change and the need to learn anew. This state of mind is understandable and we welcome this worthy desire to learn anew.

The vanguard of the Chinese proletariat learned Marxism-Leninism after the October Revolution and founded the Communist Party of China. It entered at once into political struggles and only now, after a tortuous course of twenty-eight years, has it won basic victory. From our twenty-eight years' experience we have drawn a conclusion similar to the one Sun Yat-sen drew in his testament from his 'experience of forty years'; that is, we are deeply convinced that to win victory, 'we must arouse the masses of the people and unite in a common struggle with those nations of the world which treat us as equals'. Sun Yat-sen had a world outlook different from ours and started from a different class standpoint in studying and tackling problems; yet, in the 1920s he reached a conclusion basically the same as ours on the question of how to struggle against imperialism.

Twenty-four years have passed since Sun Yat-sen's death, and the Chinese revolution, led by the Communist Party of China, has made tremendous advances both in theory and practice and has radically changed the face of China. Up to now the principal and fundamental experience the Chinese people have gained is twofold:

(1) Internally, arouse the masses of the people. That is, unite the working class, the peasantry, the urban petty bourgeoisie and the national bourgeoisie, form a domestic united front under the leadership

of the working class, and advance from this to the establishment of a state which is a people's democratic dictatorship under the leadership of the working class and based on the alliance of workers and peasants.

(2) Externally, unite in a common struggle with those nations of the world which treat us as equals and unite with the peoples of all countries. That is, ally ourselves with the Soviet Union, with the People's Democracies and with the proletariat and the broad masses of the people in all other countries, and form an international united front.

You are leaning to one side.' Exactly. The forty years' experience of Sun Yat-sen and the twenty-eight years' experience of the Communist Party have taught us to lean to one side, and we are firmly convinced that in order to win victory and consolidate it we must lean to one side. In the light of the experiences accumulated in these forty years and these twenty-eight years, all Chinese without exception must lean either to the side of imperialism or to the side of socialism. Sitting on the fence will not do, nor is there a third road. We oppose the Chiang Kai-shek reactionaries who lean to the side of imperialism, and we also oppose the illusions about a third road.

'You are too irritating.' We are talking about how to deal with domestic and foreign reactionaries, the imperialists and their running dogs, not about how to deal with anyone else. With regard to such reactionaries, the question of irritating them or not does not arise. Irritated or not irritated, they will remain the same because they are reactionaries. Only if we draw a clear line between reactionaries and revolutionaries, expose the intrigues and plots of the reactionaries, arouse the vigilance and attention of the revolutionary ranks, heighten our will to fight and crush the enemy's arrogance can we isolate the reactionaries, vanquish them or supersede them. We must not show the slightest timidity before a wild beast. We must learn from Wu Sung on the Chingyang Ridge. As Wu Sung saw it, the tiger on Chingyang Ridge was a man-eater, whether irritated or not. Either kill the tiger or be eaten by him – one or the other.

'We want to do business.' Quite right, business will be done. We are against no one except the domestic and foreign reactionaries who hinder us from doing business. Everybody should know that it is none other than the imperialists and their running dogs, the Chiang Kai-shek reactionaries, who hinder us from doing business and also from establishing diplomatic relations with foreign countries. When we have beaten the internal and external reactionaries by uniting all domestic and international forces, we shall be able to do business and establish diplomatic relations with all foreign countries on the basis of equality, mutual benefit and mutual respect for territorial integrity and sovereignty.

Victory is possible even without international help.' This is a mistaken idea. In the epoch in which imperialism exists, it is impossible for a genuine people's revolution to win victory in any country without various forms of help from the international revolutionary forces, and even if victory were won, it could not be consolidated. This was the case with the victory and consolidation of the great October Revolution, as Lenin and Stalin told us long ago. This was also the case with the overthrow of the three imperialist powers in World War II and the establishment of the People's Democracies. And this is also the case with the present and the future of People's China. Just imagine! If the Soviet Union had not existed, if there had been no victory in the anti-fascist Second World War, if Japanese imperialism had not been defeated, if the People's Democracies had not come into being, if the oppressed nations of the East were not rising in struggle and if there were no struggle of the masses of the people against their reactionary rulers in the United States, Britain, France, Germany, Italy, Japan and other capitalist countries – if not for all these in combination, the international reactionary forces bearing down upon us would certainly be many times greater than now. In such circumstances, could we have won victory? Obviously not. And even with victory, there could be no consolidation. The Chinese people have had more than enough experience of this kind. This experience was reflected long ago in Sun Yat-sen's death-bed statement on the necessity of uniting with the international revolutionary forces.

'We need help from the British and U.S. governments.' This, too, is a naive idea in these times. Would the present rulers of Britain and the United States, who are imperialists, help a people's state? Why do these countries do business with us and, supposing they might be willing to lend us money on terms of mutual benefit in the future, why would they do so? Because their capitalists want to make money and their bankers want to earn interest to extricate themselves from their own crisis – it is not a matter of helping the Chinese people. The Communist Parties and progressive groups in these countries are urging their governments to establish trade and even diplomatic relations with us. This is goodwill, this is help, this cannot be mentioned in the same breath with the conduct of the bourgeoisie in the same countries. Throughout his life, Sun Yat-sen appealed countless times to the capitalist countries for help and got nothing but heartless rebuffs. Only once in his whole life did Sun Yat-sen receive foreign help, and that was Soviet help. Let readers refer to Dr. Sun Yat-sen's testament; his earnest advice was not to look for help from the imperialist countries but to 'unite with those nations of the world which treat us as equals'. Dr. Sun had experience; he had suffered, he had been deceived. We should remember his words and not allow ourselves to be deceived again. Internationally, we belong to the side of the anti-imperialist front headed by the Soviet Union, and so we can turn only to this side for genuine and friendly help, not to the side of the imperialist front.

'You are dictatorial.' My dear sirs, you are right, that is just what we are. All the experience the Chinese people have accumulated through several decades teaches us to enforce the people's democratic dictatorship, that is, to deprive the reactionaries of the right to speak and let the people alone have that right.

Who are the people? At the present stage in China, they are the working class, the peasantry, the urban petty bourgeoisie and the national bourgeoisie. These classes, led by the working class and the Communist Party, unite to form their own state and elect their own government; they enforce their dictatorship over the running dogs of imperialism – the landlord class and bureaucrat-bourgeoisie, as well as the representatives of those classes, the Kuomintang reactionaries and their accomplices – suppress them, allow them only to behave themselves and not to be unruly in word or deed. If they speak or act in an unruly way, they will be promptly stopped and punished. Democracy is practised within the ranks of the people, who enjoy the rights of freedom of speech, assembly, association and so on. The right to vote belongs only to the people, not to the reactionaries. The combination of these two aspects, democracy for the people and dictatorship over the reactionaries, is the people's democratic dictatorship.

Why must things be done this way? The reason is quite clear to everybody. If things were not done this way, the revolution would fail, the people would suffer, the country would be conquered.

'Don't you want to abolish state power?' Yes, we do, but not right now; we cannot do it yet. Why? Because imperialism still exists, because domestic reaction still exists, because classes still exist in our country. Our present task is to strengthen the people's state apparatus – mainly the people's army, the people's police and the people's courts – in order to consolidate national defence and protect the people's interests. Given this condition, China can develop steadily, under the leadership of the working class and the Communist Party, from an agricultural into an industrial country and from a new-democratic into a socialist and communist society, can abolish classes and realize the Great Harmony. The state apparatus, including the army, the police and the courts, is the instrument by which one class oppresses another. It is an instrument for the oppression of antagonistic classes; it is violence and not 'benevolence'. 'You are not benevolent!' Quite so. We definitely do not apply a policy of benevolence to the reactionaries and towards the reactionary activities of the reactionary classes. Our policy of benevolence is applied only within the ranks of the people, not beyond them to the reactionaries or to the reactionary activities of reactionary classes.

The people's state protects the people. Only when the people have such a state can they educate and remould themselves by democratic methods on a country-wide scale, with everyone taking part, and shake off the influence of domestic and foreign reactionaries (which is still very strong, will survive for a long time and cannot be quickly destroyed), rid themselves of the bad habits and ideas acquired in the old society, not allow themselves to be led astray by the reactionaries, and continue to advance – to advance towards a socialist and communist soci Here, the method we employ is democratic, the method of persuasion, not of compulsion. When anyone among the people breaks the law, he too should be punished, imprisoned or even sentenced to death; but this is a matter of a few individual cases, and it differs in principle from the dictatorship exercised over the reactionaries as a class.

As for the members of the reactionary classes and individual reactionaries, so long as they do not rebel, sabotage or create trouble after their political power has been overthrown, land and work will be given to them as well in order to allow them to live and remould themselves through labour into new people. If they are not willing to work, the people's state will compel them to work. Propaganda and educational work will be done among them too and will be done, moreover, with as much care and thoroughness as among the captured army officers in the past. This, too, may be called a 'policy of benevolence' if you like, but it is imposed by us on the members of the enemy classes and cannot be mentioned in the same breath with the work of self-education which we carry on within the ranks of the revolutionary people.

Such remoulding of members of the reactionary classes can be accomplished only by a state of the people's democratic dictatorship under the leadership of the Communist Party. When it is well done, China's major exploiting classes, the landlord class and the bureaucrat-bourgeoisie (the monopoly capitalist class), will be eliminated for good. There remain the national bourgeoisie; at the present stage, we can already do a good deal of suitable educational work with many of them. When the time comes to realize socialism, that is, to nationalize private enterprise, we shall carry the work of educating and remoulding them a step further. The people have a powerful state apparatus in their hands – there is no need to fear rebellion by the national bourgeoisie.

The serious problem is the education of the peasantry. The peasant economy is scattered, and the socialization of agriculture, judging by the Soviet Union's experience, will require a long time and painstaking work. Without socialization of agriculture, there can be no complete, consolidated socialism. The steps to socialize agriculture must be co-ordinated with the development of a powerful industry having state enterprise as its backbone. The state of the people's democratic dictatorship must systematically solve the problems of industrialization. Since it is not proposed to discuss economic problems in detail in this article, I shall not go into them further.

In 1924 a famous manifesto was adopted at the Kuomintang's First National Congress, which Sun Yat-sen himself led and in which Communists participated. The manifesto stated: 'The so-called democratic system in modern states is usually monopolized by the bourgeoisie and has become simply an instrument for oppressing the common people. On the other hand, the Kuomintang's Principle of Democracy means a democratic system shared by all the common people and not privately owned by the few.'

Apart from the question of who leads whom, the Principle of Democracy stated above corresponds as a general political programme to what we call People's Democracy or New Democracy. A state system which is shared only by the common people and which the bourgeoisie is not allowed to own privately – add to this the leadership of the working class, and we have the state system of the people's democratic dictatorship.

Chiang Kai-shek betrayed Sun Yat-sen and used the dictatorship of the bureaucrat-bourgeoisie and the landlord class as an instrument for oppressing the common people of China. This counter-revolutionary dictatorship was enforced for twenty-two years and has only now been overthrown by the common people of China under our leadership.

The foreign reactionaries who accuse us of practising 'dictatorship' or 'totalitarianism' are the very persons who practise it. They practise the dictatorship or totalitarianism of one class, the bourgeoisie, over the proletariat and the rest of the people. They are the very persons Sun Yat-sen spoke of as the bourgeoisie of modern states who oppress the common people. And it is from these reactionary scoundrels that Chiang Kai-shek learned his counter-revolutionary dictatorship.

Chu Hsi, a philosopher of the Sung Dynasty, wrote many books and made many remarks which are now forgotten, but one remark is still remembered, 'Deal with a man as he deals with you.' This is just what we do; we deal with the imperialists and their running dogs, the Chiang Kai-shek reactionaries, as they deal with us. That is all there is to it!

Revolutionary dictatorship and counter-revolutionary dictatorship are by nature opposites, but the former was learned from the latter. Such learning is very important. If the revolutionary people do not master this method of ruling over the counter-revolutionary classes, they will not be able to maintain their state power, domestic and foreign reaction will overthrow that power and restore its own rule over China, and disaster will befall the revolutionary people.

The people's democratic dictatorship is based on the alliance of the working class, the peasantry and the urban petty bourgeoisie, and mainly on the alliance of the workers and the peasants, because these two classes comprise 80 to 90 per cent of China's population. These two classes are the main force in overthrowing imperialism and the Kuomintang reactionaries. The transition from New Democracy to socialism also depends mainly upon their alliance.

The people's democratic dictatorship needs the leadership of the working class. For it is only the working class that is most far-sighted, most selfless and most thoroughly revolutionary. The entire history of revolution proves that without the leadership of the working class revolution fails and that with the leadership of the working class revolution triumphs. In the epoch of imperialism, in no country can any other class lead any genuine revolution to victory. This is clearly proved by the fact that the many revolutions led by China's petty bourgeoisie and national bourgeoisie all failed.

The national bourgeoisie at the present stage is of great importance. Imperialism, a most ferocious enemy, is still standing alongside us. China's modern industry still forms a very small proportion of the national economy. No reliable statistics are available, but it is estimated, on the basis of certain data, that before the War of Resistance Against Japan the value of output of modern industry constituted only about 10 per cent of the total value of output of the national economy. To counter imperialist oppression and to raise her backward economy to a higher level, China must utilize all the factors of urban and rural capitalism that are beneficial and not harmful to the national economy and the people's livelihood, and we must unite with the national bourgeoisie in common struggle. Our present policy is to regulate capitalism, not to destroy it. But the national bourgeoisie cannot be the leader of the revolution, nor should it have the chief role in state power. The reason it cannot be the leader of the revolution and should not have the chief role in state power is that the social and economic position of the national bourgeoisie determines its weakness; it lacks foresight and sufficient courage and many of its members are afraid of the masses.

Sun Yat-sen advocated 'arousing the masses of the people' or 'giving assistance to the peasants and workers'. But who is to 'arouse' them or 'give assistance' to them? Sun Yat-sen had the petty bourgeoisie and the national bourgeoisie in mind. As a matter of fact, they cannot do so. Why did forty years of revolution under Sun Yat-sen end in failure? Because in the epoch of imperialism the petty bourgeoisie and the national bourgeoisie cannot lead any genuine revolution to victory.

Our twenty-eight years have been quite different. We have had much valuable experience. A well-disciplined Party armed with the theory of Marxism-Leninism, using the method of self-criticism and linked with the masses of the people; an army under the leadership of such a Party; a united front of all revolutionary classes and all revolutionary groups under the leadership of such a Party – these are the three main weapons with which we have defeated the enemy. They distinguish us from our predecessors. Relying on them, we have won basic victory. We have travelled a tortuous road. We have struggled against opportunist deviations in our Party, both Right and 'Left'. Whenever we made serious mistakes on these three matters, the revolution suffered setbacks. Taught by mistakes and setbacks, we have become wiser and handle our affairs better. It is hard for any political party or person to avoid mistakes, but we should make as few as possible. Once a mistake is made, we should correct it, and the more quickly and thoroughly the better.

To sum up our experience and concentrate it into one point, it is: the people's democratic dictatorship under the leadership of the working class (through the Communist Party) and based upon the alliance of workers and peasants. This dictatorship must unite as one with the international revolutionary forces. This is our formula, our principal experience, our main programme.

Twenty-eight years of our Party are a long period, in which we have accomplished only one thing – we have won basic victory in the revolutionary war. This calls for celebration, because it is the people's victory, because it is a victory in a country as large as China. But we still have much work to do; to use the analogy of a journey, our past work is only the first step in a long march of ten thousand *li*. Remnants of the enemy have yet to be wiped out. The serious task of economic construction lies before us. We shall soon put aside some of the things we know well and be compelled to do things we don't know well. This means difficulties. The imperialists reckon that we will not be able to manage our economy; they are standing by and looking on, awaiting our failure.

We must overcome difficulties, we must learn what we do not know. We must learn to do economic work from all who know how, no matter who they are. We must esteem them as teachers, learning from them respectfully and conscientiously. We must not pretend to know when we do not know. We must not put on bureaucratic airs. If we dig into a subject for several months, for a year or two, for three or five years, we shall eventually master it. At first some of the Soviet Communists also were not very good at handling economic matters and the imperialists awaited their failure too. But the Communist Party of the Soviet Union emerged victorious and, under the leadership of Lenin and Stalin, it learned not only how to make the revolution but also how to carry on construction. It has built a great and splendid socialist state. The Communist Party of the Soviet Union is our best teacher and we must learn from it. The situation both at home and abroad is in our favour, we can rely fully on the weapon of the people's democratic dictatorship, unite the people throughout the country, the reactionaries excepted, and advance steadily to our goal.

Part Two

Africa's Experience

W.E.B. DuBois
The Birth of African Unity
(First published in 1947)

The idea of one Africa uniting the thought and ideals of all native peoples of the dark continent belongs to the twentieth century, and stems naturally from the West Indies and the United States. Here various groups of Africans, quite separate in origin, became so united in experience, and so exposed to the impact of a new culture, that they began to think of Africa as one idea and one land. Thus, late in the eighteenth century, when a separate Negro Church was formed in Philadelphia, it called itself 'African'; and there were various 'African' societies in many parts of the United States.

It was not, however, until 1900 that a black West Indian barrister, H. Sylvester-Williams, of Trinidad, practising in London, called together a 'Pan-African' Conference. This meeting attracted attention, put the word 'Pan-African' in the dictionaries for the first time, and had some 30 delegates, mainly from England and the West Indies, with a few coloured Americans. The Conference was welcomed by the Lord Bishop of London, and a promise was obtained from Queen Victoria through Joseph Chamberlain not to 'overlook the interests and welfare of the native races'.

This meeting had no deep roots in Africa itself, and the movement and the idea died for a generation. Then came the First World War and among African Negroes at its close there was determined agitation for the rights of Negroes throughout the world, particularly in Africa. Meetings were held, a petition was sent to President Wilson, and finally, by indirection, I secured passage on the Creel press boat, the 'Orizaba', and landed in France in December, 1918.

I went with the idea calling a 'Pan-African Congress' and trying to impress upon the members of the Peace Congress sitting at Versailles the importance of Africa in the future world. I was without credentials or influence, but the idea took on.

I tried to get a conference with President Wilson, but only got as far as Colonel House, who was sympathetic but non-committal. The Chicago

Tribune said, January 19, 1919, in a dispatch from Paris dated December 30, 1918:

> An Ethiopian Utopia, to be fashioned out of the German colonies, is the latest dream of leaders of the Negro race who are here at the invitation of the United States Government as part of the extensive entourage of the American peace delegation. Robert R. Moton, successor of the late Booker Washington as head of Tuskegee Institute, and Dr. William E.B. DuBois, Editor of the *Crisis*, are promoting a Pan-African Conference to be held here during the winter while the Peace Conference is on full blast. It is to embrace Negro leaders from America, Abyssinia, Liberia, Haiti, and the French and British colonies and other parts of the black world. Its object is to get out of the Peace Conference an effort to modernize the dark continent, and in the world reconstruction to provide international machinery looking toward the civilization of the African natives.
>
> The Negro leaders are not agreed upon any definite plan, but Dr. DuBois has mapped out a scheme which he has presented in the form of a memorandum to President Wilson. It is quite Utopian, and it has less than a Chinaman's chance of getting anywhere in the Peace Conference, but it is nevertheless interesting. As 'self-determination' is one of the words to conjure with in Paris nowadays, the Negro leaders are seeking to have it applied, if possible, in a measure to their race in Africa.
>
> Dr. DuBois sets forth that while the principle of self-determination cannot be applied to uncivilized peoples, yet the educated blacks should have some voice in the disposition of the German colonies. He maintains that in settling what is to be done with the German colonies the Peace Conference might consider the wishes of the intelligent Negroes in the colonies themselves, the Negroes of the United States and of South America and the West Indies, the Negro Governments of Abyssinia, Liberia and Haiti, the educated Negroes in French West Africa and Equatorial Africa, and in British Uganda, Nigeria, Basutoland, Swaziland, Sierra Leone, Gold Coast, Gambia and Bechuanaland and in the Union of South Africa.
>
> Dr. DuBois' dream is that the Peace Conference could form an internationalized Africa, to have as its basis the former German colonies, with their 1,000,000 square miles and 12,500,000 population.

'To this', his plan reads, 'could be added by negotiation the 800,000 square miles and 9,000,000 inhabitants of Portuguese Africa. It is not impossible that Belgium could be persuaded to add to such a State the 900,000 square miles and 9,000,000 natives of the Congo, making an international Africa with over 2,500,000 square miles of land and over 20,000,000 people.

'This Africa for the Africans could be under the guidance of international organization. The governing international commission should represent not simply Governments, but modern culture, science, commerce, social reform, and religious philanthropy. It must represent not simply the white world, but the civilized Negro world.

'With these two principles the practical policies to be followed out in the government of the new States should involve a thorough and complete system of modern education, built upon the present government, religion, and customary law of the churches. Within ten years 20,000,000 black children ought to be in school. Within a generation young Africa should know the essential outlines of modern culture. From the beginning the actual general government should use both coloured and white officials.

'We can, if we will, inaugurate on the dark continent a last great crusade for humanity. With Africa redeemed, Asia would be safe and Europe indeed triumphant.'

Members of the American delegation and associated experts assured me that no congress on this matter could be held in Paris because France was still under martial law; but the ace that I had up my sleeve was Blaise Diagne, the black deputy from Senegal and Commissaire-Général in charge of recruiting native African troops. I went to Diagne and sold him the idea of a Pan-African Congress. He consulted Clemenceau, and the matter was held up two wet, discouraging months. But finally we got permission to hold the Congress in Paris. 'Don't advertise it,' said Clemenceau, 'but go ahead.' Walter Lippmann wrote me in his crabbed hand, February 20, 1919: 'I am very much interested in your organization of the Pan-African Conference, and glad that Clemenceau has made it possible. Will you send me whatever reports you may have on the work?'

The *Dispatch*, Pittsburgh, Pennsylvania, February 16, 1919, said: 'Officials here are puzzled by the news from Paris that plans are going forward there for a Pan-African Conference to be held February 19. Acting Secretary Polk said today the State Department had been officially advised by the French Government that no such Conference would be held. It was announced recently that no passports would be issued for American delegates desiring to attend the meeting.' But at the very time that Polk was assuring American Negroes that no Congress would be held, the Congress actually assembled in Paris.

First Pan-African Congress

This Congress represented Africa partially. Of the 57 delegates from 15 countries, nine were African countries with 12 delegates. The other delegates came from the United States, which sent 16, and the West Indies with 21. Most of these delegates did not come to France for this meeting, but happened to be residing there, mainly for reasons connected with the war. America and all the colonial powers refused to issue special visas.

The Congress influenced the Peace Conference. The New York *Evening Globe*, February 22, 1919, described it as 'the first assembly of the kind in history, and has for its object the drafting of an appeal to the Peace Conference to give the Negro race of Africa a chance to develop unhindered by other races. Seated at long green tables in the council room today were Negroes in the trim uniform of American Army officers, other American coloured men in frock coats or business suits, polished French Negroes who hold public office, Senegalese who sit in the French Chamber of Deputies.'

The Congress specifically asked that the German colonies be turned over to an international organization instead of being handled by the various colonial powers. Out of this idea came the Mandates Commission. The resolutions of the Congress said in part:

(1) That the Allied and Associated Powers establish a code of law for the international protection of the natives of Africa, similar to the proposed international code for labour.

(2) That the League of Nations establish a permanent Bureau charged with the special duty of over-seeing the application of these laws to the political, social, and economic welfare of the natives.

(3) The Negroes of the world demand that hereafter the natives of Africa and the peoples of African Descent be governed according to the following principles:
    1. The land and its natural resources shall be held in trust for the natives and at all times they shall have effective ownership of as much land as they can profitably develop.
    2. Capital. The investment of capital and granting of concessions

shall be so regulated as to prevent the exploitation of the natives and the exhaustion of the natural wealth of the country. Concessions shall always be limited in time and subject to State control. The growing social needs of the natives must be regarded and the profits taxed for social and material benefit of the natives.
3. Labour: Slavery and corporal punishment shall be abolished and forced labour except in punishment for crime; and the general conditions of labour shall be prescribed and regulated by the State.
4. Education: It shall be the right of every native child to learn to read and write his own language, and the language of the trustee nation, at public expense, and to be given technical instruction in some branch of industry. The State shall also educate as large a number of natives as possible in higher technical instruction in some branch of industry. The State shall also educate as large a number of natives as possible in higher technical and cultural training and maintain a corps of native teachers ...
5. The State: The natives of Africa must have the right to participate in the Government as far as their development permits in conformity with the principle that the Government exists for the natives, and not the natives for the Government. They shall at once be allowed to participate in local and tribal government according to ancient usage, and this participation shall gradually extend, as education and experience proceeds, to the higher offices of State, to the end that, in time, Africa be ruled by consent of the Africans ... Whenever it is proven that African natives are not receiving just treatment at the hands of any State or that any State deliberately excludes its civilized citizens or subjects of Negro descent from its body politic and cultural, it shall be the duty of the League of Nations to bring the matter to the civilized World.

The New York *Herald,* Paris, February 24, 1919, said: 'There is nothing unreasonable in the programme, drafted at the Pan-African Congress which was held in Paris last week. It calls upon the Allied and Associated Powers to draw up an international code of law for the protection of the nations of Africa, and to create, as a section of the League of Nations, a permanent bureau to ensure observance of such laws and thus further the racial, political and economic interests of the natives.'

Second Pan-African Congress

The idea of Pan-Africa having been thus established, we attempted to build a real organization. We went to work first to assemble a more authentic Pan-African Congress and movement. We corresponded with Negroes in all parts of Africa and in other parts of the world, and finally arranged for a Congress to meet in London, Brussels, and Paris, in August and September, 1921. Of the hundred and thirteen delegates to this Congress, forty-one were from Africa, thirty-five from the United States, twenty-four represented Negroes living in Europe, and seven were from the West Indies. Thus the African element showed growth. They came for the most part, but not in all cases, as individuals, and more seldom as the representatives of organizations or of groups.

The Pan-African movement thus began to represent a growth and development; but it immediately ran into difficulties First of all, there was the natural reaction of war and the determination on the part of certain elements in England, Belgium, and elsewhere, to recoup their war losses by intensified exploitation of colonies. They were suspicious of native movements of any sort. Then, too, there came simultaneously another movement, stemming from the West Indies, which accounted for our small West Indian representation. This was in its way a people's movement rather than a movement of the intellectuals. It was led by Marcus Garvey, and it represented a poorly conceived but intensely earnest determination to unite the Negroes of the world, more especially in commercial enterprise. It used all the nationalist and racial paraphernalia of popular agitation, and its strength lay in its backing by the masses of West Indians and by increasing numbers of American Negroes. Its weakness lay in its demagogic leadership, its intemperate propaganda, and the natural fear which it threw into the colonial powers.

The London meetings of the Congress were held in Central Hall, opposite Westminster Abbey, August 28th and 29th, 1921. They were preceded by conference with the International Department of the English Labour Party, where the question of the relation of white and coloured labour was discussed. Beatrice Webb, Leonard Woolf, Mr Gillies, Norman Leys, and others were present.

Paul Otlet, once called Father of the League of Nations, wrote me in April, 1921: 'I am very happy to learn your decision. We can put at your disposal the Palais Mondial for your Pan-African Conference, August 31st and September 1st and 2nd.' Otlet and La Fontaine, the Belgian leaders of internationalism, welcomed the meeting warmly to Belgium, but strong opposition arose. The movement was immediately confounded by the press and others as a part of, if not the real, Garvey Movement.

The Brussels *Neptune* wrote, June 14th: 'Announcement has been made ... of a Pan-African Congress organized at the instigation of the National Association for the Advancement of Coloured People of New York. It is interesting to note that this association is directed by personages who it is said in the United States have received remuneration from Moscow (Bolsheviki). The association has already organized its propaganda in the lower Congo, and we must not be astonished if some day it causes grave difficulties in the Negro village of Kinshasa, composed of all the ne'er-do-wells of the various tribes of the Colony, aside from some hundreds of labourers.'

Nevertheless, meetings of interest and enthusiasm were held. The *Crisis* reported:

'The Congress itself was held in the marvellous Palais Mondial, the World Palace situated in the Cinquantenaire Park. We could not have asked for a better setting. But there was a difference. In the first place, there were many more white than coloured people – there are not many of us in Brussels – and it was not long before we realized that their interest was deeper, more immediately significant, than that of the white people we had found elsewhere. Many of Belgium's economic and material interests centre in Africa in the Belgian Congo. Any interference with the natives might result in an interference with the sources from which so many Belgian capitalists drew their prosperity.'

Resolutions which were passed without dissent at the meeting in London contained a statement concerning Belgium, criticizing her colonial regime although giving her credit for plans of reform for the future. This aroused bitter apposition in Brussels, and an attempt was made to substitute an innocuous statement concerning good will and investigation which Diagne declared adopted in the face of a clear majority in opposition.

At the Paris meeting the original London resolutions, with some minor corrections, were adopted. They were in part:

> To the World: The absolute equality of races, physical, political, and social, is the founding stone of world and human advancement. No one denies great differences of gift, capacity, and attainment among individuals of all races, but the voice of Science, Religion, arid practical Politics is one in denying the God-appointed existence of super-races, or of races naturally and inevitably and eternally inferior.
>
> That in the vast range of time, one group should in its industrial

technique, or social organization, or spiritual vision, lag a few hundred years behind another, or forge fitfully ahead, or come to differ decidedly in thought, deed and ideal, is proof of the essential richness and variety of human nature, rather than proof of the co-existence of demigods and apes in human form. The doctrine of racial equality does not interfere with individual liberty: rather it fulfils it. And of all the various criteria of which masses of men have in the past been prejudged and classified, that of the colour of the skin and texture of the hair is surely the most adventitious and idiotic ...

The beginning of wisdom in inter-racial contact is the establishment of political institutions among suppressed peoples. The habit of democracy must be made to encircle the earth. Despite the attempts to prove that its practice is the secret and divine gift of the few, no habit is more natural or more widely spread among primitive people, or more easily capable of development among masses. Local self-government with a minimum of help and oversight can be established tomorrow in Asia, in Africa, America, and the Isles of the sea. It will in many instances need general control and guidance, but it will fail only when that guidance seeks ignorantly and consciously its own selfish ends and not the people's liberty and good.

Surely in the twentieth century of the Prince of Peace, in the millennium of Mohammed, and in the mightiest Age of Human Reason, there can be found in the civilized world enough of altruism, yearning, and benevolence to develop native institutions whose aim is not profit and power of the few ...

What, then, do those demand who see these evils of the colour line and racial discrimination, and who believe in the divine right of suppressed and backward people to learn and aspire and be free? The Negro race through their thinking intelligentsia demand:

1. The recognition of civilized men as civilized despite their race or colour.
2. Local self-government for backward groups, deliberately rising as experience and knowledge grow to complete self-government under the limitation of a self-governed world.
3. Education in self-knowledge, in scientific truth, and in industrial technique, undivorced from the art of beauty.
4. Freedom in their own religion and social customs and with the right to be different and nonconformist.

> 5. Co-operation with the rest of the world in government, industry, and art on the bases of Justice, Freedom, and Peace.
> 6. The return to Negroes of their land and its natural fruits, and defence against the unrestrained greed of invested capital.
> 7. The establishment under the League of Nations of an international institution for study of the Negro problems.
> 8. The establishment of an international section of the Labour Bureau of the League of Nations, charged with the protection of native labour.

In some such words and thoughts as these we seek to express our will and ideal, and the end of our untiring effort. To our aid, we call all men of the earth who love justice and mercy. Out of the depths we have cried unto the deaf and dumb masters of the world. Out of the depths we cry to our own sleeping souls. The answer is written in the stars.

The whole press of Europe took notice of these meetings, and more especially of the ideas behind the meeting. Gradually they began to distinguish between the Pan-African Movement and the Garvey agitation. They praised and criticized. Sir Harry Johnston wrote: 'This is the WEAKNESS of all the otherwise grand efforts of the Coloured People in the United States to pass on their own elevation and education and political significance to the Coloured Peoples of Africa: they know so LITTLE ABOUT REAL Africa.'

Even *Punch* took a good-natured jibe (September 7th, 1921): '"A PAN AFRICAN MANIFESTO", "NO ETERNALLY INFERIOR RACES" (headlines in *The Times*) No, but in the opinion of our coloured brothers some infernally superior ones!'

The Second Pan-African Congress had sent me with a committee to interview the officials of the League of Nations in Geneva. I talked with Rappard, who headed the Mandates Commission; I saw the first meeting of the Assembly; and especially I had an interesting interview with Albert Thomas, head of the ILO. Working with Monsieur Bellegarde of Haiti, a member of the Assembly, we brought the status of Africa to the attention of the League. The League published our petition as an official document, saying in part:

> The Second Pan-African Congress wishes to suggest that the spirit of the world moves toward self-government as the ultimate aim of all men and nations, and that consequently the mandated areas, being peopled as they are so largely by black folk, have a right to ask that a man of Negro descent, properly fitted in character and

training, be appointed a member of the Mandates Commission so soon as a vacancy occurs.

The Second Pan-African Congress desires most earnestly and emphatically to ask the good offices and careful attention of the League of Nations to the condition of civilised persons of Negro descent throughout the world. Consciously and sub-consciously, there is in the world today a widespread and growing feeling that it is permissible to treat civilized men as uncivilized if they are coloured and more especially of Negro descent. The result of this attitude and many consequent laws, customs, and conventions, is that a bitter feeling of resentment, personal insult, and despair is widespread in the world among those very persons whose rise is the hope of the Negro race.

We are fully aware that the League of Nations has little, if any, direct power to adjust these matters, but it has the vast moral power of public world opinion, and as a body conceived to promote Peace and Justice among men. For this reason we ask and urge that the League of Nations take a firm stand on the absolute equality of races, and that it suggest to the colonial powers connected with the League of Nations to form an International Institute for the study of the Negro problem, and for the evolution and protection of the Negro race.

Later, Bellegarde revealed to the world the disgrace of the bombing of the African Bondelschwartz, and in retaliation was recalled by the American forces then in power in Haiti.

We sought to have these meetings result in a permanent organization. A secretariat was set up in Paris and functioned for a couple of years, but it was not successful. Just as the Garvey movement made its thesis industrial co-operation, so the new young secretary of the Pan-African movement, a coloured Paris public school teacher, wanted to combine investment and profit with the idea of Pan-Africa. He wanted American Negro capital for this end. We had other ideas.

Third Pan-African Congress
This crucial difference of aim and method between our Paris office and the American Negro interested in the movement nearly ruined the organization. The Third Pan-African Congress was called for 1923, but the Paris secretary postponed it. We persevered, and finally without proper notice or preparation, met in London and Lisbon late in the year. The

London session was small and was addressed by Harold Laski and Lord Olivier and attended by H.G. Wells. Ramsay MacDonald was kept from attending only by the pending election, but wrote: 'Anything I can do to advance the cause of your people on your recommendation, I shall always do gladly.'

The meeting of the Congress in Lisbon was more successful. Eleven countries were represented there, and especially Portuguese Africa. The Liga Africana was in charge. 'The great association of Portuguese Negroes with headquarters at Lisbon which is called the Liga Africana is an actual federation of all the indigenous associations scattered throughout the five provinces of Portuguese Africa and representing several million individuals … This Liga Africana which functions at Lisbon in the very heart of Portugal, so to speak, has a commission from all the other native organizations and knows how to express to the Government in no ambiguous terms but in a highly dignified manner all that should be said to avoid injustice or to bring about the repeal of harsh laws. That is why the Liga Africana of Lisbon is the director of the Portuguese African movement; but not only in the good sense of the word, but without making any appeal to violence and without leaving constitutional limits.'

Two former colonial ministers spoke, and the following demands were made for Africans:

1. A voice in their own government.
2. The right of access to the land and its resources.
3. Trial by juries of their peers under established forms of law.
4. Free elementary education for all; broad training in modern industrial technique; and higher training of selected talent.
5. The development of Africa for the benefit of Africans, and not merely for the profit of Europeans.
6. The abolition of the slave trade and of the liquor traffic.
7. World disarmament and the abolition of war; but failing this, and as long as white folk bear arms against black folk, the right of blacks to bear arms in their own defence.
8. The organization of commerce and industry so as to make the main objects of capital and labour the welfare of the many rather than the enriching of the few …

In fine, we ask in all the world that black folk be treated as men. We can see no other road to Peace and Progress. What more paradoxical figure today fronts the world than the official head of a great South African state striving blindly to build Peace and Good Will in Europe by standing on the necks and hearts of millions of black Africans?

From that Lisbon meeting I went to Africa for the first time, to see the land whose history and development I had so long been studying. I held from President Coolidge of the United States status as Special Minister Plenipotentiary and Envoy Extraordinary to represent him at the second inaugural of President King of Liberia.

So far, the Pan-African idea was still American rather than African, but it was growing, and it expressed a real demand for examination of the African situation and a plan of treatment from the native African point of view. With the object of moving the centre of this agitation nearer other African centres of population I planned a Fourth Pan-African Congress in the West Indies in 1925. My idea was to charter a ship and sail down the Caribbean, stopping for meetings in Jamaica, Haiti, Cuba, and the French islands. But here I reckoned without my steamship lines. At first the French Line replied that they could 'easily manage the trip', but eventually no accommodation could be found on any line except at the prohibitive price of fifty thousand dollars. I suspect that colonial powers spiked this plan.

Fourth Pan-African Congress

Two years later, in 1927, a Fourth Pan-African Congress was held in New York. Thirteen countries were represented, but direct African participation lagged. There were two hundred and eight delegates from twenty-two American states and ten foreign countries. Africa was sparsely represented by representatives from the Gold Coast, Sierra Leone, Liberia, and Nigeria. Chief Amoah III of the Gold Coast spoke; Herskovits then of Columbia, Mensching of Germany, and John Vandercook were on the programme. Negroes everywhere need:

1. A voice in their own government.
2. Native rights to the land and its natural resources.
3. Modern education for all children.
4. The development of Africa for the Africans and not merely for the profit of Europeans.
5. The reorganization of commerce and industry so as to make the main object of capital and labour the welfare of the many rather than the enriching of the few.
6. The treatment of civilized men as civilized despite difference of birth, race, or colour.

The Pan-African Movement had been losing ground since 1921. In 1929, to remedy this, we made desperate efforts to hold the Fifth Pan-African Congress on the continent of Africa itself, and selected Tunis because of its accessibility. Elaborate preparations were begun. It looked as though at last the movement was going to be geographically African. But two insuperable difficulties intervened: first, the French Government very politely but firmly informed us that the Congress could take place at Marseilles or any French city, but not in Africa; and finally, there came the Great Depression.

Fifth Pan-African Congress

The Pan-African idea died, apparently, until fifteen years afterwards, in the midst of the Second World War, when it leaped to life again in an astonishing manner. At the Trades Union Conference in London in the winter of 1945 there were black labour representatives from Africa and the West Indies. Among these, aided by coloured persons resident in England, there came a spontaneous call for the assembling of another Pan-African Congress in 1945, when the International Trades Union had their meeting in Paris.

After consultation and correspondence a Pan-African Federation was organized.

> On August eleventh and twelfth there was convened at Manchester, the headquarters of the Pan-African Federation, a Delegate Conference representing all of the organizations which have been invited to participate in the forthcoming Congress. At that ad hoc meeting a review of the preparatory work was made. From the reports it revealed that the position was as follows:
>
> A number of replies had been received from Labour, Trade Union, Co-operative, and other progressive organizations in the West Indies, West Africa, South and East Africa, in acknowledgment of the formal invitation to attend the Conference. Host of these bodies not only approved and endorsed the agenda, making minor modifications and suggestions here and there, but pledged themselves to send delegates. In cases where either the time is too short or the difficulties of transport at the present time too great to be overcome at such short notice, the organizations will give mandates to the natives of the territories concerned who are travelling to Paris to attend the World Trades Union Conference. Where territories will not be sending delegates to the Trades Union

Conference, organizations will mandate individuals already in Great Britain to represent them.

In this way we are assured of the widest representation, either through people travelling directly from the colonial areas to Britain, or individuals from those territories who are already in the British Isles. Apart from these overseas delegates, more than fourteen organizations of Africans and peoples of African descent in Great Britain and Ireland will participate in the Conference.

There is no organization in the British colonial empire which has not been invited. The philosophy behind this meeting has been expressed by the West African Students Union of London in a letter to me:

> The idea of a Congress of African nations and all peoples of African descent throughout the world is both useful and timely. Perhaps it is even long overdue. But we observe that four of such Pan-African Congresses had been held in the past, all within recent memory, and that the one at present under discussion will be the fifth. It is unfortunate that all these important conferences should have been held outside Africa, but in European capitals. This point is significant, and should deserve our careful attention ...
>
> Our Executive Committee are certainly not in favour of this or any future Pan-African Congress being held anywhere in Europe. We do rather suggest the Republic of Liberia as perhaps an ideal choice. All considerations seem to make that country the most favourable place for our Fifth Pan-African Congress. And, especially, at a time like this when Liberia is planning to celebrate the centenary of the founding of the Republic two years hence, the holding of our Congress there seems most desirable. We have good reason to believe that the Government of Liberia would welcome this idea, and would give us the encouragement and diplomatic assistance that might be necessary to ensure success.

The convening committee agrees that: 'After reviewing the situation, we do feel, like you, that our Conference should be merely a preliminary one to a greater, more representative Congress to be held some time next year, especially as a new Government has come into being in Britain since we started planning the forthcoming Conference.' But they decided to call a congress this year in Manchester, since 'it is now officially announced that the World Trades Union Conference will begin on September twenty-fifth and close on October ninth, we are planning to convene the Pan-African Congress on October fifteenth. It should last a week. This will enable the colonial delegates to get from France to England between the ninth and fifteenth of October. It will also enable us to hold some informal meetings and finish off our plans.'

Difficulties of transportation and passport restrictions may make attendance at this Congress limited. At the same time there is real hope here, that out of Africa itself, and especially out of its labouring masses, has come a distinct idea of unity in ideal and co-operation in action which will lead to a real Pan-African movement.

Singularly enough, there is another 'Pan-African' movement. I thought of it as I sat recently in San Francisco and heard Jan Smuts plead for an article on 'human rights' in the preamble of the Charter of the United Nations. It was an astonishing paradox. The Pan-African movement which he represents is a union of the white rulers of Kenya, Rhodesia, and Union of South Africa, to rule the African continent in the interest of its white investors and exploiters. This plan has been incubating since 1921, but has been discouraged by the British Colonial Office. Smuts is now pushing it again, and the white legislatures in Africa have asked for it. The San Francisco trusteeship left a door open for this sort of thing. Against this upsurges the movement of black union delegates working in co-operation with the labour delegates of Russia, Great Britain, and the United States in order to build a new world which includes black Africa. We may yet have to see Pan-Africa as a real movement.

Frantz Fanon
'The Pitfalls of National Consciousness' *from* The Wretched of the Earth
(First published in French in 1961)

History teaches us clearly that the battle against colonialism does not run straight away along the lines of nationalism. For a very long time the native devotes his energies to ending certain definite abuses: forced labour, corporal punishment, inequality of salaries, limitation of political rights, etc. This fight for democracy against the oppression of mankind will slowly leave the confusion of neo-liberal universalism to emerge, sometimes laboriously, as a claim to nationhood. It so happens that the unpreparedness of the educated classes, the lack of practical links between them and the mass of the people, their laziness, and, let it be said, their cowardice at the decisive moment of the struggle will give rise to tragic mishaps.

National consciousness, instead of being the all-embracing crystallization of the innermost hopes of the whole people, instead of being the immediate and most obvious result of the mobilization of the people, will be in any case only an empty shell, a crude and fragile travesty of what it might have been. The faults that we find in it are quite sufficient explanation of the facility with which, when dealing with young and independent nations, the nation is passed over for the race, and the tribe is preferred to the state. These are the cracks in the edifice which show the process of retrogression that is so harmful and prejudicial to national effort and national unity. We shall see that such retrograde steps with all the weaknesses and serious dangers that they entail are the historical result of the incapacity of the national middle class to rationalize popular action, that is to say their incapacity to see into the reasons for that action.

This traditional weakness, which is almost congenital to the national consciousness of under-developed countries, is not solely the result of the mutilation of the colonized people by the colonial regime. It is also the result of the intellectual laziness of the national middle class, of its spiritual penury, and of the profoundly cosmopolitan mould that its mind is set in.

The national middle class which takes over power at the end of the colonial regime is an under-developed middle class. It has practically no economic power, and in any case it is in no way commensurate with the bourgeoisie of the mother country which it hopes to replace. In its wilful narcissism, the national middle class is easily convinced that it can advantageously replace the middle class of the mother country. But that same independence which literally drives it into a corner will give rise within its ranks to catastrophic reactions, and will oblige it to send out frenzied appeals for help to the former mother country. The university and merchant classes which make up the most enlightened section of the new state are in fact characterized by the smallness of their number and their being concentrated in the capital, and the type of activities in which they are engaged: business, agriculture and the liberal professions. Neither financiers nor industrial magnates are to be found within this national middle class. The national bourgeoisie of under-developed countries is not engaged in production, nor in invention, nor building, nor labour; it is completely canalized into activities of the intermediary type. Its innermost vocation seems to be to keep in the running and to be part of the racket. The psychology of the national bourgeoisie is that of the businessman, not that of a captain of industry; and it is only too true that the greed of the settlers and the system of embargoes set up by colonialism has hardly left them any other choice.

Under the colonial system, a middle class which accumulates capital is an impossible phenomenon. Now, precisely, it would seem that the historical vocation of an authentic national middle class in an under-developed country is to repudiate its own nature in so far as it is bourgeois, that is to say in so far as it is the tool of capitalism, and to make itself the willing slave of that revolutionary capital which is the people.

In an under-developed country an authentic national middle class ought to consider as its bounden duty to betray the calling fate has marked out for it, and to put itself to school with the people: in other words to put at the people's disposal the intellectual and technical capital that it has snatched when going through the colonial universities. But unhappily we shall see that very often the national middle class does not follow this heroic, positive, fruitful and just path; rather, it disappears with its soul set at peace into the shocking ways – shocking because anti-national – of a traditional bourgeoisie, of a bourgeoisie which is stupidly, contemptibly, cynically bourgeois.

The objective of nationalist parties as from a certain given period is, we have seen, strictly national. They mobilize the people with slogans of independence, and for the rest leave it to future events. When such parties are questioned on the economic programme of the state that they are clamouring for, or on the nature of the regime which they propose to install, they are incapable of replying, because, precisely, they are completely ignorant of the economy of their own country.

This economy has always developed outside the limits of their knowledge. They have nothing more than an approximate, bookish acquaintance with the actual and potential resources of their country's soil and mineral deposits; and therefore they can only speak of these resources on a general and abstract plane. After independence this under-developed middle class, reduced in numbers and without capital, which refuses to follow the path of revolution, will fall into deplorable stagnation. It is unable to give free rein to its genius, which formerly it was wont to lament, though rather too glibly, was held in check by colonial domination. The precariousness of its resources and the paucity of its managerial class force it back for years into an artisan economy. From its point of view, which is inevitably a very limited one, a national economy is an economy based on what may be called local products. Long speeches will be made about the artisan class. Since the middle classes find it impossible to set up factories that would be more profit-earning both for themselves and for the country as a whole, they will surround the artisan class with a chauvinistic tenderness in keeping with the new awareness of national dignity, and which moreover will bring them in quite a lot of money. This cult of local products and this incapability to seek out new systems of management will be equally manifested by the bogging down of the national middle class in the methods of agricultural production which were characteristic of the colonial period.

The national economy of the period of independence is not set on a new footing. It is still concerned with the ground-nut harvest, with the cocoa crop and the olive yield. In the same way there is no change in the marketing of basic products, and not a single industry is set up in the country. We go on sending out raw materials; we go on being Europe's small farmers who specialize in unfinished products.

Yet the national middle class constantly demands the nationalization of the economy and of the trading sectors. This is because, from their point of view, nationalization does not mean placing the whole economy at the service of the nation and deciding to satisfy the needs of the nation. For them, nationalization does not mean governing the state with regard to the new social relations whose growth it has been decided to encourage. To them, nationalization quite simply means the transfer into native hands of those unfair advantages which are a legacy of the colonial period.

Since the middle class has neither sufficient material nor intellectual resources (by intellectual resources we mean engineers and technicians), it limits its claims to the taking over of business offices and commercial houses formerly occupied by the settlers. The national bourgeoisie steps into the shoes of the former European settlement: doctors, barristers, traders, commercial travellers, general agents and transport agents. It considers that the dignity of the country and its own welfare require that it should occupy all these posts. From now on it will insist that all the big foreign companies should pass through its hands, whether these companies wish to keep on their connections with the country, or to open it up. The national middle class discovers its historic mission: that of intermediary.

Seen through its eyes, its mission has nothing to do with transforming the nation; it consists, prosaically, of being the transmission line between the nation and a capitalism, rampant though camouflaged, which today puts on the mask of neocolonialism. The national bourgeoisie will be quite content with the role of the Western bourgeoisie's business agent, and it will play its part without any complexes in a most dignified manner. But this same lucrative role, this cheap-jack's function, this meanness of outlook and this absence of all ambition symbolize the incapability of the national middle class to fulfil its historic role of bourgeoisie. Here, the dynamic, pioneer aspect, the characteristics of the inventor and of the discoverer of new worlds which are found in all national bourgeoisies, are lamentably absent. In the colonial countries, the spirit of indulgence is dominant at the core of the bourgeoisie; and this is because the national bourgeoisie identifies itself with the Western bourgeoisie, from whom it has learnt its lessons. It follows the Western bourgeoisie along its path of negation and decadence without ever having emulated it in its first stages of exploration and invention, stages which are an acquisition of that Western bourgeoisie whatever the circumstances. In its beginnings, the national bourgeoisie of the colonial countries identifies itself with the decadence of the bourgeoisie of the West. We need not think that it is jumping ahead; it is in fact beginning at the end. It is already senile before it has come to know the petulance, the fearlessness or the will to succeed of youth ...

The racial prejudice of the young national bourgeoisie is a racism of defence, based on fear. Essentially it is no different from vulgar tribalism, or the rivalries between septs or confraternities. We may understand why keen-witted international observers have hardly taken seriously the great flights of oratory about African unity, for it is true that there are so many cracks in that unity visible to the naked eye that it is only reasonable to insist that all these contradictions ought to be resolved before the day of unity can come.

The people of Africa have only recently come to know themselves. They have decided, in the name of the whole continent, to weigh in strongly against the colonial regime. Now the nationalist bourgeoisies, who in region after region hasten to make their own fortunes and to set up a national system of exploitation, do their utmost to put obstacles in the path of this 'Utopia'. The national bourgeoisies, who are quite clear as to what their objectives are, have decided to bar the way to that unity, to that coordinated effort on the part of two hundred and fifty million men to triumph over stupidity, hunger and inhumanity at one and the same time. This is why we must understand that African unity can only be achieved through the upward thrust of the people, and under the leadership of the people, that is to say, in defiance of the interests of the bourgeoisie.

As regards internal affairs and in the sphere of institutions, the national bourgeoisie will give equal proof of its incapacity. In a certain number of under-developed countries the parliamentary game is faked from the beginning. Powerless economically, unable to bring about the existence of coherent social relations, and standing on the principle of its domination as a class, the bourgeoisie chooses the solution that seems to it the easiest, that of the single party. It does not yet have the quiet conscience and the calm that economic power and the control of the state machine alone can give. It does not create a state that reassures the ordinary citizen, but rather one that rouses his anxiety.

The state, which by its strength and discretion ought to inspire confidence and disarm and lull everybody to sleep, on the contrary seeks to impose itself in spectacular fashion. It makes a display, it jostles people and bullies them, thus intimating to the citizen that he is in continual danger. The single party is the modern form of the dictatorship of the bourgeoisie, unmasked, unpainted, unscrupulous and cynical.

It is true that such a dictatorship does not go very far. It cannot halt the processes of its own contradictions. Since the bourgeoisie has not the economic means to ensure its domination and to throw a few crumbs to the rest of the country; since, moreover, it is preoccupied with filling its pockets as rapidly as possible but also as prosaically as possible, the country sinks all the more deeply into stagnation. And in order to hide this stagnation and to mask this regression, to reassure itself and to give itself something to boast about, the bourgeoisie can find nothing better to do than to erect grandiose buildings in the capital and to lay out money on what are called prestige expenses.

The national bourgeoisie turns its back more and more on the interior and on the real facts of its undeveloped country, and tends to look towards the former mother country and the foreign capitalists who count on its obliging compliance. As it does not share its profits with the people and in no way allows them to enjoy any of the dues that are paid to it by the big foreign companies, it will discover the need for a popular leader to whom will fall the dual role of stabilizing the regime and of perpetuating the domination of the bourgeoisie. The bourgeois dictatorship of underdeveloped countries draws its strength from the existence of a leader. We know that in the well-developed countries the bourgeois dictatorship is the result of the economic power of the bourgeoisie. In the under-developed countries, on the contrary, the leader stands for moral power, in whose shelter the thin and poverty-stricken bourgeoisie of the young nation decides to get rich.

The people who for years on end have seen this leader and heard him speak, who from a distance in a kind of dream have followed his contests with the colonial power, spontaneously put their trust in this patriot. Before independence, the leader generally embodies the aspirations of the people for independence, political liberty and national dignity. But as soon as independence is declared, far from embodying in concrete form the needs of the people in what touches bread, land and the restoration of the country to the sacred hands of the people, the leader will reveal his inner purpose: to become the general president of that company of profiteers impatient for their returns which constitutes the national bourgeoisie.

In spite of his frequently honest conduct and his sincere declarations, the leader as seen objectively is the fierce defender of these interests, today combined, of the national bourgeoisie and the ex-colonial companies. His honesty, which is his soul's true bent, crumbles away little by little. His contact with the masses is so unreal that he comes to believe that his authority is hated and that the services that he has rendered his country are being called in question. The leader judges the ingratitude of the masses harshly, and every day that passes ranges himself a little more resolutely on the side of the exploiters. He therefore knowingly becomes the aider and abettor of the young bourgeoisie which is plunging into the mire of corruption and pleasure.

The economic channels of the young state sink back inevitably into neo-colonialist lines. The national economy, formerly protected, is today literally controlled. The budget is balanced through loans and gifts, while every three or four months the chief ministers themselves or else their governmental delegations come to the erstwhile mother countries or elsewhere, fishing for capital.

The former colonial power increases its demands, accumulates concessions and guarantees, and takes fewer and fewer pains to mask the hold it has over the national government. The people stagnate deplorably in unbearable poverty; slowly they awaken to the unutterable treason of their leaders. This awakening is all the more acute in that the bourgeoisie is incapable of learning its lesson. The distribution of wealth that it effects is not spread out between a great many sectors; it is not ranged among different levels, nor does it set up a hierarchy of half-tones. The new caste is an affront all the more disgusting in that the immense majority, nine-tenths of the population, continue to die of starvation. The scandalous enrichment, speedy and pitiless, of this caste is accompanied by a decisive awakening on the part of the people, and a growing awareness that promises stormy days to come. The bourgeois caste, that section of the nation which annexes for its own profit all the wealth of the country, by a kind of unexpected logic will pass disparaging judgements upon the other Negroes and the other Arabs that more often than not are reminiscent of the racist doctrines of the former representatives of the colonial power. At one and the same time the poverty of the people, the immoderate money-making of the bourgeois caste, and its widespread scorn for the rest of the nation will harden thought and action.

But such threats will lead to the re-affirmation of authority and the appearance of dictatorship. The leader, who has behind him a lifetime of political action and devoted patriotism, constitutes a screen between the people and the rapacious bourgeoisie since he stands surety for the ventures of that caste and closes his eyes to their insolence, their mediocrity and their fundamental immorality. He acts as a braking-power on the awakening consciousness of the people. He comes to the aid of the bourgeois caste and hides his manoeuvres from the people, thus becoming the most eager worker in the task of mystifying and bewildering the masses. Every time he speaks to the people he calls to mind his often heroic life, the struggles he has led in the name of the people and the victories in their name he has achieved, thereby intimating clearly to the masses that they ought to go on putting their confidence in him. There are plenty of examples of African patriots who have introduced into the cautious political advance of their elders a decisive style characterized by its nationalist outlook. These men came from the backwoods, and they proclaimed, to the scandal of the dominating power and the shame of the nationals of the capital, that they came from the backwoods and that they spoke in the name of the Negroes. These men, who have sung the praises of their race, who have taken upon themselves the whole burden of the past, complete with cannibalism and degeneracy, find themselves today, alas, at the head of a team of administrators who turn their back on the jungle and who proclaim that the vocation of their people is to obey, to go on obeying and to be obedient till the end of time.

The leader pacifies the people. For years on end after independence has been won, we see him, incapable of urging on the people to a concrete task, unable really to open the future to them or of flinging them into the path of national reconstruction, that is to say, of their own reconstruction; we see him reassessing the history of independence and recalling the sacred unity of the struggle for liberation. The leader, because he refuses to break up the national bourgeoisie, asks the people to fall back into the past and to become drunk on the remembrance of the epoch which led up to independence. The leader, seen objectively, brings the people to a halt and persists in either expelling them from history or preventing them from taking root in it. During the struggle for liberation the leader awakened the people and promised them a forward march, heroic and unmitigated. Today, he uses every means to put them to sleep, and three or four times a year asks them to remember the colonial period and to look back on the long way they have come since then.

Now it must be said that the masses show themselves totally incapable of appreciating the long way they have come. The peasant who goes on scratching out a living from the soil, and the unemployed man who never finds employment, do not manage, in spite of public holidays and flags, new and brightly-coloured though they may be, to convince themselves that anything has really changed in their lives. The bourgeoisie who are in power vainly increase the number of processions; the masses have no illusions. They are hungry; and the police officers, though now they are Africans, do not serve to reassure them particularly. The masses begin to sulk; they turn away from this nation in which they have been given no place and begin to lose interest in it.

From time to time, however, the leader makes an effort; he speaks on the radio or makes a tour of the country to pacify the people, to calm them and bemuse them. The leader is all the more necessary in that there is no party. During the period of the struggle for independence there was one right enough, a party led by the present leader. But since then this party has sadly disintegrated; nothing is left but the shell of a party, the name, the emblem and the motto. The living party, which ought to make possible the free exchange of ideas which have been elaborated according to the real needs of the mass of the people, has been transformed into a trade union of individual interests. Since the proclamation of independence the party no longer helps the people to set out its demands, to become more aware of its needs and better able to establish its power. Today, the party's mission is to deliver to the people the instructions which issue from the summit. There no longer exists the fruitful give-and-take from the bottom to the top and from the top to the bottom which creates and guarantees democracy in a party. Quite on the contrary, the party has made itself into a screen between the masses and the leaders. There is no longer any party life, for the branches which were set up during the colonial period are today completely demobilized.

The militant champs on his bit. Now it is that the attitude taken up by certain militants during the struggle for liberation is seen to be justified, for the fact is that in the thick of the fight more than a few militants asked the leaders to formulate a dogma, to set out their objectives and to draw up a programme. But under the pretext of safeguarding national unity, the leaders categorically refused to attempt such a task. The only worthwhile dogma, it was repeatedly stated, is the union of the nation against colonialism. And on they went, armed with an impetuous slogan which stood for principles, while their only ideological activity took the form of a series of variants on the theme of the right of peoples to self-determination, borne on the wind of history which would inevitably sweep away colonialism. When the militants asked whether the wind of history couldn't be a little more clearly analysed, the leaders gave them instead hope and trust, the necessity of decolonization and its inevitability, and more to that effect.

After independence, the party sinks into an extraordinary lethargy. The militants are only called upon when so-called popular manifestations are afoot, or international conferences, or independence celebrations. The local party leaders are given administrative posts, the party becomes an administration, and the militants disappear into the crowd and take the empty title of citizen. Now that they have fulfilled their historical mission of leading the bourgeoisie to power, they are firmly invited to retire so that the bourgeoisie may carry out *its* mission in peace and quiet. But we have seen that the national bourgeoisie of under-developed countries is incapable of carrying out any mission whatsoever. After a few years, the break-up of the party becomes obvious, and any observer, even the most superficial, can notice that the party, today the skeleton of its former self, only serves to immobilize the people. The party, which during the battle had drawn to itself the whole nation, is falling to pieces. The intellectuals, who on the eve of independence rallied to the party, now make it clear by their attitude that they gave their support with no other end in view than to secure their slices of the cake of independence. The party is becoming a means of private advancement.

There exists inside the new regime, however, an inequality in the acquisition of wealth and in monopolization. Some have a double source of income and demonstrate that they are specialized in opportunism. Privileges multiply and corruption triumphs, while morality declines. Today the vultures are too numerous and too voracious in proportion to the lean spoils of the national wealth. The party, a true instrument of power in the hands of the bourgeoisie, reinforces the machine, and ensures that the people are hemmed in and immobilized. The party helps the government to hold the people down. It becomes more and more clearly anti-democratic, an implement of coercion. The party is objectively, sometimes subjectively, the accomplice of the merchant bourgeoisie. In the same way that the national bourgeoisie conjures away its phase of construction in order to throw itself into the enjoyment of its wealth, in parallel fashion in the institutional sphere it jumps the parliamentary phase and chooses a dictatorship of the national-socialist type. We know today that this fascism at high interest which has triumphed for half a century in Latin America is the dialectic result of states which were semi-colonial during the period of independence.

In these poor, under-developed countries, where the rule is that the greatest wealth is surrounded by the greatest poverty, the army and the police constitute the pillars of the regime; an army and a police force (another rule which must not be forgotten) which are advised by foreign experts. The strength of the police force and the power of the army are proportionate to the stagnation in which the rest of the nation is sunk. By dint of yearly loans, concessions are snatched up by foreigners; scandals are numerous, ministers grow rich, their wives doll themselves up, the members of parliament feather their nests and there is not a soul down to the simple policeman or the customs officer who does not join in the great procession of corruption ...

It is clear that the national bourgeoisie hardly worries at all about such an indictment. With its wave-lengths tuned in to Europe, it continues firmly and resolutely to make the most of the situation. The enormous profits which it derives from the exploitation of the people are exported to foreign countries. The young national bourgeoisie is often more suspicious of the regime that it has set up than are the foreign companies. The national bourgeoisie refuses to invest in its own country and behaves towards the state that protects and nurtures it with, it must be remarked, astonishing ingratitude. It acquires foreign securities in the European markets, and goes off to spend the week-end in Paris or Hamburg. The behaviour of the national bourgeoisie of certain under-developed countries is reminiscent of the members of a gang, who after every hold-up hide their share in the swag from the other members who are their accomplices and prudently start thinking about their retirement. Such behaviour shows that more or less consciously the national bourgeoisie is playing to lose if the game goes on too long.

They guess that the present situation will not last indefinitely but they intend to make the most of it. Such exploitation and such contempt for the state, however, inevitably give rise to discontent among the mass of the people. It is in these conditions that the regime becomes harsher. In the absence of a parliament it is the army that becomes the arbiter: but sooner or later it will realize its power and will hold over the government's head the threat of a manifesto.

As we see it, the national bourgeoisie of certain under-developed countries has learned nothing from books. If they had looked closer at the Latin American countries they doubtless would have recognized the dangers which threaten them. We may thus conclude that this bourgeoisie in miniature that thrusts itself into the forefront is condemned to mark time, accomplishing nothing. In under-developed countries the bourgeois phase is impossibly arid. Certainly, there is a police dictatorship and a profiteering caste, but the construction of an elaborate bourgeois society seems to be condemned to failure. The ranks of decked-out profiteers, whose grasping hands scrape up the bank-notes from a poverty-stricken country, will sooner or later be men of straw in the hands of the army, cleverly handled by foreign experts. In this way the former mother country practises indirect government, both by the bourgeoisie that it upholds and also by the national army led by its experts, an army that pins the people down, immobilizing and terrorizing them.

The observations that we have been able to make about the national bourgeoisie bring us to a conclusion which should cause no surprise. In under-developed countries, the bourgeoisie should not be allowed to find the conditions necessary for its existence and its growth. In other words, the combined effort of the masses led by a party and of intellectuals who are highly conscious and armed with revolutionary principles ought to bar the way to this useless and harmful middle class.

The theoretical question that for the last fifty years has been raised whenever the history of under-developed countries is under discussion – whether or not the bourgeois phase can be skipped – ought to be answered in the field of revolutionary action, and not by logic. The bourgeois phase in under-developed countries can only justify itself in so far as the national bourgeoisie has sufficient economic and technical strength to build up a bourgeois society, to create the conditions necessary for the development of a large-scale proletariat, to mechanize agriculture and finally to make possible the existence of an authentic national culture.

A bourgeoisie similar to that which developed in Europe is able to elaborate an ideology and at the same time strengthen its own power. Such a bourgeoisie, dynamic, educated and secular, has fully succeeded in its undertaking of the accumulation of capital and has given to the nation a minimum of prosperity. In under-developed countries, we have seen that no true bourgeoisie exists; there is only a sort of little greedy caste, avid and voracious, with the mind of a huckster, only too glad to accept the dividends that the former colonial power hands out to it. This get-rich-quick middle class shows itself incapable of great ideas or of inventiveness. It remembers what it has read in European textbooks and imperceptibly it becomes not even the replica of Europe, but its caricature.

The struggle against the bourgeoisie of under-developed countries is far from being a theoretical one. It is not concerned with making out its condemnation as laid down by the judgement of history. The national bourgeoisie of under-developed countries must not be opposed because it threatens to slow down the total, harmonious development of the nation. It must simply be stoutly opposed because, literally, it is good for nothing. This bourgeoisie, expressing its mediocrity in its profits, its achievements and in its thought, tries to hide this mediocrity by buildings which have prestige value at the individual level, by chromium plating on big American cars, by holidays on the Riviera and week-ends in neon-lit night-clubs.

This bourgeoisie, which turns its back more and more on the people as a whole, does not even succeed in extracting spectacular concessions from the West, such as investments which would be of value for the country's economy or the setting up of certain industries. On the contrary, assembly plants spring up and consecrate the type of neo-colonialist industrialization in which the country's economy flounders. Thus it must not be said that the national bourgeoisie retards the country's evolution, that it makes it lose time or that it threatens to lead the nation up blind alleys. In fact, the bourgeois phase in the history of under-developed countries is a completely useless phase. When this caste has vanished, devoured by its own contradictions, it will be seen that nothing new has happened since independence was proclaimed, and that everything must be started again from scratch. The change-over will not take place at the level of the structures set up by the bourgeoisie during its reign, since that caste has done nothing more than take over unchanged the legacy of the economy, the thought and the institutions left by the colonialists.

It is all the easier to neutralize this bourgeois class in that, as we have seen, it is numerically, intellectually and economically weak. In the colonized territories, the bourgeois caste draws its strength after independence chiefly from agreements reached with the former colonial power. The national bourgeoisie has all the more opportunity to take over from the oppressor since it has been given time for a leisurely *tête-à-tête* with the ex-colonial power. But deep-rooted contradictions undermine the ranks of that bourgeoisie; it is this that gives the observer an impression of instability. There is not as yet a homogeneity of caste. Many intellectuals, for example, condemn this regime based on the domination of the few. In under-developed countries, there are certain members of the elite, intellectuals and civil servants, who are sincere, who feel the necessity for a planned economy, the outlawing of profiteers and the strict prohibition of attempts at mystification. In addition, such men fight in a certain measure for the mass participation of the people in the ordering of public affairs.

In those under-developed countries which accede to independence, there almost always exists a small number of honest intellectuals, who have no very precise ideas about politics, but who instinctively distrust the race for positions and pensions which is symptomatic of the early days of independence in colonized countries. The personal situation of these men (bread-winners of large families) or their background (hard struggles and a strictly moral upbringing) explain their manifest contempt for profiteers and schemers. We must know how to use these men in the decisive battle that we mean to engage upon which will lead to a healthier outlook for the nation. Closing the road to the national bourgeoisie is, certainly, the means whereby the vicissitudes of new-found independence may be avoided, and with them the decline of morals, the installing of corruption within the country, economic regression, and the immediate disaster of an anti-democratic regime depending on force and intimidation. But it is also the only means towards progress.

What holds up the taking of a decision by the profoundly democratic elements of the young nation and adds to their timidity is the apparent strength of the bourgeoisie. In newly independent under-developed countries, the whole of the ruling class swarms into the towns built by colonialism. The absence of any analysis of the total population induces onlookers to think that there exists a powerful and perfectly organized bourgeoisie. In fact, we know today that the bourgeoisie in under-developed countries is non-existent. What creates a bourgeoisie is not the bourgeois spirit, nor its taste or manners, nor even its aspirations. The bourgeoisie is above all the direct product of precise economic conditions.

Now, in the colonies, the economic conditions are conditions of a foreign bourgeoisie. Through its agents, it is the bourgeoisie of the mother country that we find present in the colonial towns. The bourgeoisie in the colonies is, before independence, a Western bourgeoisie, a true branch of the bourgeoisie of the mother country, that derives its legitimacy, its force and its stability from the bourgeoisie of the homeland. During the period of unrest that precedes independence, certain native elements, intellectuals and traders, who live in the midst of that imported bourgeoisie, try to identify themselves with it. A permanent wish for identification with the bourgeois representatives of the mother country is to be found among the native intellectuals and merchants ...

From the beginning the national bourgeoisie directs its efforts towards activities of the intermediary type. The basis of its strength is found in its aptitude for trade and small business enterprises, and in securing commissions. It is not its money that works, but its business acumen. It does not go in for investments and it cannot achieve that accumulation of capital necessary to the birth and blossoming of an authentic bourgeoisie. At that rate it would take centuries to set on foot an embryonic industrial revolution, and in any case it would find the way barred by the relentless opposition of the former mother country, which will have taken all precautions when setting up neo-colonialist trade conventions.

If the government wants to bring the country out of its stagnation and set it well on the road towards development and progress, it must first and foremost nationalize the middle-man's trading sector. The bourgeoisie, who wish to see both the triumph of the spirit of money-making and the enjoyment of consumer goods, and at the same time the triumph of their contemptuous attitude towards the mass of the people and the scandalous aspect of profit-making (should we not rather call it robbery?), in fact invest largely in this sector. The intermediary market, which formerly was dominated by the settlers, will be invaded by the young national bourgeoisie. In a colonial economy the intermediary sector is by far the most important. If you want to progress, you must decide in the first few hours to nationalize this sector. But it is clear that such a nationalization ought not to take on a rigidly state-controlled aspect. It is not a question of placing at the head of these services citizens who have had no political education. Every time such a procedure has been adopted it has been seen that the government has in fact contributed to the triumph of a dictatorship of civil servants who had been set in the mould of the former mother country, and who quickly showed themselves incapable of thinking in terms of the nation as a whole. These civil servants very soon began to sabotage the national economy and to throw its structure out of joint; under them, corruption, prevarication, the diversion of stocks and the black market came to stay. Nationalizing the intermediary sector means organizing wholesale and retail cooperatives on a democratic basis; it also means decentralizing these cooperatives by getting the mass of the people interested in the ordering of public affairs. You will not be able to do all this unless you give the people some political education. Previously, it was realized that this key problem should be clarified once and for all. Today, it is true that the principle of the political education of the masses is generally subscribed to in under-developed countries. But it does not seem that this primordial task is really taken to heart. When people stress the need to educate the people politically, they decide to point out at the same time that they want to be supported by the people in the action that they are taking. A government which declares that it wishes to educate the people politically thus expresses its desire to govern with the people and for the people. It ought not to speak a language destined to camouflage a bourgeois administration. In the capitalist countries, the bourgeois governments have long since left this infantile stage of authority behind. To put it bluntly, they govern with the help of their laws, their economic strength and their police. Now that their power is firmly established they no longer need to lose time in striking demagogic attitudes. They govern in their own interests, and they have the courage of their own strength. They have created legitimacy, and they are strong in their own right.

The bourgeois caste in newly independent countries have not yet the cynicism or the unruffled calm which are founded on the strength of long-established bourgeoisies. From this springs the fact that they show a certain anxiety to hide their real convictions, to side-track, and in short to set themselves up as a popular force. But the inclusion of the masses in politics does not consist in mobilizing three or four times a year ten thousand or a hundred thousand men and women. These mass meetings and spectacular gatherings are akin to the old tactics that date from before independence, whereby you exhibited your forces in order to prove to yourself and to others that you had the people behind you. The political education of the masses proposes not to treat the masses as children but to make adults of them.

This brings us to consider the role of the political party in an under-developed country. We have seen in the preceding pages that very often simple souls, who moreover belong to the newly born bourgeoisie, never stop repeating that in an under-developed country the direction of affairs by a strong authority, in other words a dictatorship, is a necessity. With this in view the party is given the task of supervising the masses. The party plays understudy to the administration and the police, and controls the masses, not in order to make sure that they really participate in the business of governing the nation, but in order to remind them constantly that the government expects from them obedience and discipline. That famous dictatorship, whose supporters believe that it is called for by the historical process and consider it an indispensable prelude to the dawn of independence, in fact symbolizes the decision of the bourgeois caste to govern the under-developed country first with the help of the people, but soon against them. The progressive transformation of the party into an information service is the indication that the government holds itself more and more on the defensive. The incoherent mass of the people is seen as a blind force that must be continually held in check either by mystification or by the fear inspired by the police force. The party acts as a barometer and as an information service. The militant is turned into an informer. He is entrusted with punitive expeditions against the villages. The embryo opposition parties are liquidated by beatings and stonings. The opposition candidates see their houses set on fire. The police increase their provocations. In these conditions, you may be sure, the party is unchallenged and 99.99 per cent of the votes are cast for the government candidate. We should add that in Africa a certain number of governments actually behave in this way. All the opposition parties, which moreover are usually progressive and would therefore tend to work for the greater influence of the masses in the conduct of public matters, and who desire that the proud, money-making bourgeoisie should be brought to heel, have been by dint of baton charges and prisons condemned first to silence and then to a clandestine existence.

The political party in many parts of Africa which are today independent is puffed up in a most dangerous way. In the presence of a member of the party, the people are silent, behave like a flock of sheep and publish panegyrics in praise of the government of the leader. But in the street when evening comes, away from the village, in the cafés or by the river, the bitter disappointment of the people, their despair but also their unceasing anger makes itself heard. The party, instead of welcoming the expression of popular discontentment, instead of taking for its fundamental purpose the free flow of ideas from the people up to the government, forms a screen, and forbids such ideas. The party leaders behave like common sergeant-majors, frequently reminding the people of the need for 'silence in the ranks'. This party, which used to call itself the servant of the people, which used to claim that it worked for the full expression of the people's, will, as soon as the colonial power puts the country into its control, hasten to send the people back to their caves ...

Kwame Nkrumah
Africa Must Unite
(First published in London, 1963)

6. FREEDOM FIRST

It is my deep conviction that all peoples wish to be free, and that the desire for freedom is rooted in the soul of every one of us. A people long subjected to foreign domination, however, does not always find it easy to translate that wish into action. Under arbitrary rule, people are apt to become lethargic; their senses are dulled. Fear becomes the dominant force in their lives; fear of breaking the law, fear of the punitive measures which might result from an unsuccessful attempt to break loose from their shackles. Those who lead the struggle for freedom must break through this apathy and fear. They must give active expression to the universal longing to be free. They must strengthen the people's faith in themselves, and encourage them to take part in the freedom struggle. Above all, they must declare their aims openly and unmistakably, and organise the people towards the achievements of their goal of self-government.

The essential forger of the political revolution is a strong, well-organised, broadly based political party, knit together by a programme that is accepted by all the members, who also submit themselves to the party's discipline. Its programme should aim for 'Freedom first'. 'Seek ye first the political kingdom' became the principal slogan of the Convention People's Party, for without political independence none of our plans for social and economic development could be put into effect.

There has been a good deal of talk about dependent territories making themselves viable before attempting to take upon themselves the responsibilities of self-government. That is precisely what they cannot do. As long as the government of less developed countries remains in the hands of colonial administrators, their economies are set to a pattern determined by the interests, not of the indigenous inhabitants but of the national beneficiaries of the ruling country. Improvement in living conditions for the people will not come until political power passes into their hands.

Thus, every movement for independence in a colonial situation contains two elements: the demand for political freedom and the revolt against poverty and exploitation. Resolute leadership is required to subordinate the understandable desire of the people for better living conditions to the achievement of the primary aim of the abolition of colonial rule.

Before the Second World War, a number of political demonstrations and strikes took place in various parts of colonial Africa. The common demands were for reforms; few people envisaged at that time the emergence of national political parties demanding independence.

During the 1940s, however, many African national organizations were formed. For example, in 1944, the National Council of Nigeria and the Cameroons was founded, and, in the same year, the Nyasaland National Congress. (This was banned in 1958 and the Malawi Congress Party set up in its place.) Two years later, the Kenya African Union was formed; and the Rassemblement Democratique Africain, a federation of the various organizations which had developed throughout the French colonies in West and Equatorial Africa. There followed, in 1947, the formation of the Northern Rhodesian African National Congress; and, in our country the United Gold Coast Convention, with its aim: self-government in the shortest possible time. On 12 June 1949 came the split with the U.G.C.C. when I founded the Convention People's Party with the declared aim of achieving 'Self-Government Now'.

The 1950s saw the emergence of the Uganda National Congress (1952), the Tanganyika African National Union (1953), and the African National Congress in Southern Rhodesia. There were also national organizations formed in the Congo. In Portuguese Africa, the União dos Populaçãos de Angola and the Movimento Popular de Libertação de Angola were formed. Eventually, in 1959, they merged to form the African Revolutionary Front Against Portuguese Colonialism. This organization includes supporters in Mozambique and Portuguese Guinea.

I have mentioned only a few of the many African political organizations formed during and after the Second World War. There are many others. Their structure, organization, and the quality of their leadership have varied, but all have had in common the determination to struggle for the abolition of colonial rule and the improvement of economic and social conditions.

On the eve of the Second World War, only Liberia, Ethiopia and Egypt were independent. But by the end of 1959, that is 20 years later, there were nine independent African states: Egypt, Sudan, Morocco, Tunisia, Libya, Liberia, Ethiopia, Ghana and Guinea. In 1960_s Nigeria, the Congo,

French Togoland, French Cameroons and Somalia achieved independence. They were followed, in 1961, by Sierra Leone, Tanganyika, Uganda and Nyasaland. The independence of Kenya, Northern Rhodesia and Zanzibar cannot long be delayed.

This fundamental change in the African situation has been brought about by the struggles and sacrifices of the African peoples themselves, and nothing can now stop the rushing tide of nationalism. As long as a single foot of African soil remains under foreign domination, the battle must continue.

It may be that the time has come to have a common political party with a common aim and programme. For instance, instead of the Convention People's Party in Ghana, there might be the Ghana People's Party. In Kenya, the progressive party could be the Kenya People's Party; in Guinea, the Guinea People's Party, and so on; each party having one common aim and objective, the freedom and unity of Africa.

The various People's Parties, with their common aim, would cooperate with each other. A central organisation would undoubtedly be necessary, and also a highly-trained headquarters staff. If this kind of solidarity on the party political level could be achieved, it would surely strengthen African continental freedom and unity.

Party leaders in countries which are still not free would be able to derive strength and inspiration from close association with their opposite numbers in independent countries. Though beset by difficulties, they would gain confidence from being part of a strong continental organisation with immense resources, which they could draw upon in time of need. From its inception, the Convention People's Party declared in its constitution that it would 'seek to establish fraternal relations with, and offer guidance and support to all nationalist, democratic and socialist movements, in Africa and elsewhere, which are fighting for national independence and self-determination'.

Among independent countries the common party would act as a unifying force. Also, if a common domestic policy could be worked out it would help immeasurably in the planning and development of the African continent as a whole, in the economic and social spheres.

The unevenness of development in Africa both political and economic, is a major problem. Some countries are poor in natural resources, others rich. Some achieved independence comparatively easily, and peacefully; others are still struggling. The obvious solution is unity, so that development can be properly and cohesively planned.

Countries under alien rule achieve independence in different ways.

India was promised freedom by 'steady evolution towards self-government in ordered constitutional stages'. In fact it took 27 years of civil commotion and passive disobedience for India to achieve her aim. Libya was granted independence by the United Nations Organization as a direct result of Italy's defeat in the Second World War. The Portuguese colony of Goa was liberated by India. Several countries in the Middle East owe their existence as separate states to the Western powers, when they carved up the Ottoman Empire after the First World War.

In Africa, the nature of the freedom struggle has varied according to the background conditions against which it has had to operate and the position of the international scene at a given time.

Generally, in territories where there is a settler problem, the struggle has been more prolonged and sometimes violent, as in Kenya during the Mau Mau period. Where there is no settler problem, as in West Africa, the struggle has been hard, though on the whole peaceful and constitutional. I have already told how independence was achieved in Ghana in my autobiography, *Ghana* (1957).

Looking back, and trying to determine the reasons for the successful outcome of our struggle for freedom, one factor stands out above all others, namely, the strength of a well-organised political party, representing the broad mass of the people. The Convention People's Party represented the ordinary, common folk who wanted social justice and a higher standard of living. It kept in daily, living touch with the ordinary mass of people it represented, unlike the opposition, which was supported by a galaxy of lawyers and members of other conservative professions the self-styled 'aristocracy' of the Gold Coast. They did not understand the new mood of the people, the growing nationalism and the revolt against economic hardship.

A popular anti-colonial press developed in Africa during the 1930s. In 1932, Habib Bourguiba founded the *Action Tunisienne.* In Morocco the *Action du Peuple* edited by Mohamed Hassan el-Ouazzani appeared in August 1938; the editorial committee contained the nucleus of the leadership of Morocco's Comité d'Action Marocaine. In the Ivory Coast *L'Eclaireur de la Côte d'Ivoire* began in 1935. Three years later, in 1938, Dr Nnamdi Azikiwe's *West African Pilot* prepared the ground for the independence movement in Nigeria. These, and other newspapers, have undoubtedly helped in the spread of African nationalism. They have emphasized the need for 'freedom first' and then development. If we are to banish colonialism utterly from our continent, every African must be made aware of his part in the struggle. Freedom involves the untiring efforts of everyone engaged in the struggle for it. The vast African majority must be accepted as the basis of government in Africa.

15. TOWARDS AFRICAN UNITY

There are those who maintain that Africa cannot unite because we lack the three necessary ingredients for unity, a common race, culture and language. It is true that we have for centuries been divided. The territorial boundaries dividing us were fixed long ago, often quite arbitrarily, by the colonial powers. Some of us are Moslems, some Christians; many believe in traditional, tribal gods. Some of us speak French, some English, and some Portuguese, not to mention the millions who speak only one of the hundreds of different African languages. We have acquired cultural differences which affect our outlook and condition our political development.

All this is inevitable, due to our historical background. Yet in spite of this I am convinced that the forces making for unity far outweigh those which divide us. In meeting fellow Africans from all parts of the continent I am constantly impressed by how much we have in common. It is not just our colonial past, or the fact that we have aims in common; it is something which goes far deeper. I can best describe it as a sense of one-ness in that we are Africans.

In practical terms, this deep-rooted unity has shown itself in the development of Pan-Africanism and, more recently, in the projection of what has been called the African Personality in world affairs.

The expression 'Pan-Africanism' did not come into use until the beginning of the 20th century when Henry Sylvester-Williams of Trinidad, and William Edward Burghardt DuBois of the United States of America, both of African descent, used it at several Pan-African Congresses which were mainly attended by scholars of African descent of the New World. A notable contribution to African nationalism and Pan-Africanism was the 'Back to Africa' movement of Marcus Garvey.

The First Pan-African Congress was held in Paris in 1919 while the peace conference was in session. The French Prime Minister, Clemenceau, when asked what he thought of the holding of a Pan-African Congress, remarked: 'Don't advertise it, but go ahead.' His reaction was fairly typical among Europeans at the time. The very idea of Pan-Africanism was so strange that it seemed unreal and yet at the same time perhaps potentially dangerous. 57 representatives from various African colonies and from the United States of America and the West Indies attended. They drafted various proposals, though nothing much came of them. For example, they proposed that the Allied and associated powers should establish a code of law 'for international protection of the natives of Africa'.

The Second Pan-African Congress was held in London in 1921. The British Government, if not sympathetic, was tolerant, and 113 delegates attended. This Congress, though far from being truly representative of African opinion, nevertheless went some way towards putting the African case to the world. In a *Declaration to the World* drafted at the closing session, it was stated that 'the absolute equality of races, physical, political and social, is the founding stone of world and human advancement'. They were more concerned in those days with social than with political improvement, not yet recognising the pre-emption of the latter in order to engage the former.

Two years later, in 1923, a Third Pan-African Congress was held in London. Among the resolutions passed was one which asked for a voice for Africans in their own governments; and another which asked for the right of access to land and its resources. The political aspect of social justice was beginning to be understood. But in spite of the work of DuBois and others, progress was slow. The movement lacked funds and membership was limited. The delegates were idealists rather than men of action. However, a certain amount of publicity was achieved and Africans and men of African descent for the first time gained valuable experience in working together.

A Fourth Pan-African Congress was held in New York in 1927, which 208 delegates attended, but after that the movement seemed to fade out for a time.

A non-party organisation, the International African Service Bureau, was set up in 1937, and this was the forerunner of the Pan-African Federation, the British section of the Pan-African Congress movement. Its aim was 'to promote the well-being and unity of African peoples and peoples of African descent throughout the world', and also 'to strive to cooperate between African peoples and others who share our aspirations'.

Pan-Africanism and African nationalism really took concrete expression when the Fifth Pan-African Congress met in Manchester in 1945. For the first time the necessity for well-organised, firmly-knit movements as a primary condition for the success of the national liberation struggle in Africa was stressed.

The Congress was attended by more than two hundred delegates from all over the world. George Padmore and I had been joint secretaries of the organisational committee which planned the Congress and we were delighted with the results of our work. Among the declarations addressed to the imperialist powers asserting the determination of the colonial people to be free was the following:

> The Fifth Pan-African Congress calls on intellectuals and professional classes of the Colonies to awaken to their responsibilities. The long, long night is over. By fighting for trade union rights, the right to form cooperatives, freedom of the press, assembly, demonstration and strike, freedom to print and read the literature which is necessary for the education of the masses, you will be using the only means by which your liberties will be won and maintained. Today there is only one road to effective action – the organisation of the masses.

A definite programme of action was agreed upon. Basically, the programme centred around the demand for constitutional change, providing for universal suffrage. The methods to be employed were based on the Gandhist technique of non-violent non-cooperation, in other words, the withholding of labour, civil disobedience and economic boycott. There were to be variations of emphasis from territory to territory according to the differing circumstances. The fundamental purpose was identical: national independence leading to African unity. The limited objective was combined with the wider perspective.

Instead of a rather nebulous movement, concerned vaguely with black nationalism, the Pan-African movement had become an expression of African nationalism. Unlike the first four Congresses, which had been supported mainly by middle-class intellectuals, and bourgeois reformists, the Fifth Pan-African Congress was attended by workers, trade unionists, farmers and students, most of whom came from Africa.

When the Congress ended, having agreed on the programme for Pan-African nationalism, a working committee was set up with DuBois as chairman and myself as general secretary. The Congress headquarters were moved to London, where shortly afterwards the West African National Secretariat was also established. Its purpose was to put into action, in West Africa, the policies agreed upon in Manchester. I was offered, and accepted, the secretaryship.

We published a monthly paper called the *New African*, and called two West African Conferences in London. By this time the political conscience of African students was thoroughly aroused, and they talked of little else but the colonial liberation movement. The more enthusiastic among us formed a kind of inner group which we called the Circle. Only those working genuinely for West African freedom and unity were admitted, and we began to prepare ourselves actively for revolutionary work in any part of the African continent.

When I returned to West Africa in 1947, it was with the intention of using the Gold Coast as a starting-off point for African independence and unity. I at once made it clear that there would be no meaning to the national independence of Ghana unless it was linked with the total liberation of the African continent.

The first Conference of Independent African States met in Accra in April 1958. There were then only eight, namely, Egypt, Ghana, Sudan, Libya, Tunisia, Liberia, Morocco and Ethiopia. Our purpose was to exchange views on matters of common interest; to explore ways and means of consolidating and safeguarding our independence; to strengthen the economic and cultural ties between our countries; to decide on workable arrangements for helping fellow Africans still subject to colonial rule; and to examine the central world problem of how to secure peace.

When, on 15 April 1958, I welcomed the representatives to the conference, I felt that at last Pan-Africanism had moved to the African continent where it really belonged. It was an historic occasion. Free Africans were actually meeting together, in *Africa*, to examine and consider African affairs. Here was a signal departure from established custom, a jar to the arrogant assumption of non-African nations that African affairs were solely the concern of states outside our continent. The African personality was making itself known. The Accra Conference resulted, as indeed I hoped it would, in a great upsurge of interest in the cause of African freedom and unity.

The will to unity which the conference expressed was at least equal to the determination to carry forward the process of independence throughout Africa. The enthusiasm generated among the delegates returning to their own countries profoundly influenced subsequent developments. The Belgian Congo, Uganda, Tanganyika, Nyasaland, Kenya, the Rhodesias, South Africa, all were affected by the coming together in Accra of representatives of the various freedom movements of the continent. The total liberation and the unity of the continent at which we aimed were evolving and gaining reality in the experience of our international gathering.

In November 1959, representatives of trade unions all over Africa met in Accra to organise an All-African Trade Union Federation. The African labour movement has always been closely associated with the struggle for political freedom, as well as with economic and social development.

A further step forward in the direction of all-African cooperation took place a few months later when the conference to discuss Positive Action and Security in Africa opened in Accra in April 1960. It was called by the government of Ghana, in consultation with other independent African states, to consider the situation in Algeria and in South Africa, and also to discuss and plan future action to prevent Africa being used as a testing ground for nuclear weapons. Equally important matters to be considered were the total liberation of Africa, and the necessity to guard against neo-colonialism and balkanisation, both of which would impede unity,

In mid-1960 a further conference of Independent African states, twelve in number, was held in Addis Ababa, and yet another all-African conference met in Accra. The latter, a conference of African women to discuss common problems, opened on 18 July. The delegates spoke of freedom and unity, and of the urgent need for social and economic progress.

Against the background of continuing struggle in the Congo, and of trouble in South Africa, Algeria, and other parts of the continent, an All-African People's Conference met in Cairo early in 1961. About 200 delegates attended. The conference warned independent African states to beware of neo-colonialism.

21. CONTINENTAL GOVERNMENT FOR AFRICA

We have seen, in the example of the United States, how the dynamic elements within society understood the need for unity and fought their bitter civil war to maintain the political union that was threatened by the reactionary forces. We have also seen, in the example of the Soviet Union, how the forging of continental unity along with the retention of national sovereignty by the federal states, has achieved a dynamism that has lifted a most backward society into a most powerful unit within a remarkably short space of time. From the examples before us, in Europe and the United States of America, it is therefore patent that we in Africa have the resources, present and potential, for creating the kind of society that we are anxious to build. It is calculated that by the end of this century the population of Africa will probably exceed five hundred millions.

Our continent gives us the second largest land stretch in the world. The natural wealth of Africa is estimated to be greater than that of almost any other continent in the world. To draw the most from our existing and potential means for the achievement of abundance and a fine social order, we need to unify our efforts, our resources, our skills and intentions.

Europe, by way of contrast, must be a lesson to us all. Too busy hugging its exclusive nationalisms, it has descended, after centuries of wars interspersed with intervals of uneasy peace, into a state of confusion, simply because it failed to build a sound basis of political association and understanding.

Only now, under the necessities of economic stringency and the threat of the new German industrial and military rehabilitation, is Europe trying

– unsuccessfully – to find a modus operandi for containing the threat. It is deceptively hoped that the European Community will perform this miracle. It has taken two world wars and the break-up of empires to press home the lesson, still only partly digested that strength lies in unity.

While we in Africa, for whom the goal of unity is paramount, are striving to concert our efforts in this direction, the neo-colonialists are straining every nerve to upset them by encouraging the formation of communities based on the languages of their former colonizers. We cannot allow ourselves to be so disorganised and divided. The fact that I speak English does not make me an Englishman. Similarly, the fact that some of us speak French or Portuguese does not make us Frenchmen or Portuguese. We are Africans first and last, and as Africans our best interests can only be served by uniting within an African Community. Neither the Commonwealth nor a Franco-African Community can be a substitute.

To us, Africa with its islands is just one Africa. We reject the idea of any kind of partition. From Tangier or Cairo in the North to Cape Town in the South, from Cape Guardafui in the East to Cape Verde Islands in the West, Africa is one and indivisible.

I know that when we speak of political union, our critics are quick to observe an attempt to impose leadership and to abrogate sovereignty. But we have seen from the many examples of union put forward, that equality of the states is jealously guarded in every single constitution and that sovereignty is maintained. There are differences in the powers allotted to the central government and those retained by the states, as well as in the functions of the executive, legislature and judiciary. All of them have in common trade and economic policy. All of them are secular, in order that religion might not be dragged across the many problems involved in maintaining unity and securing the greatest possible development.

We in Africa who are pressing now for unity are deeply conscious of the validity of our purpose. We need the strength of our combined numbers and resources to protect ourselves from the very positive dangers of returning colonialism in disguised forms. We need it to combat the entrenched forces dividing our continent and still holding back millions of our brothers. We need it to secure total African liberation. We need it to carry forward our construction of a socio-economic system that will support the great mass of our steadily rising population at levels of life which will compare with those in the most advanced countries.

But we cannot mobilise our present and potential resources without concerted effort. If we developed our potentialities in men and natural resources in separate isolated groups, our energies would soon be dissipated in the struggle to outbid one another. Economic friction among us would certainly lead to bitter political rivalry, such as for many years hampered the pace of growth and development in Europe.

At present most of the independent African states are moving in directions which expose us to the dangers of imperialism and neo-colonialism. We therefore need a common political basis for the integration of our policies in economic planning, defence, foreign and diplomatic relations. That basis for political action need not infringe the essential sovereignty of the separate African states. These states would continue to exercise independent authority, except in the fields defined and reserved for common action in the interests of the security and orderly development of the whole continent.

In my view, therefore, a united Africa – that is, the political and economic unification of the African continent – should seek three objectives:

Firstly, we should have an over-all economic planning on a continental basis. This would increase the industrial and economic power of Africa. So long as we remain balkanized, regionally or territorially, we shall be at the mercy of colonialism and imperialism. The lesson of the South African Republic vis-à-vis the strength and solidarity of the United States of America is there for all to see.

The resources of Africa can be used to the best advantage and the maximum benefit to all only if they are set within an overall framework of a continentally planned development. An overall economic plan, covering an Africa united on a continental basis, would increase our total industrial and economic power. We should therefore think seriously now of ways and means of building up a Common Market of a United Africa and not allow ourselves to be lured by the dubious advantages of association with the so-called European Common Market. We in Africa have looked outward too long for the development of our economy and transportation. Let us begin to look inwards into the African continent for all aspects of its development. Our communications were devised under colonial rule to stretch outwards towards Europe and elsewhere, instead of developing internally between our cities and states. Political unity should give us the power and will to change all this. We in Africa have untold agricultural, mineral and water-power resources. These almost fabulous resources can be fully exploited and utilized in the interest of Africa and the African people, only if we develop them within a Union Government of African States. Such a Union Government will need to maintain a common currency, a monetary zone and a central bank of issue. The advantages of these financial and monetary arrangements would be inestimable, since monetary transactions between our several states would be facilitated and the pace of financial activity generally quickened. A central bank of issue is an inescapable necessity, in view of the need to re-orientate the economy of Africa and place it beyond the reach of foreign control.

Secondly, we should aim at the establishment of a unified military and defence strategy. I do not see much virtue or wisdom in our separate efforts to build up or maintain vast military forces for self-defence, which, in any case, would be ineffective in any major attack upon our separate states. If we examine this problem realistically, we should be able to ask ourselves this pertinent question: which single state in Africa today can protect its sovereignty against an imperialist aggressor? In this connection it should be mentioned that anti-apartheid leaders have alleged that South Africa is building a great military force with all the latest weapons of destruction, in order to crush nationalism in Africa. Nor is this all. There are grave indications that certain settler governments in Africa have already been caught in the dangerous arms race and are now arming themselves to the teeth. Their military activities constitute a serious threat not only to the security of Africa, but also to the peace of the world. If these reports are true, only the unity of Africa can prevent South Africa and these other governments from achieving their diabolical aims.

If we do not unite and combine our military resources for common defence, the individual states, out of a sense of insecurity, may be drawn into making defence pacts with foreign powers which may endanger the security of us all.

There is also the expenditure aspect of this problem. The maintenance of large military forces imposes a heavy financial burden on even the most wealthy states. For young African states, who are in great need of capital for internal development, it is ridiculous – indeed suicidal – for each state separately and individually to assume such a heavy burden of self-defence, when the weight of this burden could be easily lightened by sharing it among themselves. Some attempt has already been made by the Casablanca Powers and the Afro-Malagasy Union in the matter of common defence, but how much better and stronger it would be if, instead of two such ventures, there was one overall (land, sea and air) Defence Command for Africa.

The third objective which we should have in Africa stems from the first two which I have just described. If we in Africa set up a unified economic planning organisation and a unified military and defence strategy, it will be necessary for us to adopt a unified foreign policy and diplomacy to give political direction to our joint efforts for the protection and economic development of our continent. Moreover, there are some 60-odd states in Africa, about 32 of which are at present independent. The burden of separate diplomatic representation by each state on the continent of Africa alone would be crushing, not to mention representation outside Africa. The desirability of a common foreign policy which will enable us to speak with one voice in the councils of the world, is so obvious, vital and imperative that comment is hardly necessary.

I am confident that it should be possible to devise a constitutional structure applicable to our special conditions in Africa and not necessarily framed in terms of the existing constitutions of Europe, America or elsewhere, which will enable us to secure the objectives I have defined and yet preserve to some extent the sovereignty of each state within a Union of African States.

We might erect for the time being a constitutional form that could start with those states willing to create a nucleus, and leave the door open for the attachment of others as they desire to join or reach the freedom which would allow them to do so. The form could be made amenable to adjustment and amendment at any time the consensus of opinion is for it. It may be that concrete expression can be given to our present ideas within a continental parliament that would provide a lower and an upper house, the one to permit the discussion of the many problems facing Africa by a representation based on population; the other, ensuring the equality of the associated states, regardless of size and population, by a similar, limited representation from each of them, to formulate a common policy in all matters affecting the security, defence and development of Africa. It might, through a committee selected for the purpose, examine likely solutions to the problems of union and draft a more conclusive form of constitution that will be acceptable to all the independent states.

The survival of free Africa, the extending independence of this continent, and the development towards that bright future on which our hopes and endeavours are pinned, depend upon political unity.

Under a major political union of Africa there could emerge a United Africa, great and powerful, in which the territorial boundaries which are the relics of colonialism will become obsolete and superfluous, working for the complete and total mobilization of the economic planning organisation under a unified political direction. The forces that unite us are far greater than the difficulties that divide us at present, and our goal must be the establishment of Africa's dignity, progress and prosperity.

Proof is therefore positive that the continental union of Africa is an inescapable desideratum if we are determined to move forward to a realisation of our hopes and plans for creating a modern society which will give our peoples the opportunity to enjoy a life which is full and satisfying. The forces that unite us are intrinsic and greater than the superimposed influences that keep us apart. These are the forces that we must enlist and cement for the sake of the trusting millions who look to us, their leaders, to take them out of the poverty, ignorance and disorder left by colonialism into an ordered unity in which freedom and amity can flourish amidst plenty.

Here is a challenge which destiny has thrown out to the leaders of Africa. It is for us to grasp what is a golden opportunity to prove that the genius of the African people can surmount the separatist tendencies in sovereign nationhood by coming together speedily, for the sake of Africa's greater glory and infinite well-being, into a Union of African States.

Amilcar Cabral
Brief Analysis of the Social Structure in Guinea
(Condensed text of an address given in Milan, 1964)

I should like to tell you something about the situation in our country, 'Portuguese' Guinea, beginning with an analysis of the social situation, which has served as the basis for our struggle for national liberation. I shall make a distinction between the rural areas and the towns, or rather the urban centres, not that these are to be considered mutually opposed.

In the rural areas we have found it necessary to distinguish between two distinct groups: on the one hand, the group which we consider semi-feudal, represented by the Fulas, and, on the other hand, the group which we consider, so to speak, without any defined form of state organisation, represented by the Balantes. There are a number of intermediary positions between these two extreme ethnic groups (as regards the social situation). I should like to point out straight away that although in general the semi-feudal groups were Muslim and the groups without any form of state organisations were animist, there was one ethnic group among the animists, the Mandjacks, which had forms of social relations which could be considered feudal at the time when the Portuguese came to Guinea.

I should now like to give you a quick idea of the social stratification among the Fulas. We consider that the chiefs, the nobles and the religious figures form one group; after them come the artisans and the Dyulas, who are itinerant traders, and then after that come the peasants properly speaking. I don't want to give a very thorough analysis of the economic situation of each of these groups now, but I would like to say that although certain traditions concerning collective ownership of the land have been preserved, the chiefs and their entourages have retained considerable privileges as regards ownership of land and the utilisation of other people's labour; this means that the peasants who depend on the chiefs are obliged to work for these chiefs for a certain period of each year. The artisans, whether blacksmiths (which is the lowest occupation) or leather-workers or whatever, play an extremely important role in the socio-economic life of the Fulas and represent what you might call the embryo of industry. The Dyulas, whom some people consider should be placed above the artisans, do not really have such importance among the Fulas; they are the people who have the potential –which they sometimes realise – of accumulating money. In general the peasants have no rights and they are the really exploited group in Fula society.

Apart from the question of ownership and property, there is another element which it is extremely interesting to compare and that is the position of women. Among the Fulas women have no rights; they take part in production but they do not own what they produce. Besides, polygamy is a highly respected institution and women are to a certain extent considered the property of their husbands.

Among the Balantes, which are at the opposite extreme, we find a society without any social stratification: there is just a council of elders in each village or group of villages who decide on the day-to-day problems. In the Balante group, property and land are considered to belong to the village, but each family receives the amount of land needed to ensure subsistence for itself, and the means of production, or rather the instruments of production, are not collective but are owned by families or individuals.

The position of women must also be mentioned when talking about the Balantes. The Balantes still retain certain tendencies towards polygamy, although it is mainly a monogamous society. Among the Balantes women participate in production, but they own what they produce, and this gives Balante women a position which we consider privileged, as they are fairly free; the only point on which they are not free is that children belong to the head of the family and the head of the family, the husband, always claims any children his wife may have; this is obviously to be explained by the actual economy of the group where a family's strength is ultimately represented by the number of hands there are to cultivate the land.

As I have said, there are a number of intermediate positions between these two extremes. In the rural areas I should mention the small African farm owners; this is a numerically small group but all the same it has a certain importance and has proved to be highly active in the national liberation struggle. In the towns (I shall not talk about the presence of Europeans in the rural areas as there are none in Guinea) we must first distinguish between the Europeans and the Africans. The Europeans can easily be classified as they retain in Guinea the social stratification of Portugal (obviously depending on the function they exercise in Guinea). In the first place, there are the high officials and the managers of enterprises who form a stratum with practically no contact with the other European strata. After that there are the medium officials, the small European traders, the people employed in commerce, and the members are mainly skilled workers.

Among the Africans we find the higher officials, the middle officials and the members of the liberal professions forming a group; then come the petty officials, those employed in commerce with a contract, who are to be distinguished from those employed in commerce without a contract, who can be fired at any moment. The small farm owners also fall into this group; by assimilation we call all these members of the African petty bourgeoisie (obviously, if we were to make a more thorough analysis the higher African officials as well as the middle officials and the members of the liberal professions should also be included in the petty bourgeoisie). Next come the wage-earners (whom we define as those employed in commerce without any contract); among these there are certain important sub-groups such as the dockworkers, the people employed on the boats carrying goods and agricultural produce; there are also the domestic servants, who are mostly men in Guinea; there are the people working in repair shops and small factories and there are also the people who work in shops as porters and such like – these all come under the heading of wage-earners. You will notice that we are careful not to call these groups the proletariat or working class.

There is another group of people whom we call the *déclassés,* in which there are two sub-groups to be distinguished; the first sub-group is easy to identify – it is what would be called the lumpenproletariat if there was a real proletariat: it consists of really *déclassé* people, such as beggars, prostitutes and so on. The other group is not really made up of *déclassé* people, but we have not yet found the exact term for it; it is a group to which we have paid a lot of attention and it has proved to be extremely important in the national liberation struggle. It is mostly made up of young people who are connected to petty bourgeois or workers' families, who have recently arrived from the rural areas and generally do not work; they thus have close relations with the rural areas, as well as with the towns (and even with the Europeans). They sometimes live off one kind of work or another, but they generally live at the expense of their families. Here I should just like to point out a difference between Europe and Africa; in Africa there is a tradition which requires that, for example, if I have an uncle living in the town, I can come in and live in his house without working and he will feed me and house me. This creates a certain stratum of people who experience urban life and who can, as we shall see, play a very important role.

That is a very brief analysis of the general situation in Guinea, but you will understand that this analysis has no value unless it is related to the actual struggle. In outline, the methodological approach we have used has been as follows: first, the position of each group must be defined – to what extent and in what way does each group depend on the colonial regime? Next we have to see what position they adopt towards the national liberation struggle. Then we have to study their nationalist capacity and, lastly, envisaging the post-independence period, their revolutionary capacity.

Among the Fulas the first group – the chiefs and their entourages – are tied to colonialism; this is particularly the case with the Fulas as in Guinea the Fulas were already conquerors (the Portuguese allied themselves with the Fulas in order to dominate Guinea at the beginning of the conquest). Thus the chiefs (and their authority as chiefs) are very closely tied to the Portuguese authorities. The artisans are extremely dependent on the chiefs; they live off what they make for the chiefs who are the only ones that can acquire their products, so there are some artisans who are simply content to follow the chiefs; then there are other people who try to break away and are well disposed towards opposition to Portuguese colonialism. The main point about the Dyulas is that their permanent preoccupation is to protect their own personal interests; at least in Guinea, the Dyulas are not settled in any one place, they are itinerant traders without any real roots anywhere and their fundamental aim is to make bigger and bigger profits. It is precisely the fact that they are almost permanently on the move which provides us with a most valuable element in the struggle. It goes without saying that there are some who have not supported our struggle and there are some who have been used as agents against us by the Portuguese, but there are some whom we have been able to use to mobilise people, at least as far as spreading the initial ideas of the struggle was concerned – all we had to do was give them some reward, as they usually would not do anything without being paid.

Obviously, the group with the greatest interest in the struggle is the peasantry, given the nature of the various different societies in Guinea (feudal, semi-feudal, etc.) and the various degrees of exploitation to which they are subjected; but the question is not simply one of objective interest.

Given the general context of our traditions, or rather the superstructure created by the economic conditions in Guinea, the Fula peasants have a strong tendency to follow their chiefs. Thorough and intensive work was therefore needed to mobilise them. Among the Balantes and the groups without any defined form of state organisation the first point to note is that there are still a lot of remnants of animist traditions even among the Muslims in Guinea; the part of the population which follows is not really

Islamic but rather Islamised; they are animists who have adopted some Muslim practices, but are still thoroughly impregnated with animist conceptions. What is more, these groups without any defined organisation put up much more resistance against the Portuguese than the others and they have maintained intact their tradition of resistance to colonial penetration. This is the group that we found most ready to accept the idea of national liberation.

Here I should like to broach one key problem, which is of enormous importance for us, as we are a country of peasants, and that is the problem of whether or not the peasantry represents the main revolutionary force. I shall confine myself to my own country, Guinea, where it must be said at once that the peasantry is not a revolutionary force – which may seem strange, particularly as we have based the whole of our armed liberation struggle on the peasantry. A distinction must be drawn between a physical force and a revolutionary force; physically, the peasantry is a great force in Guinea: it is almost the whole of the population, it controls the nation's wealth, it is the peasantry which produces; but we know from experience what trouble we had convincing the peasantry to fight. This is a problem I shall come back to later; here I should just like to refer to ... China. The conditions of the peasantry in China were very different: the peasantry had a history of revolt, but this was not the case in Guinea, and so it was not possible for our party militants and propaganda workers to find the same kind of welcome among the peasantry in Guinea for the idea of national liberation as the idea found in China. All the same, in certain parts of the country and among certain groups we found a very warm welcome, even right at the start. In other groups and in other areas all this had to be won.

Then there are the positions vis-à-vis the struggle of the various groups in the towns to be considered. The Europeans are, in general, hostile to the idea of national liberation; they are the human instruments of the colonial state in our country and they therefore reject a priori any idea of national liberation there. It has to be said that the Europeans most bitterly opposed to the idea of national liberation are the workers, while we have sometimes found considerable sympathy for our struggle among certain members of the European petty bourgeoisie.

As for the Africans, the petty bourgeoisie can be divided into three sub-groups as regards the national liberation struggle. First, there is the petty bourgeoisie which is heavily committed to and compromised with colonialism: this includes most higher officials and some members of the liberal professions. Second, there is the group which we perhaps incorrectly call the revolutionary petty bourgeoisie: this is the part of the petty bourgeoisie which is nationalist and which was the source of the idea of the national liberation struggle in Guinea. In between lies the part of the petty bourgeoisie which has never been able to make up its mind between the national liberation struggle and the Portuguese. Next come the wage-earners, which you can compare roughly with the proletariat in European societies, although they are not exactly the same thing: here, too, there is a majority committed to the struggle, but, again, many members of this group were not easy to mobilise – wage-earners who had an extremely petty bourgeois mentality and whose only aim was to defend the little they had already acquired.

Next come the *déclassés*. The really *déclassé* people, the permanent layabouts, the prostitutes and so on have been a great help to the Portuguese police in giving them information; this group has been out rightly against our struggle, perhaps unconsciously so, but nonetheless against our struggle. On the other hand, the particular group I mentioned earlier, for which we have not yet found any precise classification (the group of mainly young people recently arrived from the rural areas with contacts in both the urban and the rural areas) gradually comes to make a comparison between the standard of living of their own families and that of the Portuguese; they begin to understand the sacrifices being borne by the Africans. They have proved extremely dynamic in the struggle. Many of these people joined the struggle right from the beginning and it is among this group that we found many of the cadres whom we have since trained.

The importance of this urban experience lies in the fact that it allows comparison: this is the key stimulant required for the awakening of consciousness. It is interesting to note that Algerian nationalism largely sprang up among the émigré workers in France. As far as Guinea is concerned, the idea of the national liberation struggle was born not abroad but in our own country, in a milieu where people were subjected to close and incessant exploitation. Many people say that it is the peasants who carry the burden of exploitation: this may be true, but so far the struggle is concerned it must be realised that it is not the degree of suffering and hardship involved as such that matters: even extreme suffering in itself does not necessarily produce the *prise de conscience* required for the national liberation struggle. In Guinea the peasants are subjected to a kind of exploitation equivalent to slavery; but even if you try and explain to them that they are being exploited and robbed, it is difficult to convince them by means of an inexperienced explanation of a technico-economic kind that they are the most exploited people; whereas it is easier to convince the workers and the people employed in the towns who earn, say, 10 escudos a day for a job in which a European earns between 30 and 50 that they are being subjected to massive exploitation and injustice, because they can see. To take my own case as a member of the petty bourgeois group which launched the struggle in Guinea, I was an agronomist working under a European who everybody knew was one of the biggest idiots in Guinea; I could have taught him his job with my eyes shut but he was the boss: this is something which counts a lot, this is the confrontation which really matters. This is of major importance when considering where the initial idea of the struggle came from.

Another major task was to examine the material interests and the aspirations of each group after the liberation, as well as their revolutionary capacities. As I have already said, we do not consider that the peasantry in Guinea has a revolutionary capacity. First of all we had to make an analysis of all these groups and of the contradictions between them and within them so as to be able to locate them all vis-à-vis the struggle and the revolution.

The first point is to decide what is the major contradiction at the moment when the struggle begins. For us the main contradiction was that between, on the one hand, the Portuguese and international bourgeoisie which was exploiting our people and, on the other hand, the interests of our people. There are also major contradictions within the country itself, i.e. in the internal life of our country. It is our opinion that if we get rid of colonialism in Guinea the main contradiction remaining, the one which will then become the principal contradiction, is that between the ruling classes, the semi-feudal groups, and the members of the groups without any defined form of organisation. The first thing to note is that the conquest carried out first by the Mandingues and then by the Fulas was a struggle between two opposite poles which was blocked by the very strong structure of the animist groups. There are other contradictions, such as that between the various feudal groups and that between the upper group and the lower. All this is extremely important for the future, and even while the struggle is still going on we must begin to exploit the contradiction between the Fula people and their chiefs, who are very close to the Portuguese. There is a further contradiction, particularly among the animists, between the collective ownership of the land and the private ownership of the means of production in agriculture. I am not trying to stretch alien concepts here, this is an observation that can be made on the spot: the land belongs to the village, but what is produced belongs to whoever produces it – usually the family or the head of the family.

There are other contradictions which we consider secondary: you may be surprised to know that we consider the contradictions between the tribes a secondary one; we could discuss this at length, but we consider that there are many more contradictions between what you might call the economic tribes in the capitalist countries than there are between the ethnic tribes in Guinea. Our struggle for national liberation and the work done by our Party have shown that this contradiction is really not so important; the Portuguese counted on it a lot but as soon as we organised the liberation struggle properly the contradiction between the tribes proved to be a feeble, secondary contradiction. This does not mean that we do not need to pay attention to this contradiction; we reject both the positions which are to be found in Africa – one which says there are no tribes, we are all the same, we are all one people in one terrible unity, our party comprises everybody; the other saying tribes exist, we must base parties on tribes. Our position lies between the two, but at the same time we are fully conscious that this is a problem which must constantly be kept in mind; structural, organisational and other measures must be taken to ensure that this contradiction does not explode and become a more important contradiction.

As for contradictions between the urban and rural areas, I would say that there is no conflict between the towns and the countryside, not least because we are only town dwellers who have just moved from the country; everybody in the towns in Guinea has close relatives in the country and all town dwellers still engage in some peasant activity (growing crops etc.); all the same, there is a potential contradiction between the towns and the countryside which colonialism tries to aggravate.

That, in brief, is the analysis we have made of the situation; this has led us to the following conclusion: we must try to unite everybody in the national liberation struggle against the Portuguese colonialists: this is where our main contradiction lies, but it is also imperative to organise things so that we always have an instrument available which can solve all the other contradictions. This is what convinced us of the absolute necessity of creating a party during the national liberation struggle. There are some people who interpret our Party as a front; perhaps our Party is a front at the moment, but within the framework of the front there is our Party which is directing the front, and there are no other parties in the front. For the circumstances of the struggle we maintain a general aspect, but within the framework of the struggle we know what our party is, we know the party finishes and where the people who just rallied for the liberation struggle begin.

When we had made our analysis, there were still many theoretical and practical problems left in front of us. We had some knowledge of other experiences and we knew that a struggle of the kind we hoped to lead, and win, had to be led by the working class; we looked for the working class in Guinea and did not find it. Other examples showed us that things were begun by some revolutionary intellectuals. What then were we to do? We were just a group of petty bourgeois who were who were driven by the reality of life in Guinea, by the sufferings we had to endure, and also by the influence events in Africa and elsewhere had on us, in particular the experiences some of us acquired in Portugal and other countries in Europe, to try and do something.

And so this little group began. We first thought of a general movement of national liberation, but this immediately proved unfeasible. We decided to extend our activity to the workers in the towns, and we had some success with this; we launched moves for higher wages, better working conditions and so on. I do not want to go into details here, the only point I want to make is that we obviously did not have a proletariat. We quite clearly lacked revolutionary intellectuals, so we had to start searching, given that we rightly did not believe in the revolutionary capacity of the peasantry.

One important group in the towns were the dockworkers; another important group were the people working in the boats carrying merchandise, who mostly live in Bissau itself and travel up and down the rivers. These people proved highly conscious of their position and of their economic importance and they took the initiative of launching strikes without any trade union leadership at all. We therefore decided to concentrate all our work on this group. This gave excellent results and this group soon came to form a kind of nucleus which influenced the attitudes of other wage-earning groups in the towns – workers proper and drivers, who form two other important groups. Moreover, if I may put it this way, we thus found our little proletariat.

We also looked for intellectuals, but there were none, because the Portuguese did not educate people. In any case, what is an intellectual in our country? It could probably be someone who knew the general situation very well, who had some knowledge, not profound theoretical knowledge, but concrete knowledge of the country itself and of its life as well as of our enemy. We, the people I have talked about, the engineers, doctors, bank clerks and so on, joined together to form a group of *interlocuteurs valables.*

There was also this other group of people in the towns, which we have been unable to classify precisely, which was still closely connected to the rural areas and contained people who spoke almost all the languages that are used in Guinea. They knew all the customs of the rural areas while at the same time possessing a solid knowledge of the European urban centres. They also had a certain degree of self-confidence, they knew how to read and write (which makes a person an intellectual in our country) and so we concentrated our work on these people and immediately started giving them some preparatory training.

We were faced with another difficult problem: we realised that we needed to have people with a mentality which could transcend the context of the national liberation struggle, and so we prepared a number of cadres from the group I have just mentioned, some from the people employed in commerce and other wage-earners, and even some peasants, so that they could acquire what you might call a working-class mentality. You may think this is absurd – in any case it is very difficult; in order for there to be a working-class mentality the material conditions of the working class should exist, a working class should exist. In fact we managed to inculcate these ideas into a large number of people – the kind of ideas, that is, which there would be if there were a working class. We trained about 1,000 cadres at our party school in Conakry, in fact for about two years this was about all we did outside the country. When these cadres returned to the rural areas they inculcated a certain mentality into the peasants and it is among these cadres that we have chosen the people who are now leading the struggle; we are not a Communist party or a Marxist-Leninist party, but the people now leading the peasants in the struggle in Guinea are mostly from the urban milieu and connected with the urban wage-earning group. When I hear that only the peasantry can lead the struggle, am I supposed to think we have made a mistake? All I can say is that at the moment our struggle is going well.

There are all sorts of other generalisations of a political nature, like this generalisation about the peasantry which keeps on cropping up. There are a number of key words and concepts, there is a certain conditioning in the reasoning of our European friends: for example, when someone thinks 'revolution', he thinks of the bourgeoisie falling, etc.; when someone thinks 'party', he forgets many things. Yesterday a friend asked me a number of questions about our party and several times I had to say to him, 'But it isn't a European party'; the concept of a party and the creation of parties did not occur spontaneously in Europe, they resulted from a long process of class struggle. When we in Africa think of creating a party now, we find ourselves in very different conditions from those in which parties appeared as historico-social phenomena in Europe. This has a number of consequences, so when you think 'party', 'single party', etc., you must connect all these things up with the history and conditions of Africa.

A rigorous historical approach is similarly needed when examining another problem related to this – how can the underdeveloped countries evolve towards revolution, towards socialism? There is a preconception held by many people, even on the left, that imperialism made us enter history at the moment when it began its adventure in our countries. This preconception must be denounced: for somebody on the left, and for Marxists in particular, history obviously means the class struggle. Our opinion is exactly the contrary. We consider that when imperialism arrived in Guinea it made us leave history – our history. We agree that history in our country is the result of class struggle, but we have our own class struggles in our own country; the moment imperialism arrived and colonialism arrived, it made us leave our history and enter another history. Obviously we agree that the class struggle has continued, but it has continued in a very different way: our whole people are struggling against the ruling class of the imperialist countries, and this gives a completely different aspect to the historical evolution of our country. Somebody has asked which class is the 'agent' of history; here a distinction must be drawn between colonial history and our history and our history as human societies; as a dominated people we only present an ensemble vis-à-vis the oppressor. Each of our peoples or groups of peoples has been subjected to different influences by the colonisers; when there is a developed national consciousness one may ask which social stratum is the agent of history, of colonial history; which is the stratum which will be able to take power into its hands when it emerges from colonial history?

Our answer is that it is *all* the social strata, if the people who have carried out the national revolution (i.e. the struggle against colonialism) have worked well, since unity of all the social strata is a prerequisite for the success of the national liberation struggle. As we see it, in colonial conditions no one stratum can succeed in the struggle for national liberation on its own, and therefore it is all the strata of society which are the agents of history. This brings us to what should be a void – but in fact it is not. What commands history in colonial conditions is not the class struggle. I do not mean that the class struggle in Guinea stopped completely during the colonial period; it continued, but in a muted way. In the colonial period it is the colonial state which commands history.

Our problem is to see who is capable of taking control of the state apparatus when the colonial power is destroyed. In Guinea the peasants cannot read or write, they have almost no relations with the colonial forces during the colonial period except for paying taxes, which is done indirectly. The working class hardly exists as a defined class, it is just an embryo. There is no economically viable bourgeoisie because imperialism prevented it being created. What there is, is a stratum of people in the service of imperialism who have learned how to manipulate the apparatus of the state – the African petty bourgeoisie: this is the only stratum capable of controlling or even utilising the instruments which the colonial state used against our people. So we come to the conclusion that in colonial conditions it is the petty bourgeoisie which is. the inheritor of state power (though I wish we could be wrong). The moment national liberation comes and the petty bourgeoisie takes power, we enter, or rather return to history, and thus the internal contradictions break out again.

When this happens, and particularly as things are now, there will be powerful external contradictions conditioning the internal situation, and not just internal contradictions as before. What attitude can the petty bourgeoisie adopt? Obviously people on the left will call for the revolution; the right will call for the 'non-revolution', i.e. a capitalist road or something like that. The petty bourgeoisie can either ally itself with imperialism and the reactionary strata in its own country to try and preserve itself as a petty bourgeoisie or ally itself with the workers and peasants, who must themselves take power or control to make the revolution. We must be very clear exactly what we are asking the petty bourgeoisie to do. Are we asking it to commit suicide? Because if there is a revolution, then the petty bourgeoisie will have to abandon power to the workers and the peasants and cease to exist qua petty bourgeoisie. For a revolution to take place depends on the nature of the party (and its size), the character of the struggle which led up to liberation, whether there was an armed struggle, what the nature of this armed struggle was and how it developed and, of course, on the nature of the state.

Here I would like to say something about the position of our friends on the left; if a petty bourgeoisie comes to power, they obviously demand of it that it carry out a revolution. But the important thing is whether they took the precaution of analysing the position of the petty bourgeoisie during the struggle; did they examine its nature, see how it worked, see what instruments it used and see whether this bourgeoisie committed itself with the left to carrying out a revolution, before the liberation? As you can see, it is the struggle in the underdeveloped countries which endows the petty bourgeoisie with a function; in the capitalist countries the petty bourgeoisie is only a stratum which serves, it does not determine the historical orientation of the country; it merely allies itself with one group or another. So that to hope that the petty bourgeoisie will just carry out a revolution when it comes to power in an underdeveloped country is to hope for a miracle, although it is true that it could do this.

This connects with the problem of the true nature of the national liberation struggle. In Guinea, as in other countries, the implantation of imperialism by force and the presence of the colonial system considerably altered the historical conditions and aroused a response – the national liberation struggle – which is generally considered a revolutionary trend; but this is something which I think needs further examination. I should like to formulate this question: is the national liberation movement something which has simply emerged from within our country, is it a result of the internal contradictions created by the presence of colonialism, or are there external factors which have determined it? And here we have some reservations; in fact I would even go so far as to ask whether, given the advance of socialism in the world, the national liberation movement is not an imperialist initiative. Is the judicial institution which serves as a reference for the right of all peoples to struggle to free themselves a product of the peoples who are trying to liberate themselves? Was it created by the socialist countries who are our historical associates? It is signed by the imperialist countries, it is the imperialist countries who have recognised the right of all peoples to national independence, so I ask myself whether we may not be considering as an initiative of our people what is in fact an initiative of the enemy. Even Portugal, which is using napalm bombs against our people in Guinea, signed the declaration of the right of all peoples to independence. One may well ask oneself why they were so mad as to do something which goes against their own interests; whether or not it was partly forced on them, the real point is that they signed it. This is where we think there is something wrong with the simple interpretation of the national liberation movement as a revolutionary trend. The objective of the imperialist countries was to prevent the enlargement of the socialist camp, to liberate the reactionary forces in our countries which were being stifled by colonialism and to enable these forces to ally themselves with the international bourgeoisie. The fundamental objective was to create a bourgeoisie where one did not exist, in order specifically to strengthen the imperialist and the capitalist camp. This rise of the bourgeoisie in the new countries, far from being at all surprising, should be considered absolutely normal, it is something that has to be faced by all those struggling against imperialism. We are therefore faced with the problem of deciding whether to engage in an out-and-out struggle against the bourgeoisie right from the start or whether to try and make an alliance with the national bourgeoisie, to try to deepen the absolutely necessary contradiction between the national bourgeoisie and the international bourgeoisie which has promoted the national bourgeoisie to the position it holds.

To return to the question of the nature of the petty bourgeoisie and the role it can play after the liberation, I should like to put a question to you. What would you have thought if Fidel Castro had come to terms with the Americans? Is this possible or not? Is it possible or impossible that the Cuban petty bourgeoisie, which set the Cuban people marching towards revolution, might have come to terms with the Americans? I think this helps to clarify the character of the revolutionary petty bourgeoisie. If I may put it this way, I think one thing that can be said is this: the revolutionary petty bourgeoisie is honest: i.e. in spite of all the hostile conditions, it remains identified with the fundamental interests of the popular masses. To do this it may have to commit suicide, but it will not lose; by sacrificing itself it can reincarnate itself, but in the condition of workers or peasants. In speaking of honesty I am not trying to establish moral criteria for judging the role of the petty bourgeoisie when it is in power; what I mean by honesty, in a political context, is total commitment and total identification with the toiling masses.

Again, the role of the petty bourgeoisie ties up with the possible social and political transformations that can be effected after liberation. We have heard a great deal about the state of national democracy, but although we have made every effort, we have thus far been unable to understand what this means; even so, we should like to know what it is all about, as we want to know what we are going to do when we have driven out the Portuguese. Likewise, we have to face the question whether or not socialism can be established immediately after the liberation. This depends on the instruments used to effect the transition to socialism; the essential factor is the nature of the state, bearing in mind that after the liberation there will be people controlling the police, the prisons, the army and so on, and a great deal depends on who they are and what they try to do with these instruments. Thus we return again to the problem of which class is the agent of history and who are the inheritors of the colonial state in our specific conditions.

I mentioned briefly earlier the question of the attitude of the European left towards the underdeveloped countries, in which there is a good deal of criticism and a good deal of optimism. The criticism reminds me of a story about some lions: there is a group of lions who are shown a picture of a lion lying on the ground and a man holding a gun with his foot on the lion (as everybody knows, the lion is proud of being king of the jungle); one of the lions looks at the picture and says, 'If only we lions could paint.' If one of the leaders of one of the new African countries could take time off from the terrible problems in his own country and become a critic of the European left and say all he had to say about the retreat of the revolution in Europe, of a certain apathy in some European countries and of the false hopes which we have all had in certain European groups ...

What really interests us here is neocolonialism. After the Second World War, imperialism entered on a new phase: on the one hand, it worked out the new policy of aid, i.e. granted independence to the occupied countries plus 'aid' and, on the other hand, concentrated on preferential investment in the European countries; this was, above all, an attempt at rationalising imperialism. Even if it has not yet provoked reactions of a nationalist kind in the European countries, we are convinced that it will soon do so. As we see it, neocolonialism (which we may call rationalised imperialism) is more a defeat for the international working class than for the colonised peoples. Neocolonialism is at work on two fronts – in Europe as well as in the underdeveloped countries. Its current framework in the underdeveloped countries is the policy of aid, and one of the essential aims of this policy is to create a false bourgeoisie to put a brake on the revolution and to enlarge the possibilities of the petty bourgeoisie as a neutraliser of the revolution; at the same time it invests capital in France, Italy, Belgium, England and so on. In our opinion the aim of this is to stimulate the growth of a workers' aristocracy, to enlarge the field of action of the petty bourgeoisie so as to block the revolution. In our opinion it is under this aspect that neocolonialism and the relations between the international working-class movement and our movements must be analysed.

If there have ever been any doubts about the close relations between our struggle and the struggle of the international working-class movement, neocolonialism has proved that there need not be any. Obviously I don't think it is possible to forge closer relations between the peasantry in Guinea and the working-class movement in Europe; what we must do first is try and forge closer links between the peasant movement and the wage-earners' movement in our own country. The example of Latin America gives you a good idea of the limits on closer relations; in Latin America you have an old neocolonial situation and a chance to see clearly the relations between the North American proletariat and the Latin American masses. Other examples could be found nearer home.

There is, however, another aspect I should like to raise and that is that the European left has an intellectual responsibility to study the concrete conditions in our country and help us in this way, as we have very little documentation, very few intellectuals, very little chance to do this kind of work ourselves, and yet it is of key importance: this is a major contribution you can make. Another thing you can do is to support the really revolutionary national liberation movements by all possible means, you must analyse and study these movements and combat in Europe, by all possible means, everything which can be used to further the repression against our peoples. I refer especially to the sale of arms. I should like to say to our Italian friends that we have captured a lot of Italian arms from the Portuguese, not to mention French arms, of course. Moreover, you must unmask courageously all the national liberation movements which are under the thumb of imperialism. People whisper that so-and-so is an American agent, but nobody in the European left has taken a violent and open attitude against these people; it is we ourselves who have to try and denounce these people, who are sometimes even those accepted by the rest of Africa, and this creates a lot of trouble for us.

I think that the left and the international working-class movement should confront those states which claim to be socialist with their responsibilities; this does not, of course, mean cutting off all their possibilities of action, but it does mean denouncing all those states which are neocolonialist.

To end, I should just like to make one last point about solidarity between the international working-class movement and our national liberation struggle. There are two alternatives: either we admit that there really is a struggle against imperialism which interests everybody, or we deny it. If, as would seem from all the evidence, imperialism exists and is trying simultaneously to dominate the working class in all the advanced countries and smother the national liberation movements in all the underdeveloped countries, then there is only one enemy against whom we are fighting. If we are fighting together, then I think the main aspect of our solidarity is extremely simple: it is to fight – I don't think there is any need to discuss this very much. We are struggling in Guinea with guns in our hands, you must struggle in your countries as well – I don't say with guns in your hands, I'm not going to tell you how to struggle, that's your business; but you must find the best means and the best forms of fighting against our common enemy: this is the best form of solidarity …

Amilcar Cabral
Tell No Lies, Claim No Easy Victories
(Extract from PAIGC directive, 1965)

Always bear in mind that the people are not fighting for ideas, for the things in anyone's head. They are fighting to win material benefits, to live better and in peace, to see their lives go forward, to guarantee the future of their children ...

We should recognise as a matter of conscience that there have been many faults and errors in our action whether political or military: an important number of things we should have done we have not done at the right times, or not done at all.

In various regions – and indeed everywhere in a general sense – political work among the people and among our armed forces has not been done appropriately: responsible workers have not carried or have not been able to carry through the work of mobilisation, formation and political organisation defined by the party leadership. Here and there, even among responsible workers, there has been a marked tendency to let things slide ... and even a certain demobilisation which has not been fought and eliminated ...

On the military plane, many plans and objectives established by the Party leadership have not been achieved. With the means we have, we could do much more and better. Some responsible workers have misunderstood the functions of the army and guerrilla forces, have not made good co-ordination between these two and, in certain cases, have allowed themselves to be influenced by preoccupation with the defence of our positions, ignoring the fact that, for us, attack is the best means of defence ...

And with all this as a proof of insufficient political work among our armed forces, there has appeared a certain attitude of 'militarism' which has caused some fighters and even some leaders to forget the fact that we are armed militants and not militarists. This tendency must be urgently fought and eliminated within the army ...

If ten men go to a rice field and do the day's work of eight, there's no reason to be satisfied. It's the same in battle. Ten men fight like eight; that's not enough ... One can always do more. Some people get used to the war, and once you get used to a thing it's the end: you get a bullet up the spout of your gun and you walk around. You hear the motor on the river and you don't use the bazooka that you have, so the Portuguese boats pass unharmed. Let me repeat: one can do more. We have to throw the Portuguese out ...

Create schools and spread education in all liberated areas. Select young people between 14 and 20, those who have at least completed their fourth year, for further training. Oppose without violence all prejudicial customs, the negative aspects of the beliefs and traditions of our people. Oblige every responsible and educated member of our Party to work daily for the improvement of their cultural formation ...

Oppose among the young, especially those over 20, the mania for leaving the country so as to study elsewhere, the blind ambition to acquire a degree, the complex of inferiority and the mistaken idea which leads to the belief that those who study or take courses will thereby become privileged in our country tomorrow ... But also oppose any ill will towards those who study or wish to study – the complex that students will be parasites or future saboteurs of the Party ...

In the liberated areas, do everything possible to normalise the political life of the people. Section committees of the Party (*tabanca* committees), zonal committees, regional committees, must be consolidated and function normally. Frequent meetings must be held to explain to the population what is happening in the struggle, what the Party is endeavouring to do at any given moment, and what the criminal intentions of the enemy may be.

In regions still occupied by the enemy, reinforce clandestine work, the mobilisation and organisation of the populations, and the preparation of militants for action and support of our fighters ...

Develop political work in our armed forces, whether regular or guerrilla, wherever they may be. Hold frequent meetings. Demand serious political work from political commissars. Start political committees, formed by the political commissar and commander of each unit in the regular army.

Oppose tendencies to militarism and make each fighter an exemplary militant of our Party.

Educate ourselves, educate other people, the population in general, to fight fear and ignorance, to eliminate little by little the subjection to nature and natural forces which our economy has not yet mastered. Convince little by little, in particular the militants of the Party, that we shall end by conquering the fear of nature, and that man is the strongest force in nature.

Demand from responsible Party members that they dedicate themselves seriously to study, that they interest themselves in the things and problems of our daily life and struggle in their fundamental and essential aspect, and not simply in their appearance ... Learn from life, learn from our people, learn from books, learn from the experience of others. Never stop learning.

Responsible members must take life seriously, conscious of their responsibilities, thoughtful about carrying them out, and with a comradeship based on work and duty done ... Nothing of this is incompatible with the joy of living, or with love for life and its amusements, or with confidence in the future and in our work ...

Reinforce political work and propaganda within the enemy's armed forces. Write posters, pamphlets, letters. Draw slogans on the roads. Establish cautious links with enemy personnel who want to contact us. Act audaciously and with great initiative in this way ... Do everything possible to help enemy soldiers to desert. Assure them of security so as to encourage their desertion. Carry out political work among Africans who are still in enemy service, whether civilian or military. Persuade these brothers to change direction so as to serve the Party within enemy ranks or desert with arms and ammunition to our units.

We must practise revolutionary democracy in every aspect of our Party life. Every responsible member must have the courage of his responsibilities, exacting from others a proper respect for his work and properly respecting the work of others. Hide nothing from the masses of our people. Tell no lies. Expose lies whenever they are told. Mask no difficulties, mistakes, failures. Claim no easy victories ...

A.G. Frank
The Development of Underdevelopment
(First published in *Monthly Review*, September 1966)

We cannot hope to formulate adequate development theory and policy for the majority of the world's population who suffer from underdevelopment without first learning how their past economic and social history gave rise to their present underdevelopment. Yet most historians study only the developed metropolitan countries and pay scant attention to the colonial and underdeveloped lands. For this reason most of our theoretical categories and guides to development policy have been distilled exclusively from the historical experience of the European and North American advanced capitalist nations.

Since the historical experience of the colonial and underdeveloped countries has demonstrably been quite different, available theory therefore fails to reflect the past of the underdeveloped part of the world entirely, and reflects the past of the world as a whole only in part. More important, our ignorance of the underdeveloped countries' history leads us to assume that their past and indeed their present resemble earlier stages of the history of the now developed countries. This ignorance and this assumption lead us into serious misconceptions about contemporary underdevelopment and development. Further, most studies of development and underdevelopment fail to take account of the economic and other relations between the metropolis and its economic colonies throughout the history of the world-wide expansion and development of the mercantilist and capitalist system. Consequently, most of our theory fails to explain the structure and development of the capitalist system as a whole and to account for its simultaneous generation of underdevelopment in some of its parts and economic development in others.

It is generally held that economic development occurs in a succession of capitalist stages and that today's underdeveloped countries are still in a stage, sometimes depicted as an original stage of history, through which the now developed countries passed long ago. Yet even a modest acquaintance with history shows that underdevelopment is not original or traditional and that neither the past nor the present of the underdeveloped countries resembles in any important respect the past of the now developed countries. The now developed countries were never underdeveloped, though they may have been undeveloped. It is also widely believed that the contemporary underdevelopment of a country can be understood as the product or reflection solely of its own economic, political, social, and cultural characteristics or structure. Yet historical research demonstrates that contemporary underdevelopment is in large part the historical product of past and continuing economic and other relations between the satellite underdeveloped and the now developed metropolitan countries. Furthermore, these relations are an essential part of the structure and development of the capitalist system on a world scale as a whole. A related and also largely erroneous view is that the development of these underdeveloped countries and, within them, of their most underdeveloped domestic areas, must and will be generated or stimulated by diffusing capital, institutions, values, etc., to them from the international and national capitalist metropoles. Historical perspective based on the underdeveloped countries' past experience suggests that, on the contrary, in the underdeveloped countries economic development can now occur only independently of most of these relations of diffusion.

Evident inequalities of income and differences in culture have led many observers to see 'dual' societies and economies in the underdeveloped countries. Each of the two parts is supposed to have a history of its own, a structure, and a contemporary dynamic largely independent of the other. Supposedly, only one part of the economy and society has been importantly affected by intimate economic relations with the 'outside' capitalist world; and that part, it is held, became modern, capitalist, and relatively developed precisely because of this contact. The other part is widely regarded as variously isolated, subsistence-based, feudal, or precapitalist, and therefore more underdeveloped.

I believe on the contrary that the entire 'dual society' thesis is false and that the policy recommendations to which it leads will, if acted upon, serve only to intensify and perpetuate the very conditions of underdevelopment they are supposedly designed to remedy.

A mounting body of evidence suggests, and I am confident that future historical research will confirm, that the expansion of the capitalist system over the past centuries effectively and entirely penetrated even the apparently most isolated sectors of the underdeveloped world. Therefore, the economic, political, social, and cultural institutions and relations we now observe there are the products of the historical development of the capitalist system no less than are the seemingly more modern or capitalist features of the national metropoles of these underdeveloped countries. Analogously to the relations between development and underdevelopment on the international level, the contemporary underdeveloped institutions of the so-called backward or feudal domestic areas of an underdeveloped country are no less the product of the single historical process of capitalist development than are the so-called capitalist institutions of the supposedly more progressive areas. In this paper I should like to sketch the kinds of evidence which support this thesis and at the same time indicate lines along which further study and research could fruitfully proceed.

II

The Secretary General of the Latin American Center for Research in the Social Sciences writes in that Center's journal: 'The privileged position of the city has its origin in the colonial period. It was founded by the Conqueror to serve the same ends that it still serves today; to incorporate the indigenous population into the economy brought and developed by that Conqueror and his descendants. The regional city was an instrument of conquest and is still today an instrument of domination.' The Instituto Nacional Indigenista (National Indian Institute) of Mexico confirms this observation when it notes that 'the mestizo population, in fact, always lives in a city, a center of an intercultural region, which acts as the metropolis of a zone of indigenous population and which maintains with the underdeveloped communities an intimate relation which links the center with the satellite communities'. The Institute goes on to point out that 'between the mestizos who live in the nuclear city of the region and the Indians who live in the peasant hinterland there is in reality a closer economic and social interdependence than might at first glance appear' and that the provincial metropoles 'by being centers of intercourse are also centers of exploitation'.

Thus these metropolis–satellite relations are not limited to the imperial or international level but penetrate and structure the very economic, political, and social life of the Latin American colonies and countries. Just as the colonial and national capital and its export sector become the satellite of the Iberian (and later of other) metropoles of the world economic system, this satellite immediately becomes a colonial and then a national metropolis with respect to the productive sectors and population of the interior. Furthermore, the provincial capitals, which thus are themselves satellites of the national metropolis – and, through the latter, of the world metropolis – are in turn provincial centers around which their own local satellites orbit.

Thus, a whole chain of constellations of metropoles and satellites relates all parts of the whole system from its metropolitan center in Europe or the United States to the farthest outpost in the Latin American countryside.

When we examine this metropolis–satellite structure, we find that each of the satellites, including now-underdeveloped Spain and Portugal, serves as an instrument to suck capital or economic surplus out of its own satellites and to channel part of this surplus to the world metropolis of which all are satellites. Moreover, each national and local metropolis serves to impose and maintain the monopolistic structure and exploitative relationship of this system (as the Instituto Nacional Indigenista of Mexico calls it) as long as it serves the interests of the metropoles, which take advantage of this global, national, and local structure to promote their own development and the enrichment of their ruling classes.

These are the principal and still surviving structural characteristics which were implanted in Latin America by the Conquest. Beyond examining the establishment of this colonial structure in its historical context, the proposed approach calls for study of the development – and underdevelopment – of these metropoles and satellites of Latin America throughout the following and still continuing historical process. In this way we can understand why there were and still are tendencies in the Latin American and world capitalist structure which seem to lead to the development of the metropolis and the underdevelopment of the satellite and why, particularly, the satellized national, regional, and local metropoles in Latin America find that their economic development is at best a limited or underdeveloped development.

That present underdevelopment of Latin America is the result of its centuries-long participation in the process of world capitalist development, I believe I have shown in my case studies of the economic and social histories of Chile and Brazil. My study of Chilean history suggests that the Conquest not only incorporated this country fully into the expansion and development of the world mercantile and later industrial capitalist system but that it also introduced the monopolistic metropolis–satellite structure and development of capitalism into the Chilean domestic economy and society itself. This structure then penetrated and permeated all of Chile very quickly. Since that time and in the course of world and Chilean history during the epochs of colonialism, free trade, imperialism, and the present, Chile has become increasingly marked by the economic, social, and political structure of satellite underdevelopment. This development of underdevelopment continues today, both in Chile's still increasing satellization by the world metropolis and through the ever more acute polarization of Chile's domestic economy.

The history of Brazil is perhaps the clearest case of both national and regional development of underdevelopment. The expansion of the world economy since the beginning of the sixteenth century successively converted the Northeast, the Minas Gerais interior, the North, and the Center-South (Rio de Janeiro, São Paulo, and Parana) into export economies and incorporated them into the structure and development of the world capitalist system. Each of these regions experienced what may have appeared as economic development during the period of its respective golden age. But it was a satellite development which was neither self-generating nor self-perpetuating. As the market or the productivity of the first three regions declined, foreign and domestic economic interest in them waned; and they were left to develop the underdevelopment they live today. In the fourth region, the coffee economy experienced a similar though not yet quite as serious fate (though the development of a synthetic coffee substitute promises to deal it a mortal blow in the not too distant future). All of this historical evidence contradicts the generally accepted theses that Latin America suffers from a dual society or from the survival of feudal institutions and that these are important obstacles to its economic development.

During the First World War, however, and even more during the Great Depression and the Second World War, São Paulo began to build up an industrial establishment which is the largest in Latin America today. The question arises whether this industrial development did or can break Brazil out of the cycle of satellite development and underdevelopment which has characterized its other regions and national history within the capitalist system so far. I believe that the answer is no. Domestically the evidence so far is fairly clear. The development of industry in São Paulo has not brought greater riches to the other regions of Brazil. Instead, it converted them into internal colonial satellites, de-capitalized them further, and consolidated or even deepened their underdevelopment. There is little evidence to suggest that this process is likely to be reversed in the foreseeable future except insofar as the provincial poor migrate and become the poor of the metropolitan cities. Externally, the evidence is that although the initial development of São Paulo's industry was relatively autonomous, it is being increasingly satellized by the world capitalist metropolis and its future development possibilities are increasingly restricted. This development, my studies lead me to believe, also appears destined to limited or underdeveloped development as long as it takes place in the present economic, political, and social framework.

IV

We must conclude, in short, that underdevelopment is not due to the survival of archaic institutions and the existence of capital shortage in regions that have remained isolated from the stream of world history. On the contrary, underdevelopment was and still is generated by the very same historical process which also generated economic development: the development of capitalism itself. This view, I am glad to say, is gaining adherents among students of Latin America and is proving its worth in shedding new light on the problems of the area and in affording a better perspective for the formulation of theory and policy.

The same historical and structural approach can also lead to better development theory and policy by generating a series of hypotheses about development and underdevelopment such as those I am testing in my current research. The hypotheses are derived from the empirical observation and theoretical assumption that within this world-embracing metropolis–satellite structure the metropoles tend to develop and the satellites to underdevelop. The first hypothesis has already been mentioned above: that in contrast to the development of the world metropolis which is no one's satellite, the development of the national and other subordinate metropoles is limited by their satellite status. It is perhaps more difficult to test this hypothesis than the following ones because part of its confirmation depends on the test of the other hypotheses. Nonetheless, this hypothesis appears to be generally confirmed by the non-autonomous and unsatisfactory economic and especially industrial development of Latin America's national metropoles, as documented in the studies already cited. The most important and at the same time most confirmatory examples are the metropolitan regions of Buenos Aires and São Paulo whose growth only began in the nineteenth century, was therefore largely untrammeled by any colonial heritage, but was and remains a satellite development largely dependent on the outside metropolis, first of Britain and then of the United States.

A second hypothesis is that the satellites experience their greatest economic development and especially their most classically capitalist industrial development if and when their ties to their metropolis are weakest. This hypothesis is almost diametrically opposed to the generally accepted thesis that development in the underdeveloped countries follows from the greatest degree of contact with and diffusion from the metropolitan developed countries. This hypothesis seems to be confirmed by two kinds of relative isolation that Latin America has experienced in the course of its history. One is the temporary isolation caused by the crises of war or depression in the world metropolis. Apart from minor ones, five periods of such major crises stand out and seem to confirm the hypothesis. These are: the European (and especially Spanish) depression of the seventeenth century, the Napoleonic Wars, the First World War, the depression of the 1930s, and the Second World War. It is clearly established and generally recognized that the most important recent industrial development – especially of Argentina, Brazil, and Mexico, but also of other countries such as Chile – has taken place precisely during the periods of the two World Wars and the intervening depression. Thanks to the consequent loosening of trade and investment ties during these periods, the satellites initiated marked autonomous industrialization and growth. Historical research demonstrates that the same thing happened in Latin America during Europe's seventeenth-century depression. Manufacturing grew in the Latin American countries, and several of them such as Chile became exporters of manufactured goods. The Napoleonic Wars gave rise to independence movements in Latin America, and these should perhaps also be interpreted as confirming the development hypothesis.

The other kind of isolation which tends to confirm the second hypothesis is the geographic and economic isolation of regions which at one time were relatively weakly tied to and poorly integrated into the mercantilist and capitalist system. My preliminary research suggests that in Latin America it was these regions which initiated and experienced the most promising self-generating economic development of the classical industrial capitalist type. The most important regional cases probably are Tucumán and Asunción, as well as other cities such as Mendoza and Rosario, in the interior of Argentina and Paraguay during the end of the eighteenth and the beginning of the nineteenth centuries. Seventeenth- and eighteenth-century São Paulo, long before coffee was grown there, is another example. Perhaps Antioquia in Colombia and Puebla and Querétaro in Mexico are other examples. In its own way, Chile was also an example since, before the sea route around the Horn was opened, this country was relatively isolated at the end of the long voyage from Europe via Panama. All of these regions became manufacturing centers and even exporters, usually of textiles, during the periods preceding their effective incorporation as satellites into the colonial, national, and world capitalist system.

Internationally, of course, the classic case of industrialization through non-participation as a satellite in the capitalist world system is obviously that of Japan after the Meiji Restoration. Why, one may ask, was resource-poor but unsatellized Japan able to industrialize so quickly at the end of the century while resource-rich Latin American countries and Russia were not able to do so and the latter was easily beaten by Japan in the War of 1904 after the same forty years of development efforts? The second hypothesis suggests that the fundamental reason is that Japan was not satellized either during the Tokugawa or the Meiji period and therefore did not have its development structurally limited as did the countries which were so satellized.

VI

A corollary of the second hypothesis is that when the metropolis recovers from its crisis and re-establishes the trade and investment ties which fully reincorporate the satellites into the system, or when the metropolis expands to incorporate previously isolated regions into the world-wide system, the previous development and industrialization of these regions are choked off or channelled into directions which are not self-perpetuating and promising. This happened after each of the five crises cited above. The renewed expansion of trade and the spread of economic liberalism in the eighteenth and nineteenth centuries choked off and reversed the manufacturing development which Latin America had experienced during the seventeenth century, and in some places at the beginning of the nineteenth. After the First World War, the new national industry of Brazil suffered serious consequences from American economic invasion. The increase in the growth rate of Gross National Product and particularly of industrialization throughout Latin America was again reversed and industry became increasingly satellized after the Second World War and especially after the post-Korean War recovery and expansion of the metropolis. Far from having become more developed since then, industrial sectors of Brazil and most conspicuously of Argentina have become structurally more and more underdeveloped and less and less able to generate continued industrialization and/or sustain development of the economy. This process, from which India also suffers, is reflected in a whole gamut of balance of payments, inflationary, and other economic and political difficulties, and promises to yield to no solution short of far-reaching structural change.

Our hypothesis suggests that fundamentally the same process occurred even more dramatically with the incorporation into the system of previously unsatellized regions. The expansion of Buenos Aires as a satellite of Great Britain and the introduction of free trade in the interest of the ruling groups of both metropoles destroyed the manufacturing and much of the remainder of the economic base of the previously relatively prosperous interior almost entirely. Manufacturing was destroyed by foreign competition, lands were taken and concentrated into latifundia by the rapaciously growing export economy, intra-regional distribution of income became much more unequal, and the previously developing regions became simple satellites of Buenos Aires and, through it, of London. The provincial centers did not yield to satellization without a struggle. This metropolis–satellite conflict was much of the cause of the long political and armed struggle between the Unitarists in Buenos Aires and the Federalists in the provinces, and it may be said to have been the sole important cause of the War of the Triple Alliance in which Buenos Aires, Montevideo, and Rio de Janeiro, encouraged and helped by London, destroyed not only the autonomously developing economy of Paraguay but killed off nearly all of its population which was unwilling to give in. Though this is no doubt the most spectacular example which tends to confirm the hypothesis, I believe that historical research on the satellization of previously relatively independent yeoman-farming and incipient manufacturing regions such as the Caribbean islands will confirm it further. These regions did not have a chance against the forces of expanding and developing capitalism, and their own development had to be sacrificed to that of others. The economy and industry of Argentina, Brazil, and other countries which have experienced the effects of metropolitan recovery since the Second World War are today suffering much the same fate, if fortunately still in lesser degree.

VII

A third major hypothesis derived from the metropolis–satellite structure is that the regions which are the most underdeveloped and feudal-seeming today are the ones which had the closest ties to the metropolis in the past. They are the regions which were the greatest exporters of primary products to and biggest sources of capital for the world metropolis and which were abandoned by the metropolis when for one reason or another business fell off. This hypothesis also contradicts the generally held thesis that the source of a region's underdevelopment is its isolation and its pre-capitalist institutions.

This hypothesis seems to be amply confirmed by the former supersatellite development and present ultra-underdevelopment of the once sugar-exporting West Indies, Northeastern Brazil, the ex-mining districts of Minas Gerais in Brazil, highland Peru, and Bolivia, and the central Mexican states of Guanajuato, Zacatecas, and others whose names were made world famous centuries ago by their silver. There surely are no major regions in Latin America which are today more cursed by underdevelopment and poverty; yet all of these regions, like Bengal in India, once provided the life blood of mercantile and industrial capitalist development – in the metropolis. These regions' participation in the development of the world capitalist system gave them, already in their golden age, the typical structure of underdevelopment of a capitalist export economy. When the market for their sugar or the wealth of their mines disappeared and the metropolis abandoned them to their own devices, the already existing economic, political, and social structure of these regions prohibited autonomous generation of economic development and left them no alternative but to turn in upon themselves and to degenerate into the ultra-underdevelopment we find there today.

These considerations suggest two further and related hypotheses. One is that the latifundium, irrespective of whether it appears as a plantation or a hacienda today, was typically born as a commercial enterprise which created for itself the institutions which permitted it to respond to increased demand in the world or national market by expanding the amount of its land, capital, and labor and to increase the supply of its products. The fifth hypothesis is that the latifundia which appear isolated, subsistence-based, and semi-feudal today saw the demand for their products or their productive capacity decline and that they are to be found principally in the above-named former agricultural and mining export regions whose economic activity declined in general. These two hypotheses run counter to the notions of most people, and even to the opinions of some historians and other students of the subject, according to whom the historical roots and socioeconomic causes of Latin American latifundia and agrarian institutions are to be found in the transfer of feudal institutions from Europe and/or in economic depression.

The evidence to test these hypotheses is not open to easy general inspection and requires detailed analyses of many cases. Nonetheless, some important confirmatory evidence is available. The growth of the latifundium in nineteenth-century Argentina and Cuba is a clear case in support of the fourth hypothesis and can in no way be attributed to the transfer of feudal institutions during colonial times. The same is evidently the case of the post-revolutionary and contemporary resurgence of latifundia particularly in the north of Mexico, which produce for the American market, and of similar ones on the coast of Peru and the new coffee regions of Brazil. The conversion of previously yeoman-farming Caribbean islands, such as Barbados, into sugar-exporting economies at various times between the seventeenth and twentieth centuries and the resulting rise of the latifundia in these islands would seem to confirm the fourth hypothesis as well. In Chile, the rise of the latifundium and the creation of the institutions of servitude which later came to be called feudal occurred in the eighteenth century and have been conclusively shown to be the result of and response to the opening of a market for Chilean wheat in Lima. Even the growth and consolidation of the latifundium in seventeenth-century Mexico – which most expert students have attributed to a depression of the economy caused by the decline of mining and a shortage of Indian labor and to a consequent turning in upon itself and ruralization of the economy – occurred at a time when urban population and demand were growing, food shortages became acute, food prices skyrocketed, and the profitability of other economic activities such as mining and foreign trade declined. All of these and other factors rendered hacienda agriculture more profitable. Thus, even this case would seem to confirm the hypothesis that the growth of the latifundium and its feudal-seeming conditions of servitude in Latin America has always been and still is the commercial response to increased demand and that it does not represent the transfer or survival of alien institutions that have remained beyond the reach of capitalist development. The emergence of latifundia, which today really are more or less (though not entirely) isolated, might then be attributed to the causes advanced in the fifth hypothesis – i.e. the decline of previously profitable agricultural enterprises whose capital was, and whose currently produced economic surplus still is, transferred elsewhere by owners and merchants, who frequently are the same persons or families. Testing this hypothesis requires still more detailed analysis, some of which I have undertaken in a study on Brazilian agriculture.

All of these hypotheses and studies suggest that the global extension and unity of the capitalist system, its monopoly structure and uneven development throughout its history, and the resulting persistence of commercial rather than industrial capitalism in the underdeveloped world (including its most industrially advanced countries) deserve much more attention in the study of economic development and cultural change than they have hitherto received. Though science and truth know no national boundaries, it is probably new generations of scientists from the underdeveloped countries themselves who most need to, and best can, devote the necessary attention to these problems and clarify the process of underdevelopment and development. It is their people who in the last analysis face the task of changing this no longer acceptable process and eliminating this miserable reality.

They will not be able to accomplish these goals by importing sterile stereotypes from the metropolis which do not correspond to their satellite economic reality and do not respond to their liberating political needs. To change their reality they must understand it. For this reason, I hope that better confirmation of these hypotheses and further pursuit of the proposed historical, holistic, and structural approach may help the peoples of the underdeveloped countries to understand the causes and eliminate the reality of their development of underdevelopment and their underdevelopment of development.

Part Three

African Socialism

Julius K. Nyerere
'Introduction' *to* Nyerere on Socialism
(First published in Dar es Salaam, 1969)

What is a Socialist Society?
What should we look for when trying to determine whether a particular society is socialist? What are the universal characteristics and values which would underlie differences of institution and organization in a socialist society?

First, and most central of all, is that under socialism Man is the purpose of all social activity. The service of man, the furtherance of his human development, is in fact the purpose of society itself. There is no other purpose above this; no glorification of 'nation', no increase in production – nothing is more central to a socialist society than an acceptance that Man is its justification for existence.

In one sense, all the other characteristics of socialism follow from this. But in view of the historical development of mankind, one more thing has to be stated categorically. The word 'man' to a socialist, means all men – all human beings. Male and female; black, white, brown, yellow; long-nosed and short-nosed; educated and uneducated; wise and stupid; strong and weak; all these, and all other distinctions between human beings, are irrelevant to the fact that all members of the society – all the human beings who are its purpose – are equal.

The equality of man may or may not be susceptible to scientific proof. But its acceptance as a basic assumption of life in society is the core and essence of socialism. No one who qualifies his belief in the equality of man is really a socialist. A society is not socialist if in its organization, or its practices, it discriminates, or allows discrimination, between its members because of their parentage, their place of birth, their appearance, their religious beliefs, or any thing other than their behaviour in relation to their fellows. The existence of racialism, of tribalism, or of religious intolerance, means that a society is not socialist – regardless of whatever other attributes it may have. A society in which all men are of equal account will probably be socialist, because socialist organization is really the means by which the diversity of mankind is harnessed to the common benefit of all men. Socialism, as a system, is in fact the organization of men's inequalities to serve their equality. Their equality is socialist belief.

The upholding of human dignity could be expected to follow automatically from these two basic characteristics of a socialist society. For a society cannot acquiesce in the abasement or humiliation of its own purpose; on the contrary, a man-centred society would promote the dignity and the growth to excellence of all the human beings who are members of it. Indeed, it could not draw boundaries around itself in this matter. A socialist society would seek to uphold human dignity everywhere; and however limited its capacity in this respect, it could never act in such a manner as to be itself responsible for the denial of any man's humanity.

Democracy is another essential characteristic of a socialist society. For the people's equality must be reflected in the political organization; everyone must be an equal participant in the government of his society. Whatever devices are used to implement this principle, the people (meaning all the members of the society equally) must be sovereign, and they must be able to exert their sovereignty without causing a break-down of the law and order or of the administration in their society. There must, in other words, be some mechanisms by which the people exert their will peacefully, and achieve changes in the laws which govern them; they must be able to change the personnel in positions of leadership within the framework of the normal workings of the social system. It is difficult to see how this could be achieved without the existence of some system of free elections if the society is so large that direct democracy (the direct government by all the people) is impossible. But elections are not the beginning and end of democracy. The freedom of the people to choose their own representatives is important, but it is equally important that the people's representatives should possess the freedom and the power to exert effective control over those sectors of the social organization for which they have been given responsibility. And none of these things is possible unless every other aspect of society – its economic, social and legal organization – is such as to emphasize and serve man's equality. A political democracy which exists in a society of gross economic inequalities, or of social inequality, is at best imperfect, and at worst a hollow sham.

A socialist society, therefore, will consist of workers – and only of workers. Every member will contribute, by his work, to the total of wealth and welfare produced by the society, and he will receive a return in proportion to his efforts and his contribution to the wellbeing of the community. Only small children, the men and women who are too old to work, and the sick, are exempt from the responsibility to work. To everyone else this duty, and this right, belongs. For work is not only a duty to society; it is also a right of every human being, and anyone who is deprived of the opportunity to do something useful for himself, his fellow citizens, and his society, needs and merits some compensation. The child needs food, love, and care; that is obvious and unquestioned. The sick and crippled need an opportunity to do whatever is within their power, and also the willing gift of such food, clothing and shelter as they are unable to provide for themselves. And the society has a responsibility also towards any person whom it deprives of an opportunity to earn his own living. Under socialism there could not be a group of 'permanently unemployed'; but technological changes, and the economic flexibility which must exist in a developing community, may mean that some individuals need support while they are receiving new training, or especially in a country like Tanzania, until the first harvest when they return to the land.

Apart from these groups, however, everyone in a socialist society will be a worker. Unless this is so, socialism cannot exist; it would collapse through its own poverty. But the word 'worker' in this context means anyone who works; he may be a peasant working on his own shamba, a member of a co-operative farming group, or a woman looking after her small children and the family home. None of these people receive wages for their activity, but they do contribute to the total output of goods and welfare. Nor is it necessary to make a distinction between a wage-earner whose work involves much physical labour, and one who works in an office or carries managerial or professional responsibilities. All who contribute to the society by their work are workers.

It follows from this that in a socialist society there will be no exploitation of one man by another. There will be no 'masters' who sit in idleness while others labour on 'their' farms or in 'their' factories. Nor will there be too great a degree of inequality between the incomes of different members of the society. It is arguable that an especially clever man, or an especially hard-working man, contributes more to the society than one who does not have these qualities, and that he is therefore entitled to receive greater remuneration. But can anyone man do work which is 100 times more valuable than that of another? It is true that for some jobs to be done effectively certain extra facilities are needed by the worker; a teacher or an administrator, for example, will need a place where he can study quietly, will need to be able to obtain books of a certain type, and so on. But does anyone need a palace while another receives only a 'bedspace'?

There is, however, another form of exploitation which a socialist society would avoid, and to which it may be especially prone. A man who cheats his fellows by dishonesty, who fails to do a full day's work, or who fails to co-operate with his fellows because he wants to bolster his own personal interests, is exploiting other men. Society has as much a right, and a duty, to prevent these kinds of exploitation as it has to prevent the exploitation which arises from individual ownership of the means of production and exchange.

For this is another characteristic of a socialist community. It would be so organized that the tools of production and the mechanisms of exchange are firmly under the control of the people. Control in this context does not only mean regulation in the negative sense of stopping people from doing certain things. It also means the power to do positive things –to expand a factory, to build a new one in a particular place, to invest in a risky enterprise, etc. It seems almost certain that this will normally involve public ownership, at least of the key points of the economy, and one would therefore expect a socialist society to be distinguished from a non-socialist society in this matter of ownership of the economy. It may be, however, that particular societies can devise some other means of securing effective and positive control over their economy in such a manner as to preclude exploitation. This would be unusual, but if they can, that society could still be recognized as socialist, provided that the other essential characteristics of socialism exist.

It may be necessary to add that public ownership can be of many types, and it has a purpose. The purpose is to ensure that there is no exploitation in the economy, and no built-in tendency towards inequalities. It could therefore be ownership by the people through the instrument of their elected central government, or their local government; or it could be expressed through co-operatives, or other group organizations. The appropriate form would vary both according to the technology concerned, and according to the other practices and desires of the society. The essential point is that no individual or group of individuals would be able to hold to ransom either the society as a whole, or other individuals, by means of their exclusive control of an instrument which is necessary to the increasing well-being of the community.

Obviously this does not preclude private ownership of the things which pertain to the individual worker, or to the family. Such a suggestion is simply put forward to frighten the timid men and to mislead those trying to find an alternative to the social evils of capitalism. A farmer can own his hoe, a carpenter can own his hand-saw; any worker can own the tools which he uses by himself as a supplement to his own hands. Similarly, a family can own the house in which it lives, the furniture and equipment which increase the comfort of its members, and so on. The question of public ownership arises when men have to co-operate together in the pursuit of a particular objective. When the tool has to be used by two men it must be owned equally; when the product is necessary for the decent life of others they must be involved in the control over it. Any suggestion that socialism involves the nationalization or community ownership of every artefact of life is the suggestion of a fool or a mischief-maker.

There is another bogeyman which is used to frighten people, and that is the suggestion that individual freedom does not exist under socialism. The purpose of socialism is to enlarge the real freedom of man, to expand his opportunity of living in dignity and well-being. An obviously essential part of this is that the laws of the society shall be known, be applied equally, and that people shall not be subject to arbitrary arrest, or persecution by the servants of the society. The Rule of Law is a part of socialism; until it prevails, socialism does not prevail. By itself the Rule of Law does not bring socialism; but you cannot have socialism without it, because it is the expression of man's equality in one facet of social living.

The final characteristic of a socialist society which must be listed here is the social values it emphasizes. In a feudal or aristocratic system, birth is a matter of the highest importance; if you are born of certain parents you have social respect as well as economic advantages accorded to you as of right. In a capitalist system, individual wealth is the most important single criterion for respect, and the competitive spirit is acclaimed as a paramount social virtue, in practice if not in theory. The social values of a socialist society will be very different from either of these. First, both the organization and the teaching will emphasize man's co-operative spirit, his desire to work in harmony with his friends and neighbours, not his personal aggressiveness. Second, it will reserve its highest respect and its highest prizes for those whose life and work demonstrate the greatest service, not the greatest personal acquisitiveness. Comparative wealth will not be the criterion on which a man is judged by his fellows. Success in a socialist society will imply that a man has earned the respect, admiration and love of his fellow citizens, by his desire to serve, and by the contribution he has made to the wellbeing of the community.

All these things together are the hallmark of a socialist society. When you find them you have found a society which is socialist. When you find some but not others, you have found a society which is partly socialist or which has the elements of socialism in it. And when you find a deliberate attempt being made to build these values and organizational systems, then you have found a society which is working towards socialism.

Socialism and the Production of Wealth

Both before and since the Arusha Declaration (1967), the Government and Party in Tanzania have been emphasizing the need to increase output – to increase the production of wealth. We shall continue to do this, because *in our circumstances* an increase in the amount of goods produced and available for social services, for distribution, and for investment, is a socialist purpose. Our country is bedevilled by its present poverty; people are sick, ignorant, and live in very poor conditions, because we do not produce enough wealth to be able to eradicate these evils. We have to increase our production of goods if we are to enable everyone to live in conditions of human dignity. At present not even complete equality in the distribution of the available wealth would do this; our national income per head is something between Shs. 400/- and Shs. 460/- per year. An increase in production must have a very high priority in our social plans; it is the cornerstone for all our other ambitions.

It is necessary to stress this because the production of wealth for its own sake is not a socialist purpose. The purpose of production must always be the greater well-being of man; goods must be produced because they are useful and make life better. To Tanzanians that looks very obvious; indeed, most Tanzanian citizens may wonder what I am talking about, because it is so obvious that extra food, bricks, roofing, ovens, chairs, tables, beds, clothing, and so on and so on, will make life better. Yet we are still in danger of being attracted by the idea of 'wealth' as represented by all the consumer goods we see advertised in foreign magazines (and even Tanzanian ones), or in the films, etc. We are still in danger of accepting the idea that the greatest production of consumer goods is the criterion by which a nation, or an economic system, should be judged.

A socialist does not look at things that way. He asks, what sort of production? What is it that is being produced? Under what conditions? And what effect does it have, on balance, on the society as a whole? To a socialist, therefore, there is no virtue in 'creating a market' for something which people have never thought of wanting and, really have no need for, but which someone hopes to make a profit by producing. This happens all the time in capitalist societies; it is an inherent part of them. There are very many examples which could be given; I will mention only two. In some societies it is a matter of pride, I am told, to buy an electric toothbrush-presumably the energy required to clean one's mouth properly is beyond the strength of well-fed men and women! An even more useless object which manufacturers were trying to persuade the people of another capitalist country to buy was something called a 'non-spill' tray, which was said to enable you to swing a tray holding glasses of liquid without spilling a drop! Advertisements to promote the sale of such things are a normal part of capitalist society; their newspapers, television, etc., make every attempt to suggest to people that they will be 'old-fashioned' if they do not acquire the object in question. In other words, an attempt is made to make people discontented without the thing which is being 'promoted', so that they will buy it – if they have enough money. This is called 'creating a market', and 'creating a market' is said to be an inherent part of 'progress', of increasing the national income, and of 'free consumer choice'.

A socialist will not be impressed by such values, nor even by the talk of people 'exercising their freedom as consumers', if, at the same time as these things are being produced and sold, other human values are being ignored or sacrificed. For the incredible thing is that in the same countries which encourage this kind of 'market creation', other people are living in conditions of great poverty, educational facilities are starved of funds, and completely free hospital care for everyone is said to be too expensive for the community to bear! The production of wealth for the benefit of man – that is production for socialist purposes – would have rather different results. Electric tooth-brushes and non-spill trays – if they were produced at all – would not be produced until after these more basic needs had been met.

To a socialist, the first priority of production must be the manufacture and distribution of such goods as will allow every member of the society to have sufficient food, clothing and shelter, to sustain a decent life. Other goods would be produced only if they in some way hastened the day when this goal was reached. Apart from these basic needs of man, a socialist society would put much emphasis on the production of socially advantageous goods. It would concentrate on better educational facilities, medical care, places of community activity like libraries, community centres, parks, etc. It would devote resources also to social values which have nothing to do with production-things like improving the hours and conditions of work, or maintaining and improving the natural beauties of the world in which we live. Of course, some care, money, and energy have to be spent on these non-consumer products even before the basic job is complete, because they affect the way people will be able to live. Thus, for example, when building new houses in a town it is necessary to plan for public spaces and leave room for community buildings even if you cannot build them immediately; it is necessary to provide minimum educational and health services as far as you can; and it is essential to spend that minimum amount of money which is necessary to prevent the destruction of that natural beauty or wild life which could never be replaced if it was once allowed to disappear.

In a socialist society, therefore, man as a consumer is not 'king'. Instead man is recognized as a human being who desires human dignity, who is a consumer both privately and socially, and who is also a producer. For socialism involves an acceptance of the fact that man's life in society cannot be divided up into bits. A man is concerned with his life as a whole; if he is starving it is no use expecting him to be happy because he has the freedom to vote every few years, or if he is well-fed it is no use expecting him to be happy as a slave. Under a socialist society men come together to try and organize the community in which they live so that all their different needs and all their co-operative social values are considered, with priority being given to those which are most urgent, but without any being destroyed.

In Tanzania the increased output of wealth so that all our people may live decently is the most urgent thing. But we cannot allow this need to destroy our belief in human equality and human dignity. On the contrary, we have to organize our expansion of wealth in such a way as to give the maximum possible emphasis to these other values.

Socialism is Secular

The fact that socialism is concerned with all aspects of man's life in society does not mean that man as an individual ceases to exist. Every person is unique; there are some things which are, and which must be, private to himself. Society has the right where necessary to regulate, encourage, or discourage those actions of individuals which affect other members of the society. It has no business in relation to things which are by nature or by method entirely personal. Once a man has fulfilled his responsibilities to the society, it is nothing to do with socialism whether he spends his spare time painting, dancing, writing poetry, playing football, or just sitting. Nor is it any business of socialism if an individual is, or is not, inspired in his daily life by a belief in God, nor if he does, or does not, attend a place of religious worship or pray elsewhere.

Socialism is concerned with man's life in *this* society. A man's relationship with his God is a personal matter for him and him alone; his beliefs about the hereafter are his own affair. These things have nothing to do with anyone else as long as he does not indulge in practices which adversely affect the similar private rights of other members of the society. Thus, for example, a man's belief that he should pray at specified hours of the day and night wherever he happens to be is a matter for him, and no one else has the right to interfere. But a religion which involved human sacrifice, or demanded the exploitation of human beings, could not be allowed to carry out these practices.

Socialism's concern about the organization of life on earth does not involve any supposition about life elsewhere, or about man's soul, or the procedures for fulfilling the will of God or Gods. Socialism is secular. It has nothing to say about whether there is a God. Certainly it rests on the assumption of the equality of man, but people can reach this conclusion by many routes. People can accept the equality of man because they believe that all men were created by God, they can believe it because they feel that the scientific evidence supports such a conclusion, or they can accept it simply because they believe it is the only basis on which life in society can be organized without injustice. It does not matter why people accept the equality of man as the basis of social organization; all that matters is that they do accept it.

This means that socialism cannot require that its adherents be atheists. There is not the slightest necessity for people to study metaphysics and decide whether there is one God, many Gods, or no God, before they can be socialist. It is not necessary to try and decide whether there is an after-life, or what kind, before you can be a socialist. These questions are important to man, but irrelevant to socialism; trying to bring them into the discussion about socialism simply causes quarrels between socialists, and thus weakens the struggle for the things they all support. What matters in socialism and to socialists is that you should care about a particular kind of social relationship on this earth. Why you care is your own affair. There is nothing incompatible between socialism and Christianity, Islam, or any other religion which accepts the equality of man on earth.

The fact that socialism and religion are two different things does not mean that socialism is anti-religious. In a socialist society the members of the community would be free to be religious, and to follow whatever religion they wish; the society would try very hard not to make a decision which outrages the religious feelings of any of its members, however small in numbers the group may be. There are times, however, when this cannot be done - for example if questions of public health arose in an urban society out of certain religious burial practices. But even then, every effort would be made to reach agreement with the people concerned; the religious feelings would always be taken into account.

This necessity for religious toleration arises out of the nature of socialism. For a man's religious beliefs are important to him, and the purpose of socialism is Man. Socialism does not just seek to serve some abstract thing called 'the people'; it seeks to maximize the benefit of society to all the individuals who are members of it. It is thus the essentially personal nature of religious beliefs which makes it necessary for socialism to leave religious questions alone as far as possible – which makes it necessary that socialism should be secular. And being secular involves trying to avoid upsetting deeply held religious beliefs, however stupid they may appear to non-believers. The wearing of long hair, the erection of statues to the religious heroes or saints, the pouring of libations, the ban on music and dancing – all these things appear at best irrelevant to those who do not follow the religion concerned, but they are important to those who do. And because they are important to these believers, a socialist society will not interfere. It will not force people to cut their hair nor allow others to be forced to wear their hair long. It will not prohibit libations, although it may ask that they be poured where they will not damage public property. It will not force people to dance, even if the society has agreed that its people should do a period of National Service which normally includes dance activity. It will protect the statues from wilful damage. It will allow genuine conscientious objection to the bearing of arms, and so on. Always socialism will try to enlarge freedom, and religious freedom is an essential part of man's liberty.

There is No Theology of Socialism

There is, however, an apparent tendency among certain socialists to try and establish a new religion – a religion of socialism itself. This is usually called 'scientific socialism' and the works of Marx .and Lenin are regarded as the holy writ in the light of which all other thoughts and actions of socialists have to be judged.

Of course, this doctrine is not presented as a religion; its proponents are often most anxious to decry religion as the 'opiate of the people', and they present their beliefs as 'science'. Yet they talk and act in the same manner as the most rigid of theologians. We find them condemning one another's actions because they do not accord with what the priests of 'scientific socialism' have decided is the true meaning, in modern terms, of books written more than 100 years ago. Indeed we are fast getting to the stage where quarrels between different Christian sects about the precise meaning of the Bible fade into insignificance when compared with the quarrels of those who claim to be the true interpreters of Marxism-Leninism!

This attempt to create a new religion out of socialism is absurd. It is not scientific, and it is almost certainly not Marxist – for however combatant and quarrelsome a socialist Marx was, he never claimed to be an infallible divinity! Marx was a great thinker. He gave a brilliant analysis of the industrial capitalist society in which he lived; he diagnosed its ills and advocated certain remedies which he believed would lead to the development of a healthy society. But he was not God. The years have proved him wrong in certain respects just as they have proved him right in others. Marx did not write revealed truth; his books are the result of hard thinking and hard work, not a revelation from God. It is therefore unscientific to appeal to his writings as Christians appeal to the Bible, or Muslims to the Koran.

The works of Marx and Lenin are useful to a socialist because these men thought about the objective conditions of their time and tried to work out the actions necessary to achieve certain ends. We can learn from their methods of analysis, and from their ideas. But the same is true of many other thinkers of the past. It is no part of the job of a socialist in 1968 to worry about whether or not his actions or proposals are in accordance with what Marx or Lenin wrote, and it is a waste of time and energy to spend hours – if not months and years – trying to prove that what you have decided is objectively necessary is really in accordance with their teachings. The task of a socialist is to think out for himself the best way of achieving desired ends under the conditions which exist now. It is his job to think how to organize society, how to solve a particular problem, or how to effect certain changes, in a manner which will emphasize the importance of man and the equality of man.

It is especially important that we in Africa should understand this. We are groping our way forward towards socialism, and we are in danger of being bemused by this new theology, and therefore of trying to solve our problems according to what the priests of Marxism say is what Marx said or meant. If we do this we shall fail: Africa's conditions are very different from those of the Europe in which Marx and Lenin wrote and worked. To talk as if these thinkers provided all the answers to our problems, or as if Marx invented socialism, is to reject both the humanity of Africa and the universality of socialism. Marx did contribute a great deal to socialist thought. But socialism did not begin with him, nor can it end in constant reinterpretations of his writings.

Speaking generally, and despite the existence of a few feudalistic communities, traditional Tanzanian society had many socialist characteristics. The people did not call themselves socialists, and they were not socialists by deliberate design. But all people were workers, there was no living off the sweat of others. There was no very great difference in the amount of goods available to the different members of the society. All these are socialist characteristics. Despite the low level of material progress, traditional African society was in practice organized on a basis which was in accordance with socialist principles.

These conditions still prevail over large areas of Tanzania – and indeed in many other parts of Africa. Even in our urban areas, the social expectation of sharing what you have with your kinsfolk is still very strong – and causes great problems for individuals! These things have nothing to do with Marx; the people have never heard of him. Yet they provide a basis on which modern socialism can be built. To reject this base is to accept the idea that Africa has nothing to contribute to the march of mankind; it is to argue that the only way progress can be achieved in Africa is if we reject our own past and impose on ourselves the doctrines of some other society.

Nor would it be very scientific to reject Africa's past when trying to build socialism in Africa. For scientific thinking means finding out all the facts in a particular situation, regardless of whether you like them or not, or whether they fit in with preconceived ideas. It means analysing these facts, and then working out solutions to the problems you are concerned with in the light of these facts, and of the objectives you are trying to achieve. This is what Marx did in Europe in the middle of the nineteenth century; if he had lived in Sukumaland, Masailand.or Ruvuma, he would have written a different book from *Das Kapital*, but he could have been just as scientific and just as socialist. For if 'scientific socialism' means anything, it can only mean that the objectives are socialist and you apply scientific methods of study in working out the appropriate policies. If the phrase does not mean that, then it is simply a trap to ensnare the unwary into a denunciation of their own nature and therefore into a new form of oppression. For a scientist works to discover truth. He does not claim to know it, nor is he seeking to discover truth as revealed – which is the job of the theologian. A scientist works on the basis of the knowledge which has been accumulated empirically, and which is held to be true until new experience demonstrates otherwise, or demonstrates a superior truth which takes precedence in particular situations.

A really scientific socialist would therefore start his analysis of the problems of a particular society from the standpoint of that society. In Tanzania he would take the existence of some socialist values as part of his material for analysis; he would study the effect of the colonial era on these attitudes and on the systems of social organization; he would take account of the world situation as it affects Tanzania. After doing all that, he would try to work out policies appropriate for the growth of a modern socialist state. And he could well finish up with the Arusha Declaration and the policies of ujamaa!

A scientific socialist could do all this with or without a knowledge and understanding of Marx and Lenin – or for that matter Saint Simon, Owen or Laski. Knowledge of the work and thinking of these and other people may help a socialist to know what to look for and how to evaluate the things he sees; but it could also mislead him if he is not careful. Equally, a knowledge of history may help him to learn from the experience of others; a knowledge of economics will help him to understand some of the forces at work in the society. But if he tries to use any of these disciplines or philosophies as a gospel according to which he must work out solutions he will go wrong. There is no substitute for his own hard work and hard thinking.

For example, a study of the work of past socialist thinkers and of history and economics appears to have led some people to argue that Tanzania can only become socialist if it first goes through the stage of capitalism. Yet it is difficult to believe that they thought about the objective conditions of this country when coming to this conclusion. (It is also difficult to believe that they understand the principles of socialism – the attitudes of mind it requires!) Certainly Tanzania was part of the Western capitalist world while it was under colonial domination, but it was very much on the fringe. Certainly our independent nation inherited a few capitalist institutions, and some of our people adopted capitalist and individualistic ideas as a result of their education or their envy of the colonial representatives whom they encountered. But the masses of the people did not become capitalist, and are not filled with capitalist ideas. By far the largest part of our economy is not organized on capitalist lines. Indeed, whenever we try to help Africans to become capitalist shopkeepers, capitalist farmers, industrialists, etc., we find that most of them fail because they cannot adopt the capitalist practices which are essential to commercial success! Yet rather than give up their theories, these dogmatists often attribute these African failures to the machinations of a racial minority – thus revealing their racialism and non-socialist beliefs – instead of recognizing that capitalism demands certain attributes among its practitioners which the majority of our people have never been forced to acquire.

Under these circumstances what would be the sense in working to create capitalism, with all the individualism, social aggressiveness, and human indignities which it involves? These attributes would have to be fought against, and the organizations of capitalism destroyed or reformed, when you finally decided that the task of building socialism could be begun. And when should opposition to capitalism be started? If capitalism must precede socialism, how far does it have to go before it can be replaced?

Capitalism would only have to precede socialism if there was some reason to believe that the people will fail to solve the problems of production except by capitalist methods. It is certainly true that capitalism can lead to the high output of goods and services – no socialist would dispute that. But there is very little evidence to support the contention that only through capitalism can a satisfactory level of production be attained; indeed there is an increasing amount of evidence with which to refute such a statement. Countries like the USSR, East Germany, China, and North Korea may differ in their approach to socialism, but they are certainly not capitalist, and they do produce the goods their people need. North Korea, for example, may not be able to compare with the state of New York in the provision of television sets, cars, and fashion clothes; but it has electrified something like 98 per cent of its villages, and 86 per cent of its farm houses, and it has built new and improved houses for about two-thirds of its rural families in the space of eight years. In other words, the priorities of production may be different, and the emphasis given to economic output as against other values may vary, but North Korea has shown that production can be organized in a non-capitalist manner. If it can be done once, what reason is there to believe that it cannot be done again?

The real truth is that the principles of socialism are relevant to all human society at all stages of technology and social organization. But their application has constantly to be worked out afresh according to the objective conditions prevailing in the time or place. There is no book which provides all the answers to these problems of application; there is no 'socialist road map' which depicts all obstacles and provides a path through or around them. In fact we have no alternative but to hold fast to the principles of socialism to understand its characteristics – and then apply the accumulated knowledge of man to the continuing and changing problems of man. And we have to do this as best we can, without the infinite knowledge which belongs to God and which would provide the answers to all our problems. There is no magic formula, and no short cut to socialism. We can only grope our way forward, doing our best to think clearly, and scientifically, about our own conditions in relation to our objectives …

The Universality and Diversity of Socialism

What does all this amount to? It is an expression of belief that man can only live in harmony with man, and can only develop to his full potential as a unique individual, in a society the purpose of which is Man, which is based on the principles of human equality, and which is so organized as to emphasize both man's equality and his control over all the instruments of his life and development. It is a statement that because men are different, and because different communities and societies have had different histories, live in different geographical conditions, and have developed different customs and systems of belief, therefore the road to socialism and the institutions through which socialism is ultimately expressed will be different. It is a statement insisting that the progress of one man or group of men does not make it unnecessary for other men and other groups to think for themselves. It is an assertion that there are no natural laws of human development which we have only to discover and apply in order to reach the Nirvana of a perfect socialist society; on the contrary, that it is by deliberate design that men will build socialist societies, and by deliberate design that they will maintain socialist principles in a form which seems to them to be good. It is an assertion of man's unity and also his diversity; the validity of certain basic principles for social living, and the variety of their expression. It is a statement that one will not recognize or define a socialist society by its institutions or its statements, but by its fundamental characteristics of equality, co-operation, and freedom.

The Transition to Socialism

By definition, however, the characteristics which identify a socialist state will not exist in their entirety in a state which is trying to build socialism. If the institutions, and the attitudes, of socialism existed it would be socialist; until then it is inevitable that at least some of the essential elements of socialist society will be missing. This is true whether the commitment to socialism is linked with revolution, or whether it follows peaceful political development socialism does not spring ready-made out of the womb of violence. Even the most successful and popular revolution inevitably leaves behind it a legacy of bitterness, suspicion and hostility between members of the society. These are not conducive to the institutions of equality, and make it difficult to build a spirit of co-operation between the whole people. In particular there is always a fear that those who suffered during the revolution may be looking for an opportunity of revenge; there is the memory of injury and bereavement deliberately inflicted, which poisons the relations between men within the society. A violent revolution may make the introduction of socialist *institutions* easier; it makes more difficult the development of the socialist *attitudes* which give life to these institutions.

This is not to say that violent revolutions are always wrong or irrelevant to socialism. Sometimes they are a regrettable necessity because they are the only way to break the power of those who prevent progress towards socialism. But violence is a short cut only to the destruction of the institutions and power groups of the old society; they are not a short cut to the building of the new. For even if change is secured through the violent overthrow of a feudal or a fascist society, the new life has still to be built by and with people who lived in the old society and who were shaped by it even if they reacted against it. The necessity for a violent revolution brings its own problems to the building of socialism; they may be different problems from those experienced by the states which are fortunate enough to be able to move peacefully from one kind of social system to another, but they are nonetheless real.

In fact those who talk as if violence must always and everywhere precede socialism, and who judge a country to be developing towards socialism only if violence has occurred, are almost certainly not socialist in their own attitudes. For violence cannot be welcomed by those who care about people. It is a very serious matter because of the misery and suffering it involves for human beings; it should only be accepted as a necessity when every other road forward is completely blocked and cannot be cleared by persistence, by public determination, or by other expressions of the majority will. Violence itself is the opposite of a socialist characteristic. Brigands can govern by violence and fear; dictatorships can establish themselves and flourish. Socialism cannot be imposed in this way, for it is based on equality. It denies the right of any individual or any small minority, to say, 'I know and the others are fools who must be led like sheep'. Leadership can be given – and indeed must be given – in a socialist state. But it must be the people's leadership, which they accept because ultimately they control it. Socialist leadership is of the people; it cannot be imposed by force or tyranny.

This means that where a violent revolution was a necessary precondition for the establishment of an opportunity to begin the work of building socialism, the early period of transition towards this goal will have certain kinds of non-socialist characteristics. There may well be suspicions, fear, illegalities, and an absence of political freedom; there may be something of a vacuum in effective administration even as brave attempts are made to create the groundwork of socialist economic organizations.

If, on the other hand, the transition out of the old society can be effected by non-violent means, different non-socialist characteristics will be evident as the work of building is in process. There will be many remnants of the preceding social organization; many old habits may continue simply because social upheaval has not forced people to think about them; and old attitudes and behaviour may still be dominant in people holding responsible positions. These things create difficulties for socialist progress just as the aftermath of a revolution creates difficulties. By whichever method the conditions for building socialism are established, a visitor could look at the society in transition and deny its socialism, or its progress, by pointing to characteristics which are non-socialist, or even anti-socialist.

This is as true in Tanzania as elsewhere, and indeed our Union provides examples of the difficulties of both kinds of transition. In Zanzibar the revolution cleared many obstacles from the path of socialism, but it created other difficulties and fears. On the mainland, where political circumstances obviated the necessity for violence, we are able to try to build socialism by evolution – by dealing with the problems one by one in accordance with the consensus of opinion and our capacity at anyone time. But this, too, has its difficulties, and the danger that self-seeking men will be able to mislead the people into opposing the struggle forward. And in both parts of the Union we have still to ensure that new privileged groups do not grow out of the post-independence and post-revolutionary forces.

The solution to all these problems depends upon the growth of socialist understanding and socialist attitudes among the people. In particular it depends upon the speed and success with which the concepts of human equality and the people's sovereignty are accepted by the society and the leadership in the society. Institutions can help to spread these ideas and encourage their expression, but they do not in themselves provide an answer. Thus, for example, the Permanent Commission of Enquiry provides machinery through which members of the public can complain against petty tyranny of leaders and officials, but its effectiveness depends upon the willingness of the people to make and to substantiate their complaints, as well as the willingness of Government and Party personnel to correct wrongs which reduce the people's sovereignty. Or, again, the leadership qualifications are aimed at emphasizing the identity of the leadership and the people, but they can only restrict behaviour negatively – and their intentions can be evaded. There is, in fact, no substitute for the individual moral courage of men; everything ultimately depends upon the determination of the people to be judges over those to whom they have entrusted positions of responsibility and leadership. The only way in which leadership can be maintained as a people's leadership is if the leaders have reason to fear the judgement of the people.

The people's purposes in society, however, will only go forward smoothly when they exercise their power over leadership in a calm and deliberate manner – and when the institutions of the society enable them to do so. And the people have to understand their own power, and its importance to their future; they have to understand the basic principles of socialism. Only then will they be able to avoid being used by the jealousies and envies of individuals who seek to exploit, for their own ambition's sake, the honest mistakes of individual leaders. Only then will the people be able to avoid the blandishments of those who, for their own benefit, pretend that there is a short cut to socialism and to prosperity which the existing leaders stand in the way of. The people's will must be sovereign; but it will only lead them to the equalities and dignities of socialism if they exert that sovereignty with an understanding of socialism.

The Problems of Building Socialism in an Ex-colonial Country

There are particular problems about this in an ex-colonial country like Tanzania. For to build socialism you must have socialists – particularly in leading positions. It is not enough that our people's traditional life should have been based upon socialist principles; that is good, but it is necessary that the leaders in modernization should also accept those principles and be able to apply them in the very different technological and international conditions of the twentieth century. Further, it is essential that the people should be aware of the new socialist objective and what it means to them.

Yet in Tanzania the great mass campaigns of the 1950s and early 1960s were for independence. We campaigned against colonialism, against foreign domination. We did not campaign against capitalism or for socialism. Creating still more difficulties was the fact that the colonialism we fought against was that of a people who happened to be of a different racial group than ourselves. It was fatally easy to identify the thing you were fighting against as people of this other race – the Europeans. It is true that we in Tanzania campaigned on the grounds of human equality; that has helped us. But the problem Africa knew was that of discrimination against the African majority. We therefore asked, 'Why are there no African District Commissioners, administrators, supervisors, secretaries, etc.?', and often this was transposed into, 'Why are there European or Asian this and that?' Humanity took second place in this struggle very often; even when political leaders said on public platforms and elsewhere that they would never countenance reverse discrimination after independence, this was sometimes interpreted as a manoeuvre designed to avoid the heavy hand of the colonial authority! Almost throughout Africa, therefore, the first and most vocal demand of the people after independence was for Africanization. They did not demand localization – indeed, the most popular thing would have been for leaders to deny citizenship to non-black residents. Still less did the people demand socialization; they simply demanded the replacement of white and brown faces by black ones: The leaders could therefore receive applause if they replaced white, or brown, capitalists by black ones. Capitalism was the system which the masses knew in the modern sector, and what they had been fighting against was that this modem sector should be in alien hands.

It was not only the masses who looked upon things in this way; many leaders of the independence struggle themselves saw things in these terms. They were not against capitalism; they simply wanted its fruits, and saw independence as the means to that end. Indeed, many of the most active fighters in the independence movement were motivated – consciously or unconsciously – by the belief that only with independence could they attain that ideal of individual wealth which their education or their experience in the modern sector had established as a worthwhile goal. It is in this fact that lies the paradox of the changing classifications given to different African leaders by the capitalists of the colonial territories. For the 'extremist' of the independence period was sometimes the man who was saying, 'Kill the whites' because he wanted what they had for himself. In such a case (if he survives) the 'extremist' may well become a great defender of capitalism after independence, and he will then probably be reclassified as a 'moderate'! Similarly, the independence campaigner who opposed the murder of non-Africans could either have been deeply religious, or he could have been a socialist. If he was the latter, his classification by the capitalists after independence is liable to change from 'moderate' to 'extremist' or 'communist'!

This lack of ideological content during the independence struggle often served to maintain unity among the anti-colonialist forces, or to prevent a diversion of energies into the difficult questions of socialist education. (It was not always selfishness which made leaders think only in terms of Africanizing the capitalist economy of the colonialists; often they had no knowledge of any alternative.) But it can present a serious problem in the post-independence period. Once they have power, some of the leaders whom the people have learned to know and trust will think their nationalism demands expropriation of non-Africans in favour of African citizens; the more sophisticated may deny this but think of economic development in terms of expanding capitalism with the participation of Africans.

Such leaders as these may well identify the progress they have promised the people with the increasing wealth of the few; they will point to African-owned large cars and luxurious houses, and so on, as evidence of growing prosperity and of their own devotion to the cause of national independence. It was on this basis, for example, that some Tanzanian leaders criticized the Arusha Declaration. They said that the leadership qualifications prevented Africans from becoming landowners and businessmen, while Asians and Europeans could continue in these fields as they had done before independence. These critics thus demonstrated their conviction, firstly, that

Asian citizens could not or should not desire to hold responsible positions in the society; and secondly, that exploitation was only wrong when carried out upon the masses by people of a different race. Incidentally, they were also showing that they wished to use positions of power for private gain, because almost the only way in which Africans could get the capital to become landlords or capitalists was by virtue of their office or their seniority in the public service. (There were exceptions to this general rule, because there had been isolated instances before independence of Africans establishing themselves in business or modern farming. But in general it was the post-independence accession to power which enabled Africans to enter the capitalist system as owners or employers instead of as workers.)

The perpetuation of capitalism, and its expansion to include Africans, will be accepted by the masses who took part in the independence struggle. They may take the new wealth of their leaders as natural and even good – for a time they may even take a reflected pride in it. This may go on for a long period if economic circumstances of the country allow a simultaneous lightening of the general poverty – or even if the conditions of the masses remain static. This public acceptance of African capitalism will be obtained because the people have learned to trust their nationalist leaders, and will wish to honour them. Also there will inevitably be new jobs and opportunities for a good number of the most active, vocal and intelligent of those who might otherwise have led criticism. And on top of that, there will be an end to stupidities like interference with traditional African customs by a foreign Government. But, sooner or later, the people will lose their enthusiasm and will look upon the independence Government as simply another new 'ruler which they should avoid as much as possible. Provided it has been possible to avoid any fundamental upset in their traditional economic and social conditions, they will then sink back into apathy –until the next time someone is able to convince them that their own efforts can lead to an improvement in their lives!

It is comparatively easy to get independence from a colonial power – especially one which claims to base its national morality on the principles of freedom and democracy. Everyone wants to be free, and the task of a nationalist is simply to rouse the people to a confidence in their own power of protest. But to build the real freedom which socialism represents is a very different thing. It demands a positive understanding and positive actions, not simply a rejection of colonialism and a willingness to co-operate in non-cooperation. And the anti-colonial struggle will almost certainly have intensified the difficulties.

During the campaign for independence a number of developments were probably inevitable, or were unavoidable except at great cost. First is the fact that racialism has been allowed to grow – and may even have been indirectly encouraged during the process of simplifying the issues at stake. In Tanzania the masses remained remarkably free from this disease – and are still free. But many of the leaders suffered from discrimination themselves, and some have been unable to achieve that degree of objectivity which would enable them to direct their hatred towards discrimination itself instead of at the racial group which the discriminators represented. Yet racialism is absolutely and fundamentally contrary to the first principle of socialism – the equality of man.

Second, the most active, and therefore the most popular, of the nationalist leaders may have been people without a socialist conviction. They may either have never had an opportunity to study the problems and possibilities of social and economic organization, or they may even have been people who were motivated by a personal desire for the fruits of capitalism.

Third, all the national Party organization and education were geared to defeating colonialism and to opposing people of another race who happened to be in positions of power. This means that once independence is achieved, and the key positions of power have been Africanized, there is a grave danger that the Party will lose support and will atrophy. The people – and even many of the leaders – may feel that the Party has achieved its purpose; once independence has been attained there is no point in the effort required to sustain it.

All these things mean that after independence the work of building socialism has to be started from the beginning. The people have to be shown another goal – the goal of socialism – and they have to learn that only by extending their efforts for this second purpose will they really benefit from the effort they have already made.

To do this new task a strong Party organization is as essential as it was before independence, but it involves a serious and conscious effort on the part of the leaders. In particular they have to act deliberately so as to emphasize their identification with the people, and so as to remain one of them. During the independence struggle this was no problem: the leaders lived with the people, and were as poor as the masses whom they led. They had no choice in the matter and no particular temptation. In the struggle for socialism the position is different: often the leaders have to live in more comfortable surroundings if they are to do their new Government tasks efficiently, and they are also faced with all the temptations of power. Yet to be effective leaders in this second phase of the freedom struggle, it is essential that they should turn their backs on these temptations; they have to act like socialists and be prepared to account to the people for all the personal wealth which they deploy.

However, it is not only leaders who must be involved in the building of socialism. There must be an active adult education system which is directed at helping the people to understand the principles of socialism and their relevance to real development and freedom. There must be local institutions of socialism – co-operative societies which are under the effective control of the members, ujamaa villages, and so on. These are as essential to the building of ujamaa as the Government action which secures control of the key points of the economy for the people at the same time as it mobilizes all the resources of skill and experience which are available. In addition, new economic, social and political institutions must be created which will stress the equality of all men regardless of race or tribe, and which will enable the people to make their voices heard throughout the society. Yet all this must be done under conditions which safeguard these infant institutions, and the young state, from subversion. These things must be achieved while the people are protected against the manipulation of those who are so arrogant that they wish to enforce their own judgement of what is 'the good life'.

This is a formidable – though not exhaustive – list of work to be done even when stated in such broad and general terms. It becomes much more difficult when translated into practice – when you begin to work out the details which appear insignificant but which can make all the difference to success or failure. The difficulties are exacerbated in Africa where the responsibilities and temptations of new nationhood coincide with a great shortage of educated people, of finance, and of committed, modern and thinking socialists. But these same difficulties also provide unique opportunities. Because a new nation has been created, the people are ready and anxious for change – they only need leadership based on human respect. And the absence of large financial resources – once it is understood and accepted – forces a concentration on the abilities and the importance of men rather than money, and thus orientates the society towards the development of man instead of material wealth. The very magnitude of the problem creates a challenge, and the major difficulty is to relate the hard, detailed work, and the long-drawn-out struggle forward, to the ultimate goal.

In Tanzania we have begun the work of building socialism. So far all that we have really achieved is some success in showing people that there is another goal to work for now that our independence exists. For the rest we have tried to prevent the growth of new and stronger groups with a vested interest in capitalism; we have established some of the institutions through which the people can speak; and we have just begun to search out and help the local experiments in modern socialism. We have defined our policies in education, in rural development, and have listed our expectations of leadership. But we are *not* a socialist society. Our work has only just begun. Of particular priority are the outstanding tasks of socialist adult education, and of strengthening the people's self-confidence and pride. These are the essential preliminaries to real freedom from the abuse of power, and from the dangers of manipulation by ambitious, dishonest and selfish men. They are also fundamental to the people's active participation in, and control of, the development of a new society.

The ultimate success in the work of building socialism in Tanzania – as elsewhere – depends upon the people of this nation. For any society is only what the people make it. The benefit to the people of a socialist society will depend upon their contribution to it-their work, their co-operation for the common good, and their acceptance of each other as equals and brothers.

To the extent that we in Tanzania succeed in the struggle to which we have committed ourselves, so we shall be taking our place in the march of humanity towards peace and human dignity. For too long we in Africa – and Tanzania as part of Africa – have slept, and allowed the rest of the world to walk round and over us. Now we are beginning to wake up and to join with our fellow human beings in deciding the destiny of the human race. By thinking out our own problems on the basis of those principles which have universal validity, Tanzania will make its contribution to the development of mankind. That is our opportunity and our responsibility.

Kwame Nkrumah
Class Struggle in Africa
(First published in London, 1970)

INTRODUCTION

In Africa where so many different kinds of political, social and economic conditions exist it is not an easy task to generalise on political and socio-economic patterns. Remnants of communalism and feudalism still remain and in parts of the continent ways of life have changed very little from traditional times. In other areas a high level of industrialisation and urbanisation has been achieved. Yet in spite of Africa's socioeconomic and political diversity it is possible to discern certain common political, social and economic conditions and problems. These derive from traditional past, common aspirations, and from shared experience under imperialism, colonialism and neocolonialism. There is no part of the continent which has not known oppression and exploitation, and no part which remains outside the processes of the African Revolution. Everywhere, the underlying unity of purpose of the peoples of Africa is becoming increasingly evident, and no African leader can survive who does not pay at least lip service to the African revolutionary objectives of total liberation, unification and socialism.

In this situation, the ground is well prepared for the next crucial phase of the Revolution, when the armed struggle which has now emerged must be intensified, expanded and effectively co-ordinated at strategic and tactical levels; and at the same time, a determined attack must be made on the entrenched position of the minority reactionary elements amongst our own peoples. For the dramatic exposure in recent years of the nature and extent of the class struggle in Africa, through the succession of reactionary military coups and the outbreak of civil wars, particularly in West and Central Africa, has demonstrated the unity between the interests of neocolonialism and the indigenous bourgeoisie.

At the core of the problem is the class struggle. For too long, social and political commentators have talked and written as though Africa lies outside the main stream of world historical development – a separate entity to which the social, economic and political patterns of the world do not apply. Myths such as 'African socialism' and 'pragmatic socialism', implying the existence of a brand or brands of socialism applicable to Africa alone, have been propagated; and much of our history has been written in terms of socio-anthropological and historical theories as though Africa had no history prior to the colonial period. One of these distortions has been the suggestion that the class structures which exist in other parts of the world do not exist in Africa.

Nothing is further from the truth. A fierce class struggle has been raging in Africa. The evidence is all around us. In essence it is, as in the rest of the world, a struggle between the oppressors and the oppressed.

The African Revolution is an integral part of the world socialist revolution, and just as the class struggle is basic to world revolutionary processes, so also is it fundamental to the struggle of the workers and peasants of Africa.

Class divisions in modem African society became blurred to some extent during the pre-independence period, when it seemed there was national unity and all classes joined forces to eject the colonial power. This led some to proclaim that there were no class divisions in Africa, and that the communalism and egalitarianism of traditional African society made any notion of a class struggle out of the question. But the exposure of this fallacy followed quickly after independence, when class cleavages which had been temporarily submerged in the struggle to win political freedom reappeared, often with increased intensity, particularly in those states where the newly independent government embarked on socialist policies.

For the African bourgeoisie, the class which thrived under colonialism is the same class which is benefiting under the post-independence, neocolonial period. Its basic interest lies in preserving capitalist social and economic structures. It is therefore in alliance with international monopoly finance capital and neocolonialism, and in direct contact with the African masses, whose aspirations can only be fulfilled through scientific socialism.

Although the African bourgeoisie is small numerically and lacks the financial and political strength of its counterparts in the highly industrialised countries, it gives the illusion of being economically strong because of its close tie-up with foreign finance capital and business interests. Many members of the African bourgeoisie are employed by foreign firms and have, therefore, a direct financial stake in the continuance of the foreign economic exploitation of Africa. Others, notably in the civil service, trading and mining firms, the armed forces, the police and in the professions, are committed to capitalism because of their background, their western education and their shared experience and enjoyment of positions of privilege. They are mesmerised by capitalist institutions and organisations. They ape the way of life of their old colonial masters, and are determined to preserve the status and power inherited from them.

Africa has in fact in its midst a hard core of bourgeoisie who are analogous to colonists and settlers in that they live in positions of privilege – a small, selfish, money-minded, reactionary minority among vast masses of exploited and oppressed people. Although apparently strong because of their support from neocolonialists and imperialists, they are extremely vulnerable. Their survival depends on foreign support. Once this vital link is broken, they become powerless to maintain their positions and privileges. They and the 'hidden hand' of neocolonialism and imperialism which supports and abets reaction and exploitation now tremble before the rising tide of worker and peasant awareness of the class struggle in Africa.

1. ORIGINS OF CLASS IN AFRICA

Africa and its islands, with a land area of some twelve million square miles and a population estimated at about 500 million, could easily contain within it, and with room to spare, the whole of India, Europe, Japan, the British Isles, Scandinavia and New Zealand. The United States of America could easily be fitted into the Sahara Desert. Africa is geographically compact, and in terms of natural resources potentially the richest continent in the world.

In Africa, where economic development is uneven, a wide variety of highly sophisticated political systems were in existence over many centuries before the colonial period began. It is here, in the so-called developing world of Africa, and in Asia and Latin America, where the class struggle and the progress towards ending the exploitation of man by man have already entered into the stage of decisive revolutionary change.

The political maturity of the African masses may to some extent be traced to economic and social patterns of traditional times. Under communalism, for example, all land and means of production belonged to the community. There was people's ownership. Labour was the need and habit of all. When a certain piece of land was allocated to an individual for his personal use, he was not free to do as he liked with it since it still belonged to the community. Chiefs were strictly controlled by counsellors and were removable.

There have been five major types of production relationships known to man – communalism, slavery, feudalism, capitalism and socialism. With the establishment of the socialist state, man has embarked on the road to communism. It was when private property relationships emerged and as communalism gave way to slavery that the class struggle began.

In general, at the opening of the colonial period, the peoples of Africa were passing through the higher stage of communalism characterised by the disintegration of tribal democracy and the emergence of feudal relationships, hereditary tribal chieftaincies and monarchical systems. With the impact of imperialism and colonialism, communalist socio-economic patterns began to collapse as a result of the introduction of export crops such as cocoa and coffee. The economies of the colonies became interconnected with world capitalist markets. Capitalism, individualism, and tendencies to private ownership grew. Gradually, primitive communalism disintegrated and the collective spirit declined. There was an expansion of private farming and the method of small commodity production.

It was a relatively easy matter for white settlers to appropriate land which was not individually owned. For example, in Malawi, by 1892, more than sixteen per cent of the land had been alienated, and three-quarters of it was under the direction of eleven big companies. When the land was seized by settlers, the African 'owners' became in some cases tenants or leaseholders, but only on land considered not fertile enough for white farmers. The latter were usually issued with certificates of ownership of land by the British consul acting on behalf of the British government; and any land not under any specific private ownership was declared 'British crown land'. Similar arrangements were made in other parts of colonial Africa.

Under colonialism, communal ownership of land was finally abolished and ownership of land imposed by law. Furthermore, through the system of 'Indirect Rule', chiefs became tools, and in many cases paid agents, of the colonial administration.

With the seizure of the land, with all its natural resources – that is, the means of production – two sectors of the economy emerged, the European and the African, the former exploiting the latter. Subsistence agriculture was gradually destroyed and Africans were compelled to sell their labour power to the colonialists, who turned their profits into capital. It was in these circumstances that the race–class struggle also emerged as part of the class struggle.

With the growth of commodity production, mainly for export, single crop economies developed completely dependent on foreign capital. The colony became a sphere for investment and exploitation. Capitalism developed with colonialism. At the same time, the spread of private enterprise, together with the needs of the colonial administrative apparatus, resulted in the emergence of first a petty bourgeois class and then an urban bourgeois class of bureaucrats, reactionary intellectuals, traders and others, who became increasingly part and parcel of the colonial economic and social structure.

To facilitate exploitation, colonialism hampered social and cultural progress in the colonies. Obsolete forms of social relations were restored and preserved. Capitalist methods of production and capitalist social relationships were introduced. Friction between tribes was in some cases deliberately encouraged when it served to strengthen the hands of colonial administrators.

But certain economic developments, such as that of the extractive industry, plantations and capitalist farming, the building of ports, roads and railways, were undertaken in the interests of capitalism. As a result, social changes occurred. Feudal and semi-feudal relationships were undermined with the emergence of an industrial and agricultural proletariat. At the same time there developed a national bourgeoisie and an intelligentsia.

In this colonialist situation, African workers regarded the colonialists, foreign firms and foreign planters, as the exploiters. Thus their class struggle became in the first instance anti-imperialist, and not directed against the indigenous bourgeoisie. It is this which has been responsible in some degree for the relatively slow awakening of the African worker and peasant to the existence of their true class enemy – the indigenous bourgeoisie.

At the end of the colonial period there was in most African states a highly developed state machine and a veneer of Parliamentary democracy concealing a coercive state run by an elite of bureaucrats with practically unlimited power. There was an intelligentsia, completely indoctrinated with western values; a virtually non-existent labour movement; a professional army and a police force with an officer corps largely trained in western military academies; and a chieftaincy used to administering at local level on behalf of the colonial government.

But on the credit side, a new grass roots political leadership emerged during the independence struggle. This was based on worker and peasant support, and committed not only to the winning of political freedom but to a complete transformation of society. This revolutionary leadership, although of necessity associated with the national bourgeoisie in the independence struggle, was quite separate from it, and proceeded to break away after independence to pursue its class socialist objectives. This struggle still continues.

2. CLASS CONCEPT

Class struggle is a fundamental theme of recorded history. In every non-socialist society there are two main categories of class, the ruling class or classes, and the subject class or classes. The ruling class possesses the major instruments of economic production and distribution, and the means of establishing its political dominance, while the subject class serves the interests of the ruling class, and is politically, economically and socially dominated by it. There is conflict between the ruling class and the exploited class. The nature and cause of the conflict is influenced by the development of productive forces. That is, in any given class formation, whether it be feudalism, capitalism, or any other type of society, the institutions and ideas associated with it arise from the level of productive forces and the mode of production. The moment private ownership of the means of production appears, and capitalists start exploiting workers, the capitalists become a bourgeois class, the exploited workers a working class. For in the final analysis, a class is nothing more than the sum total of individuals bound together by certain interests which as a class they try to preserve and protect.

Every form of political power, whether parliamentary, multi-party, one-party or open military dictatorship, reflects the interest of a certain class or classes in society. In socialist states the government represents workers and peasants. In capitalist states, the government represents the exploiting class. The state, then, is the expression 6f the domination of one class over other classes.

Similarly, political parties represent the existence of different classes. It might be assumed from this that a single party state denotes classlessness. But this is not necessarily the case. It only applies if the state represents political power held by the people. In many states, where two or more political parties exist, and where there are sharp class cleavages, there is to all intents and purposes government by a single party. In the case of the United States of America, for example, Republican and Democratic Parties may be said to be in fact a single party in that they represent a single class, the propertied class. In Britain, there is in practice little difference between the Conservative Party and the Labour Party. The Labour Party founded to promote the interests of the working class has in fact developed into a bourgeois-oriented party. Both the Conservative Party and the Labour Party are therefore expressions of the bourgeoisie and reflect its ideology.

Inequality can only be ended by the abolition of classes. The division between those who plan, organise and manage, and those who actually perform the manual labour, continually recreates the class system. The individual usually finds it very difficult, if not impossible, to break out of the sphere of life into which he is born; and even where there is 'equality of opportunity', the underlying assumption of inequality remains, where the purpose of 'opportunity' is to aspire to a higher level in a stratified society.

A ruling class is cohesive and conscious of itself as a class. It has objective interests, is aware of its position and the threat posed to its continued dominance by the rising tide of working class revolt. In Africa, the ruling classes account for approximately only one per cent of the population. Some 80–90 per cent of the population consists of peasants and agricultural labourers. Urban and industrial workers represent about five per cent. Yet because of the presence of foreigners and foreign interests, class struggle in African society has been blurred. Conflict between the African peoples and the interests of neocolonialism, colonialism, imperialism and settler regimes has concealed all other contradictory forces. This explains to some extent why class or vanguard parties have been so long emerging in Africa ...

The uneven economic development of Africa bas made for a variety of class patterns with wide differences existing between the areas of white settler minority governments, the few remaining colonial enclaves, and independent Africa.

For example, in Rhodesia, four million Africans are crowded into less than half the land acreage of the country. In other words, more than half the land is in the hands of some 500,000 white settlers. This state of affairs has resulted in an enormous social and political gulf between the rich, white estate owners and the impoverished, politically impotent African peasants and workers. Here, as in all settler areas, class is a race issue first and foremost – the 'haves' are white, the 'have-nots' are black – and all the usual arguments – the myth of racial inferiority, the need for government by the most able, and so on – are used to justify perpetuation of the enforced racialist, settler arrangement.

Again, in francophone Africa, social patterns have resulted in the emergence of class divisions peculiar to this particular colonised area. There were the 'citoyens', the French 'colons' or citizens. There were the 'assimilés', the coloured mulattos and the black intelligentsia, or those Africans who worked their way to this class through the army or the bureaucracy. Then came the 'sujets', the workers and peasants. An 'assimilé' could become a 'citoyen', but a 'sujet' could not, unless he first worked his way into the 'assimilé' class. This type of social system operated in all the French colonies. Analogous arrangements still exist in the few remaining Spanish and Portuguese territories in Africa.

The assimilation policy meant that any colonial 'subject' could be naturalised as a full French citizen. In practice, however, even those who reached a high enough level of education usually did not attempt to avail themselves of this so-called privilege, largely because, except in the Four

Communes, French citizenship was incompatible with the retention of one's personal status - that is, the right to live by African customary law as opposed to the French *code civil*. There was a certain logic in this from a strictly assimilationist point of view: if one was going to be a Frenchman in the political sense, then one should behave like one socially, and accept such institutions as monogamy and French inheritance laws. But its effect underlined the failure of assimilation, for on these terms, assimilation was not a saleable commodity; and so, outside the Four Communes, 'citizen' remained virtually synonymous with 'white Frenchman'.

While the nature of the economic relationship between the colony and its metropolitan master determined the nature of the class conflict in a particular area, other factors included the ideas and customs of the invading power, although these were attributable ultimately to changes in the structure of productive relations.

In areas colonised by the British, a certain amount of urbanisation made for the emergence of bourgeois and petty bourgeois elites, which developed their own class characteristic attitudes and organisations. To obtain a 'white collar' job became the ambition of every African aspiring to improve his prospects and social status. Manual work, particularly agricultural work, was considered beneath the dignity of anyone who had acquired even the most rudimentary degree of education.

In pre-colonial Africa, under conditions of communalism, slavery and feudalism there were embryonic class cleavages. But it was not until the era of colonial conquest that a Europeanised class structure began to develop with clearly identifiable classes of proletariat and bourgeoisie. This development has always been played down by reactionary observers, most of whom have maintained that African societies are homogeneous and without class divisions. They have even endeavoured to retain this view in the face of glaring evidence of class struggle shown in the post-independence period, when bourgeois elements have joined openly with neocolonialists, colonialists and imperialists in vain attempts to keep the African masses in permanent subjection.

9. BOURGEOISIE

Colonialism, imperialism and neocolonialism are expressions of capitalism and of bourgeois economic and political aspirations. In Africa, under colonialism, capitalist development led to the decline of feudalism and to the emergence of new class structures.

Before the colonial period, the power of the chiefs – which was generally not based on land ownership – was strictly limited and controlled. The 'stool' and not the chief was sacred. Control was exercised by a council of elders. Colonialism reinforced the power of chiefs through the system of 'Indirect Rule'. They were given new powers, were sometimes paid, and became for the most part the local agents of colonialism. In some colonised areas new chiefs were appointed by the colonial power. These became known as 'warrant chiefs'.

Imperialists utilised the feudal and tribal nobility to support their exploitation; and this resulted in a blunting of social contradictions, since the feudal and semi-feudal strata maintained a strong hold over the peasant masses and inhibited the growth of revolutionary organisations.

Relics of feudalism still exist in many parts of Africa. For example, in Northern Nigeria and in North and West Cameroon, tribal chiefs live on the exploitation of peasants who not only have to pay them tributes and taxes, but who often have to do forced labour.

But although feudal relics remain, the colonial period ushered in capitalist social structures. The period was characterised by the rise of the petty bourgeoisie, and of a small but influential national bourgeoisie consisting in the main of intellectuals, civil servants, members of the professions, and of officers in the armed forces and police. There was a marked absence of capitalists among the bourgeoisie, since local business enterprise was on the whole discouraged by the colonial power. Anyone wishing to achieve wealth and status under colonialism was therefore likely to choose a career in the professions, the civil service or the armed forces, because there were so few business opportunities. Foreigners controlled mining, industrial enterprises, banks, wholesale trade and large-scale farming. In most of Africa, the bourgeoisie was, in fact, for the most part petty bourgeoisie.

It was partly the restrictions placed on the business outlets of the African bourgeoisie which led it to oppose imperialist rule. After the end of the Second World War, when the pressure for national liberation was increased, imperialists were compelled to admit part of the African bourgeoisie to spheres from which it had previously been excluded. More Africans were allowed into the state machinery and into foreign companies. Thus, a new African elite, closely linked with foreign capital, was created. At the same time, repressive measures were taken against progressive parties and trade unions. Several colonialist wars were fought, as for example, the wars against the peoples of Madagascar, Cameroon and Algeria. It was during this period that the foundations of neocolonialism were laid.

During the national liberation struggle, the petty bourgeoisie tends to divide into three main categories. Firstly, there are those who are heavily committed to colonialism and to capitalist economic and social development. These are in the main the 'officials' and professional men, and agents of foreign firms and companies. Secondly, there are the 'revolutionary' petty bourgeoisie – the nationalists – who want to end colonial rule but who do not wish to see a transformation of society. They form part of the national bourgeoisie. Thirdly, there are those who 'sit on the fence', and are prepared to be passive onlookers.

In general, few members of the African bourgeoisie amassed sufficient capital to become significant in the business sector. The African bourgeoisie remains therefore largely a comprador class, sharing in some of the profits which imperialism drains from Africa. Under conditions of colonialism and neocolonialism, it will never be encouraged sufficiently to become strong in the economic sphere since this would mean creating business competitors. The local bourgeoisie must always be subordinate partners to foreign capitalism. For this reason, it cannot achieve power as a class or govern without the close support of reactionary feudal elements within the country, or without the political, economic and military support of international capitalism.

Imperialism may foster liberation movements in colonial areas when capitalist exploitation has reached the stage of giving rise to a labour movement which seriously threatens the interests of international capitalism. By the granting of political independence to bourgeois parties, reactionary indigenous forces can thereby be put into positions of power which enable them to cement their alliance with the international bourgeoisie. In practically every national liberation struggle, there emerge two liberation parties. One of them is the genuine people's party committed not only to national liberation but to socialism. The other aims at political independence, but intends to preserve capitalist structures, and is supported by imperialism.

In the majority of the independent African states there exist embryonic elements of a rural bourgeoisie. In Ghana, large farmers and cocoa brokers come into this category. According to the 1960 census, the rural bourgeoisie number 1.4 million, while the urban middle class was estimated at 300,000. This was in a population 24 per cent of which was defined as urban. In most cases, both urban and rural bourgeoisie are not conscious of themselves as a class, though they are very much aware of their strength and importance, and conscious of the threat to their privileged positions in society by the increasing pressure of worker–peasant resistance.

In the struggle for political independence, urban workers, peasants and the national bourgeoisie ally together to eject the colonial power. Class cleavages are temporarily blurred. But once independence is achieved, class conflicts come to the fore over the social and economic policies of the new government.

It is possible for classes to combine in the post-colonial situation, and the nature of the government is assessed by which particular class interests are dominant. Theorists arguing that proletariat and petty bourgeoisie should join together to win the peasantry, in order to attack the bourgeoisie, ignore the fact that the petty bourgeoisie will always, when it comes to the pinch, side with the bourgeoisie to preserve capitalism. It is only peasantry and proletariat working together who are wholly able to subscribe to policies of all-out socialism. Where conflict involves both political and economic interests, the economic always prevails.

The African bourgeoisie, in common with their counterpart in other parts of the world, hold the view that governments exist to protect private property, and that success is measured by wealth, the acquisition of property and social status. They set up bourgeois organisations such as clubs and professional associations on the model of those existing in the bourgeois societies of Europe and the Americas. They want politics to be confined to the struggles between various propertied groups. It is common in Africa, and in other coup areas of the world – notably Asia and Latin America – for there to be a succession of bourgeois coups d'état in a single state. The propertied fight the propertied for political supremacy. For the independent states of Africa, Asia and Latin America have a similar historical past in that they have suffered from imperialism and colonialism; and after political independence have, in almost every case, been swept into the orbit of neocolonialism. In this situation, the majority are governed by bourgeois elements who compete among themselves for political domination. For whichever group succeeds in dominating the political scene is in a position to enhance its property and status. Other factors such as regionalism and tribalism obviously enter into the struggle for power among the indigenous bourgeoisie, but the essential point remains that these struggles take place among the propertied class, and are not struggles between classes.

The tribal formula is frequently used to obscure the class forces created in African society by colonialism. In many areas, uneven economic development under colonial rule led to a differentiation of economic functions along ethnic lines. This tendency is exploited in the interests of international capitalism.

A distinction must be made between tribes and tribalism. The clan is the extended family, and the tribe is the extended clan with the same ethnic language within a territory. There were tribes in Africa before imperialist penetration, but no 'tribalism' in the modern sense. Tribalism arose from colonialism, which exploited feudal and tribal survivals to combat the growth of national liberation movements.

The formation of nationalities was retarded as a result of colonial conquest, when the imperialists carved up Africa among themselves, disregarding geographical, linguistic and ethnic realities. The normal growth of the economy and of the class structure of African society was hindered and distorted. Patriarchal and feudal structures were artificially preserved, and all possible obstacles erected to prevent the emergence of a class-conscious proletariat.

Capitalist methods of exploitation inevitably gave birth to a proletariat, particularly in areas where mines and plantations were highly developed, as in South and East Africa, and in Congo Kinshasa. Here, workers were kept in tribal or traditional structures, and in reservations, in an attempt to prevent the growth of class consciousness.

At Independence, the colonial powers again fostered separatism and tribal differences through the encouragement of federal constitutions. Genuine independence was prevented through the operation of diverse forms of neocolonialism.

In the era of neocolonialism, tribalism is exploited by the bourgeois ruling classes as an instrument of power politics, and as a useful outlet for the discontent of the masses. Many of the so-called tribal conflicts in modern Africa are in reality class forces brought into conflict by the transition from colonialism to neocolonialism. Tribalism is the result, not the cause, of underdevelopment. In the majority of 'tribal' conflicts, the source is the exploiting bourgeois or feudal minority in co-operation with imperialists and neocolonialists seeking to promote their joint class interests. Support has tended to be withdrawn from traditional rulers and transferred to the rising urban bourgeoisie, who are, under neocolonialism, in a better position to maintain and promote the interests of international capitalism. The process assumes the appearance of a tribal confrontation, but in reality is part of the class struggle.

The emergence of tribes in any country is natural, or due to historical development. Tribes, like nationalities, may always remain in a country, but it is tribalism – tribal politics – that should be fought and destroyed. Under a socialist Union Government of Africa, tribalism, not tribes, will disappear.

Certain elements among the African bourgeoisie and traditional rulers – for example, revolutionary intellectuals – may dissociate themselves from their class origin and the ideology connected with it. These are 'revolutionary outsiders' who can be absorbed into the ranks of the socialist revolution.

For the most part, however, in areas of the world where capitalist development is in its infancy, the bourgeoisie – heavily outnumbered by peasantry and proletariat – feel threatened by the rising tide of socialism. As a result, there is a close drawing together of bourgeois elite groupings, and special reliance is placed on the military. Neocolonialist, bourgeois military coups take place to forestall or to destroy the power of workers and peasants, and of socialist-oriented governments.

Such coups are strongly supported by the machinery of neocolonialism. For imperialists and neocolonialists seek, in their own interests, to support the privileged class which emerged under colonialism. Both indigenous bourgeoisie and neocolonialists have common interests in prolonging their dominance by preserving the fundamental features of the colonial state apparatus. The bureaucratic bourgeoisie, in particular, is the spoilt child of neocolonialist governments. Many African states spend ridiculously large sums of money on their bureaucrats. For example, Gabon, with a population of less than half a million, has a Parliament of 65 members each earning 165,000 francs a year. Yet the average worker in Gabon earns only 700 francs annually. In Dahomey [Benin], 60 per cent of the national income is spent on paying the salaries of government officials.

The bureaucratic bourgeoisie, the inheritors of the functions of earlier ruling classes, are closely connected with foreign firms, with the diplomats of imperialist countries, and with the African exploiting classes. Although not a cohesive elite, they are in general dedicated to the capitalist path of development, and are among the most devoted of indigenous agents of neocolonialism. Their education and class position largely isolate them from the masses.

At Independence, their position is strengthened immeasurably by the Africanisation policies of the newly independent government, and by the tremendous increase of work entailed in the large-scale economic and social planning undertaken by the new government. They provide the administrative and technical expertise required. Further, they are able to select and organise the information to be laid before ministers responsible for the formulation of policy. In this way, they play a considerable part in actual decision-making. Many top bureaucrats assume responsibilities and powers for which they are not equipped. They tend to become arrogant and isolated from the lower strata of civil servants and clerks, and submissive to foreign, neocolonialist bureaucrats. When they exert influence on policy it is likely to be along class lines. Their education and class position make them separate from the masses, and they become the willing accomplices of local capitalists, dishonest intellectuals, ambitious army and police officers, and of neocolonialists. Although subject always to the control of a political and military authority, they occupy an extremely strong position in the neocolonialist state apparatus, and exert their influence in support of the ruling classes. They become in some cases, particularly under military–police dictatorships, the de facto policy-makers, without being answerable to the public. This becomes particularly apparent when they act in league with foreign bureaucrats.

When reactionary military coups take place, whether or not they have been involved in planning them, they readily support the bourgeois coup-makers by carrying on the day-to-day work of administration, and by assisting in the drawing up and carrying out of decrees and regulations. Top bureaucrats sit on the innumerable councils, commissions of inquiry and so on which proliferate after a coup. In effect, the establishment of arbitrary military–police rule enhances their position since the reactionary new rulers are utterly dependent on them. Unlike 'civilian governments', military regimes are in a position to impose policies without having to obtain the consent of the people's representatives. They can, therefore, allow bureaucrats much greater freedom of action.

Top civil servants assist in policy-making in most countries. In the U.S.A., they change with a change of government and are very much a part of the decision-making power elite. In Britain, they are supposed to be apolitical and to serve whichever government is in power.

But in Africa, the bourgeoisie as a whole cannot be seen in isolation from imperialism, colonialism and neocolonialism. While representing only a very small fraction of the population it is nevertheless a great danger to the African masses because of the strength it derives from its dependence on foreign bourgeois capitalism, which seeks to keep the peasants and workers of Africa in a condition of perpetual subjection.

It is, in fact, impossible to separate the interests of the African bourgeoisie and those of international monopoly finance capital. The weakening of either one of them inevitably results in the weakening of the other.

The alliance between the indigenous bourgeoisie and international monopoly finance capital is being further cemented by the growing trend towards partnership between individual African governments, or regional economic organisations, and giant imperialist, multi-national corporations. African governments, some of which claim to be pursuing a socialist path of development and 'nationalising' key industries, are in fact merely 'participating' in them. They are combining with collective imperialism in the continuing exploitation of African workers and rural proletariat. The African government shields the corporations from the resistance of the working class, and bans strikes or becomes the strike-breaker; while the corporations strengthen their stranglehold of the African economy, secure in the knowledge that they have government protection. In fact, the African governments become the policemen of imperialist, multi-national corporations. There thus develops a common front to halt socialist advance.

It is the indigenous bourgeoisie who provide the main means by which international monopoly finance continues to plunder Africa and to frustrate the purposes of the African Revolution. The exposure and the defeat of the African bourgeoisie, therefore, provides the key to the successful accomplishment of the worker–peasant struggle to achieve total liberation and socialism, and to advance the cause of the entire world socialist revolution.

12. SOCIALIST REVOLUTION

The highest point of political action, when a revolution attains its excellence, is when the proletariat – comprising workers and. peasants – under the leadership of a vanguard party the principles and motivations of which are based on scientific socialism, succeeds in overthrowing all other classes.

The basis of a revolution is created when the organic structure and conditions within a given society have aroused mass consent and mass desire for positive action to change or transform that society. While there is no hard and fast dogma for socialist revolution, because no two sets of historical conditions and circumstances are exactly alike, experience has shown that under conditions of class struggle, socialist revolution is impossible without the use of force. Revolutionary violence is a fundamental law in revolutionary struggles. The privileged will not, unless compelled, surrender power. They may grant reforms, but will not yield an inch when basic pillars of their entrenched positions are threatened. They can only be overthrown by violent revolutionary action.

Great historical advance is seldom, if ever, achieved without high cost in effort and lives; and those who argue that the transition from capitalism to socialism can be accomplished without. the use of force are under a delusion. The qualitative change implicit in the socialist revolution is far more profound than that which was involved in the transition from feudalism to capitalism. Socialist revolutionaries seek a complete and fundamental transformation of society, and the total abolition of privileged classes; whereas the decline of feudalism merely ushered in a new stratification of society in which money, and not titles and land, became the basis of power and privilege. Socialist revolution opposes all concepts of elitism, and ends class antagonisms and racism. The socialist revolutionaries are fighting for a type of state which really expresses the aspirations of the masses, and which ensures their participation in every aspect of government.

Under capitalism, freedom is the right to do what the law permits, in the interests of the ruling bourgeois class. The more capitalism develops, the more anarchic it becomes; and socialist revolution is the logical and inevitable result.

Where capitalist development and industrialisation are in their infancy, and the bourgeoisie only represents a very small section of the population, socialist revolution can be achieved by workers and peasants seizing power by means of revolutionary action. Through socialist revolutionary leadership, Africa can proceed from bourgeois-capitalist ownership of property to arrive at socialist-communist ownership of property and the means of production and distribution. But in the revolutionary struggle, no reliance can be placed on any section of the bourgeoisie or petty bourgeoisie. Though these elements may join in revolutionary action during the struggle for national liberation, they will always, when it comes to the pinch, try to block the creation of a socialist state. They are committed to capitalism and dependent for their very existence on the support of imperialism and neocolonialism. It is only when the bourgeois ruling class in neocolonialist states is overthrown by class-based socialist revolution that fundamental changes in society can be accomplished.

Certain factors advance the process of socialist revolution. Foremost among them is capitalist development and industrialisation, which leads to an increase of urban workers – the sector of the population which generates the leadership of the proletarian revolution. Among other factors are the desertion of the ruling class by the intellectuals; inefficient governmental machinery, and a politically inept ruling bourgeois class. The example and the help of other socialist revolutions also assist the process. Finally, bitter class antagonism, and race–class problems, have the effect of accelerating the advance to socialism.

In the twentieth century, most forcible seizures of political power have occurred in areas of the world which have a relatively low level of industrialisation – namely areas which have a history of imperialism, colonialism and neocolonialism. These violent changes in the status quo cannot be explained in terms of the power struggles of elite groups. They represent actions of whole classes. In the case of socialist revolution, the seizure of power is by the working class; but in reactionary coups d'état, the bourgeoisie is further entrenched either by the ejection of a socialist-oriented government, or by a power struggle between different sections from within the existing bourgeois framework.

The economic, political and social ferment of Africa, Asia and Latin America must be seen in the context of the world socialist revolution. For the world revolutionary process today unites three main streams: the socialist world system, the liberation movements of the peoples of Africa, Asia and Latin America, and the working-class movement in the industrialised, capitalist countries.

The peoples of the less industrialised areas of the world are in a good strategic position to advance in the direction of socialist revolution as a result of their experience of imperialism, colonialism and neocolonialism. They see the issues clearly, since productive and distributive processes are not obscured or blurred by the trappings and diversions of the capitalist 'welfare state', and capitalist corruption.

The cause of international proletarian revolution is part and parcel of the liberation struggles of the developing world. The class antagonisms in the contemporary world are highly concentrated in these areas. They have become the storm centres of world revolution, dealing direct and deadly blows at imperialism.

The embourgeoisement of certain sections of the international working class and the economism of socialist and working-class leadership in some areas have made the socialist revolutionary struggle in the developing world of even greater importance in the world socialist revolutionary process. Thus, in some respects, the socialist revolutionary struggle has developed a class–race complexion. But while it would be harmful not to recognise the emergence of a racial factor in the revolutionary struggle, it must not be allowed to confuse or obscure the fundamental issue of socialist revolution, which is the class struggle.

The developing world is not a homogeneous bloc opposed to imperialism. The concept of the 'Third World' is illusory. At present, parts of it lie under imperialist domination. The struggle against imperialism takes place both within and outside the imperialist world. It is a struggle between socialism and capitalism, not between a so-called 'Third World' and imperialism. Class struggle is fundamental in its analysis. Furthermore, it is not possible to build socialism in the developing world in isolation from the world socialist system.

CONCLUSION

The African Revolution, while still concentrating its main effort on the destruction of imperialism, colonialism and neo-colonialism, is aiming at the same time to bring about a radical transformation of society. It is no longer a question of whether African Independent States should pursue a capitalist or non-capitalist path of development. The choice has already been made by the workers and peasants of Africa. They have chosen liberation and unification; and this can only be achieved through armed struggle under socialist direction. For the political unification of Africa and socialism are synonymous. One cannot be achieved without the other.

'People's capitalism', 'enlightened capitalism', 'class peace', 'class harmony' are all bourgeois-capitalist attempts to deceive the workers and peasants, and to poison their minds. A 'non-capitalist road' pursued by a 'united front of progressive forces', as some suggest, is not even practical politics in contemporary Africa. There are only two ways of development open to an Independent African State. Either it must remain under imperialist domination via capitalism and neocolonialism; or it must pursue a socialist path by adopting the principles of scientific socialism. It is unrealistic to assert that because industrialisation is in its infancy, and a strong proletariat is only beginning to emerge, that it is not possible to establish a socialist state. History has shown how a relatively small proletariat, if it is well organised and led, can awaken the peasantry and trigger off socialist revolution. In a neocolonialist situation, there is no half-way to socialism. Only policies of all-out socialism can end capitalist-imperialist exploitation.

Socialism can only be achieved through class struggle. In Africa, the internal enemy – the reactionary bourgeoisie – must be exposed as exploiters and parasites, and as collaborators with imperialists and neocolonialists on whom they largely depend for the maintenance of their positions of power and privilege. The African bourgeoisie provides a bridge for continued imperialist and neocolonialist domination and exploitation. The bridge must be destroyed. This can be done by worker–peasant solidarity organised and directed by a vanguard socialist revolutionary party. When the indigenous bourgeoisie and imperialism and neocolonialism are defeated, both the internal and the external enemies of the African Revolution will have been overcome, and the aspirations of the African people fulfilled.

As in other areas of the world where socialist revolution is based largely on the peasantry, African revolutionary cadres have a tremendous task ahead of them. Urban and rural proletariat must be won to the revolution, and the revolution taken to the countryside. It is only when the peasantry have been politically awakened and won to the revolution that freedom fighters – on whom the revolution largely depends in the armed phase – will be able to develop and to expand their areas of operation. At the same time, the two main internal props of bourgeois power – the bureaucrats and the police and professional armed forces – must be politicised.

The ultimate victory of the revolutionary forces depends on the ability of the socialist revolutionary party to assess the class position in society, and to see which classes and groups are for, and which against, the revolution. The party must be able to mobilise and direct the vast forces for socialist revolution already existing, and to awaken and stimulate the immense revolutionary potential which is at present lying dormant.

But as long as violence continues to be used against the African peoples, the Party cannot achieve its objectives without the use of all forms of political struggle, including armed struggle. If armed struggle is to be waged effectively, it also, like the party, must be centrally organised and directed. An All-African Military High Command under the political direction of the All-African working class party would then be able to plan unified strategy and tactics, and thus deliver the final blows at imperialism, colonialism, neocolonialism and settler minority regimes.

Armed resistance is not a new phenomenon in Africa. For hundreds of years, Africans fought against colonialist intrusion though these heroic struggles have received scant attention in the histories of Africa compiled largely by foreign bourgeois writers. Indeed, it may be said that Africans have never ceased to resist imperialist penetration and domination, though the resistance became for the most part non-violent as imperialism intensified its suppression and exploitation. For a time when colonialism was in its heyday, it seemed on the surface as though African resistance had been finally overcome and that the continent would remain indefinitely under foreign economic and political domination. But resistance was always simmering just below the surface, and after the Second World War re-emerged in a new active form in the struggles for national liberation. Though some of the liberation struggles were accomplished successfully without resort to arms, others were achieved only after years of bitter fighting.

But political independence did not bring to an end economic oppression and exploitation. Nor did it end foreign political interference. The neocolonialist period begins when international monopoly finance capital, working through the indigenous bourgeoisie, attempts to secure an even tighter stranglehold over the economic life of the continent than was exercised during the colonial period.

Under neocolonialism a new form of violence is being used against the peoples of Africa. It takes the form of indirect political domination through the indigenous bourgeoisie and puppet governments teleguided and marionetted by neo-colonialists; direct economic exploitation through an extension of the operations of giant interlocking corporations; and through all manner of other insidious ways such as the control of mass communications media, and ideological penetration.

In these circumstances, the need for armed struggle has arisen once more. For the liberation and unification of Africa cannot be achieved by consent, by moral precept or moral conquest. It is only through the resort to arms that Africa can rid itself once and for all of remaining vestiges of colonialism, and of imperialism and neocolonialism; and a socialist society be established in a free and united continent. In this the African masses have the support and assistance of the socialist world.

The African revolutionary struggle is not an isolated one. It not only forms part of the world socialist revolution, but must be seen in the context of the Black Revolution as a whole. In the U.S.A., the Caribbean, and wherever Africans are oppressed, liberation struggles are being fought. In these areas, the Black man is in a condition of domestic colonialism, and suffers both on the grounds of class and of colour. The core of the Black Revolution is in Africa, and until Africa is united under a socialist government, the Black man throughout the world lacks a national home. It is around the African peoples' struggles for liberation and unification that African or Black culture will take shape and substance. Africa is *one* continent, *one* people, and *one* nation. The notion that in order to have a nation it is necessary for there to be a common language, a common territory and a common culture has failed to stand the test of time or the scrutiny of scientific definition of objective reality. Common territory, language and culture may in fact be present in a nation, but the existence of a nation does not necessarily imply the presence of all three. Common territory and language alone may form the basis of a nation. Similarly, common territory plus common culture may be the basis. In some cases, only one of the three applies. A state may exist on a multi-national basis. The community of economic life is the major feature within a nation, and it is the economy which holds together the people living in a territory. It is on this basis that the new Africans recognise themselves as potentially one nation, whose dominion is the entire African continent.

The total liberation and the unification of Africa under an All-African socialist government must be the primary objective of all Black revolutionaries throughout the world. It is an objective which, when achieved, will bring about the fulfilment of the aspirations of Africans and people of African descent everywhere. It will at the same time advance the triumph of the international socialist revolution, and the onward progress towards world communism, under which every society is ordered on the principle of 'from each according to his ability, to each according to his needs'.

Claude Ake
'The Class Struggle' *from* Revolutionary Pressures in Africa
(First published in London, 1978)

The Class Struggle of Africa
Are there classes in Africa? What is the class structure of contemporary Africa? Objective class relations exist in Africa. There are those who effectively control the means of production, and those who effectively possess no means of production. However, each of these classes is complex and considerably heterogeneous.

Who are the members of these classes? First there js the exploiting class, which consists of the following categories of people.

(a) *Exploiters by class situation.* Everyone who is a capitalist proper. That is everyone who owns capital and employs wage labour in industry commerce or agriculture.

(b) *Exploiters by class position.* Those who, while not legally owning means of production, play a major role in administering or actualizing exploitation and maintaining its conditions. They are usually salaried people who hold important positions in the administrative, cultural and coercive apparatus of the state. Members of this category are the officer corps of the armed forces and the police, high-ranking civil servants and employees of parastatal bodies, and university teachers. There are several contradictions within this category. Perhaps the most interesting, analytically and politically, is that between those associated with the cultural apparatus of the state, particularly university teachers, and those associated with the coercive apparatus of the state, particularly the officer corps of the armed forces.

Turning to the exploited class, the picture is somewhat simpler. The members of this class are the peasants and the urban proletariat. Like the exploiter class, this exploited class is also heterogeneous although it is much less riddled with contradictions. The heterogeneity of this class arises mainly from two factors. One is the coexistence of capitalist and pre-capitalist modes of production. In this connection the major division is that between peasants and workers. However this contradiction is blunted somewhat by what I may call, for lack of a better term, the ruralization of African cities. African primordial solidaristic ties have shown a remarkable resiliency in the face of the onslaught of capitalism. Many workers remain peasants at heart, keep a foot in the village and regard the village as home. One of the striking features of urbanization in Africa is the re-creation of the village community in the city as a basis for recreational activities and for economic and social security. The other source of the incoherence of the exploited class lies in regionalism and the states of consciousness which go with it, especially tribalism.

I have usually referred to the exploited class in Africa as the African proletariat. A note on this usage is necessary; strictly speaking it is inaccurate. Only a small minority of the African masses are workers, the overwhelming majority are peasants; I am using proletariat to include not only workers but peasants. Why not simply describe the exploited class in Africa as the peasantry? I prefer the term proletariat for the following reasons. First, I wish to emphasize that this exploited class is the subordinate class in essentially capitalist economies. Second, calling the class a peasantry leads to misleading expectations of their mode of exploitation. The manner of exploitation of peasants in an economy dominated by capitalists is somewhat different from their manner of exploitation in an economy dominated by landlords. Finally, the use of the term peasantry leads to misleading expectations about the status and character of the class struggle and the prospects of socialist revolution in Africa. There is a tendency to tie the prospects of achieving socialism too rigidly to the development of productive forces and to assume that peasants are not a revolutionary force. I consider this to be a most unfortunate tendency especially when applied to the African situation, but I will hold off discussion of these issues for later.

So far I have treated the class structure of African countries in a highly undifferentiated manner as if all African countries have exactly the same type of class structure. There are in fact many differences between the class structures of African countries. But I will not try to deal with all these differences and their significance. I will limit myself to what I consider to be the most important difference, which also constitutes the basis of the most useful and most fundamental typology of African political systems.

This difference does not appear on the level of the exploited class, those

I have called the African proletariat. It lies in the extent of the development of the African bourgeoisie. We may divide African countries into two groups, with reference to this development. The first group consists of those countries in which colonial policies and/or the development of the forces of production made possible the existence of a small African bourgeoisie, that is an indigenous class of capitalists. I should emphasize that when I talk of an African bourgeoisie or an indigenous capitalist, I do not mean to suggest anything about the independence of this class, that is the lack of comprador characteristics. I am simply describing a group of people who can mobilize and deploy capital, and engage in accumulation, confronting their victims as capital against labour. Among the African countries which belong to this type are Egypt, Nigeria, Ghana, Ivory Coast, Kenya, Morocco and Senegal. The second group of African countries are those in which colonial policies and/or the development of the forces of production has not permitted the emergence of even an embryonic bourgeoisie. There is still class differentiation in these countries, but it is more accurate to describe the dominant class as a petty bourgeoisie rather than a bourgeoisie. It is, to use Cabral's phrase, a 'service class', which is not involved directly in production by mobilizing, deploying and manipulating capital for accumulation. The members of this service class include intellectuals, bureaucrats, and the managers of the coercive machinery of the state. However, the petty bourgeoisie also includes some social groups which are not strictly servicing capitalist accumulation, groups such as petty traders, middle echelon professionals, teachers, etc. Countries which fall into this category include Angola, Benin, Botswana, Burundi, Chad, Congo, Ethiopia, Guinea, Mali, Niger, Rwanda, Somalia, Sudan, Mozambique, Tanzania, Upper Volta and Togo.

I mentioned that colonial policies and the level of the development of productive forces largely account for the differences in class structure under review here. I should add that these two variables are also partially dependent on another factor, namely the natural resource endowments of the country. Countries with more substantial resource endowments tended to be the ones in which colonial policy led to a greater development of productive forces and the process of class formation. Here again there are intervening variables. To mention just one, the type of resource endowment dictated the extent of investment in infrastructures and auxiliary services. This helps to explain why Zaire and Angola do not have an indigenous bourgeoisie despite their substantial resource endowments. However, it would seem that this factor was a rather less important determinant of the class structure of these countries than the expectation on the part of the colonizing power that their colonization would be permanent – an expectation which hindered the creation of an indigenous bourgeoisie. It is difficult to be sure of the relative importance of these factors.

On balance, it would appear that the difference in class structure of the two groups of countries has not only persisted but also become accentuated in the 'post colonial era'. The 'departing' colonizing powers have tried to sustain the small momentum in the development of the productive forces in the few countries where such momentum already existed. It is being sustained to aid the process of class formation and the emergence of a comprador bourgeoisie, and by the natural course of international capital seeking safer and bigger markets and high returns. Thus Nigeria, Algeria, Egypt, Ivory Coast, Kenya, and Senegal attract more European investment than Ethiopia, Angola, Guinea, Somalia, Mali and Tanzania.

Further refinement of this classification is necessary. There is a very important difference among the countries that are under a petty bourgeoisie as opposed to those under a bourgeoisie. The former countries fall into two categories. The first comprises those countries in which the petty bourgeoisie is striving to turn itself into a bourgeoisie. The second is a residual category of those countries in which the petty bourgeoisie is not trying to transform itself into an indigenous capitalist class. Admittedly this is an unusually difficult distinction. For one thing, every ruling class in Africa has a weak material base and is engaged in consolidating it. The line between consolidating the material base of class rule and exploiting subordinate classes in order to further the development of a capitalist class is often very thin. All the more so because state power is the available instrument for promoting both ends in the particular circumstances of the African experience. Also the ruling class cannot consolidate its material base without appearing to be carrying on capitalist accumulation any more than it can use state power to further capitalist accumulation without masking some capitalist and exploitative tendencies. Nevertheless the indications are that in the vast majority of African countries under the rule of a petty bourgeoisie, the petty bourgeoisie is not both trying to consolidate its material base as well as transform itself into a bourgeoisie. The exceptions are the few countries in which the petty bourgeoisie has shown signs of rather serious commitment to socialism such as Guinea-Bissau, Angola and Mozambique. Problematic as these distinctions are, they have to be made. Their importance for understanding what is happening and what is likely to happen in Africa is considerable.

The African Bourgeoisie as an Obstacle to Progress

I will now turn to the major task of this chapter, which is to show how underdevelopment is related to the class structure of Africa and how the African bourgeoisie constitutes *the* obstacle to progress.

The hub of the relation of underdevelopment to the class structure is the fact that, with few exceptions, the ruling classes in Africa are an integral part of the structure of imperialism and of the syndrome of imperialist exploitation. I have already spelled out how the relation of the ruling classes to imperialism prevents the solution of the problem of indigenization. Up to a point, I have already dealt with the relation of underdevelopment to class structure insofar as underdevelopment is a function of exploitative links between African economies and imperialism, indigenization being the removal of these exploitative links. But this is only one aspect of a complex phenomenon.

African Ruling Classes and the Western Ideology of Development

Another aspect of the relationship of underdevelopment to the class structure of contemporary Africa is the developmental ideology of the ruling classes of Africa. They pursue the task of economic development in the context of an ideological orientation which essentially accepts the developmental precepts of the metropolitan bourgeoisie. Surprisingly enough, even the radical (socialism-oriented) African leaders are hardly an exception in this respect. In an earlier discussion, I pointed out that the bourgeois countries use the ideology of development in the global class struggle and that this ideology has come to be hegemonic. The attitude of Africa's rulers to the ideology of development is interesting for it reflects the identities and differences of their objective interests with those of the metropolitan bourgeoisie. African leaders are critical of the ideology of development and sometimes appear to reject it. They talk constantly of the uniqueness of the African experience and of following a unique path to development. An example of this attitude is to be found in Kenya's famous ideological blueprint, *Sessional Paper No. 10 of 1965: African Socialism and Its Applications to Planning in Kenya:* 'In the phrase "African Socialism", the word "Africa" is not introduced to describe a continent to which a foreign ideology is to be transplanted. It is meant to convey the African roots of a system that is itself African in its characteristics. "African Socialism" is a term describing an African political and economic system that is positively African, not being imported from any country or being a blueprint of any foreign ideology but capable of incorporating useful and compatible techniques from whatever source.'

The same type of attitude pervades Nyerere's *Freedom and Unity*. The following passage is typical of the thrust of that work: 'Ujamaa, then, or familyhood, describes our socialism. It is opposed to capitalism, which seeks to build a happy society on the basis of the exploitation of man by man; and it is equally opposed to doctrinaire socialism which seeks to build its happy society on a philosophy of inevitable conflict between man and man.'

African leaders have also been quite critical of the bourgeois countries' attitude to development, particularly for not being humanistic and for emphasizing economic growth rather than development. Tanzania's *Mwongozo*, or *TANU Guidelines*, is an excellent example of this type of criticism.

These critical attitudes express the contradiction between the African ruling classes and the metropolitan bourgeoisie on one level as well as those between the bourgeois countries and the proletarian countries. The contents of these criticisms invariably reflect a type of consciousness which is associated with colonial status. For instance, take the strident assertion of uniqueness and autonomy; that one's autonomy and uniqueness have to be asserted implies a certain insecurity about them, or at any rate the necessity of rehabilitating them, and this in turn implies their violation.

But it is just as necessary for Africa's rulers to accept the ideology of development, albeit with some modification, as it is for them to be critical of it, for the ideology of development serves their interests as a ruling class. Just how it does so will become clear shortly. Meanwhile, it is necessary to specify that what the African leaders find so congenial about the ideology of development is the very core of this ideology, namely its notion of what the obstacles to development are and how they might be overcome. The ideology of development sees the problem of achieving development as one of overcoming a series of very specific technical obstacles such as low level of savings, limited achievement motivation, low propensity to invest, low productivity, inadequate technology, low wages, regional disparities, inadequate manpower. When the problem of development is conceptualized in this manner, it is quite clear what has to be done to further development; mobilize more capital, invest more, stimulate achievement motivation, etc.

Does the ideology of development serve the objective interests of Africa's rulers? In what way? These questions are fairly easy to answer for the vast majority of the ruling classes of Africa, those we have classified as bourgeois or petty bourgeois with aspirations of becoming bourgeois. The ideology of development, particularly its analysis of the problem and process of development, helps to conceal class contradictions. The clear implication of this particular approach to development is that the class structure of a country is irrelevant to its prospects for development, and if the class structure and class struggle are irrelevant to the prospects for development then there is no need to do anything about existing relations of production. The ideology of development offers a status quo-oriented approach to development. This is precisely one of the major reasons why Western imperialism, which wants to insulate Africa against socialism, is promoting it so zealously.

Second, the ideology of development helps to legitimize dependence, especially economic dependence. The ideology of development conceptualizes development essentially as a process of becoming more like the bourgeois countries; but a proletarian country becomes more like the bourgeois countries insofar as it can acquire some of the specific goods and specific skills which they monopolize. Once the proletarian country accepts this general approach to development, it comes to regard economic dependence as inevitable and even desirable. On this view, dependence ceases to be an unpleasant necessity and a betrayal of the mandate of a leadership which came to power on the wave of a movement to liberate people from colonialism. It is the stigma of this betrayal that African leaders want to avoid and the ideology of development serves them handsomely.

Third the ideology of development excuses the painfully slow pace of economic development in Africa. As we have seen, it breaks down the process of development into the solution of very specific, largely technical problems. But it is part of the conservative thrust of this ideology that the problems are ones that are solved only in the very long run by slow incremental change. For instance, suppose Tanzania thinks in terms of acquiring the material characteristics of the United States such as sophisticated technology, a complex network of superhighways, etc. How can it possibly acquire (even assuming the best intentions on the part of its 'developed' patrons) the capital to transform its present condition into anything remotely resembling that of the United States? In effect the proletarian country which commits itself to the approach to development in question necessarily commits itself to 'slow and sober' progress. If development is accepted as something which comes by very slow progress over an extremely long time, then patience is necessary and what may seem like stagnation or intolerably slow progress passes as the normal course of things. This leaves little room for legitimately criticising the performance of those who lead the drive for development.

Now that we have seen the advantages of this particular approach to development to African leaders, it does not seem so paradoxical that even the few African leaders who have opted for socialism are not entirely immune to the influence of the ideology of development. They too benefit in the above ways although the benefits are marginally less crucial for them than for the other ruling classes of Africa.

It remains to show how the acceptance of the ideology of development by African leaders helps to perpetuate Africa's underdevelopment. The preceding discussion has already given us indications of the relation between the acceptance of this approach to development and the perpetuation of underdevelopment. So I will merely summarize and bring the important points together. To begin with, by misconceiving and distorting the problem of development, the ideology inhibits its solution. For instance the reduction of development to the solution of specific problems does not help at all, because immersion in these technical problems can only bring stagnation. Given Africa's resources these problems are intractable, and even if they were solved they would not really bring development in any sophisticated sense of the term. While energy is diverted to these technical problems, more crucial bottlenecks which prevent immediate and sizeable progress are neglected. To mention just one neglected bottleneck, there can be no development when those who are to bring development are themselves part of the structure of imperialism. Nor can there be development as long as class contradictions persist and grow. The ideology of development inhibits the development of Africa by effectively masking the link between development and revolution. The experiences of China, the Soviet Union and much of Eastern Europe underline this link. So do the experiences of Western Europe where the achievement of rapid economic growth followed in the wake of the *revolutionary* liquidation of feudalism. In Africa as elsewhere the greatest obstacles to development are social and institutional ones such as class structure, and the vested interests tied up with these obstacles are such that they cannot be removed by anything short of a revolutionary upheaval. Any approach which makes the achievement of development in Africa compatible with the maintenance of the present exploitative relations of production and with the links to imperialism can only hinder Africa. .

To sum up; the influence of the ideology of development on the pursuit of development in Africa must be considered as a hindrance to the overcoming of underdevelopment in Africa. This influence prevails mainly because of the objective class situation and class interests of the ruling classes of Africa. I will now turn to the examination of another link between underdevelopment and the class structure of contemporary Africa.

Underdevelopment and the Uniqueness of Capitalism in Africa

The link I want to examine now has to do with the peculiar characteristics of capitalism in Africa. These peculiarities go back to the colonial legacy. Colonial capitalism was a far cry from the orthodox classic capitalism of Adam Smith's *Wealth of Nations*. For classical capitalism the principle of laisser-faire was sacred. Classical capitalism rejected the authoritative allocation of rewards for work and of price levels; it only accepted the authoritative enforcement of contracts 'freely' entered into in the process of commodity exchange. For classical capitalism, the principle of. laisser-faire was important because competition was important. The doctrine of classical capitalism saw competition as the foundation of the efficiency of the capitalist system, and of its dynamism in developing the forces of production; indeed it held that self-interested competition was the means by which the public interest is served. The claim for laisser-faire and competition was of course exaggerated, for competition also leads to waste, misallocation, anarchy in production and monopoly. Nevertheless, competition was a critical element in the dynamism of capitalism. And there is no denying the fact that, in Western Europe, capitalism was a progressive force which has had a most revolutionary effect in transforming and expanding the forces of production.

The same cannot be said of colonial capitalism. An occupying power ruling by force could not institutionalize the principle of laisser-faire. Competition might distribute the wealth more than was desirable; it could lead to some concentration of wealth in the hands of some of the indigenous people and this could endanger the regime, as economic power is easily transformed into political power. If the indigenous people were allowed to compete and become successful, this would undermine the colonial doctrine which represented them as less than human in order to justify their inhuman treatment. The policy compatible with this doctrine was one which denied them access to economic advancement and kept them thoroughly wretched. So the colonial peoples largely lost the advantages of capitalism insofar as these were associated with competition. But this is putting it so mildly as to run the risk of misrepresentation. In the final analysis the colonial regime did not so much institutionalize capitalism as pillage. While classical capitalism can be dynamic and creative, pillage has no such potential. Even if the colonizers had been less inclined to rapacity, colonialism capitalism would still have been incapable of liberating the productive forces in Africa because of the external orientation of the economy. Colonial capitalism was more interested in external demand than internal demand; it was not interested in turning the primary products into manufactured goods in the colonies, and thus the development of technology was inhibited. Finally, it was not interested in ploughing back capital into the colony; this was not conducive to economic growth.

Since independence, some of the regressive characteristics of capitalism in Africa have been reinforced much to the detriment of the prospects of economic growth. The reinforcement of these characteristics has to do with the situation of the ruling classes in Africa; particularly the disparity between their economic and political power. I have mentioned earlier that the African bourgeoisie has a very weak material base even in those countries such as Nigeria and Kenya where capitalism is more established and the process of class formation considerably advanced. I have also indicated that the weakness of the material base imperils the survival of the African bourgeoisie. The strengthening of its material base has naturally become one of the major preoccupations of this bourgeoisie. It is what it is doing about strengthening its material base that interests us, for its actions in this regard are reinforcing the regressive characteristics of capitalism in Africa.

How the African Bourgeoisie Strengthens Its Material Base

If the African bourgeoisie is to strengthen its material base then it must appropriate more of the surplus value which the labour of the rest of the population produces. African bourgeoisies must find more effective ways of exploitation in addition to the usual method of private capitalist exploitation. For this classic type of exploitation by entrepreneurs who hire wage-labour and realize surplus value, is restricted in Africa by the fact that only a very small proportion of the labour force is in wage employment. Thus this form of exploitation is not the dominant form of exploitation in Africa, as it is in many other parts of the world. While, however, it would be incorrect to conclude from the relatively low incidence of this form of exploitation and the weakness of the private sector that there are no classes in Africa, it is essential for African bourgeoisies to resort to subtler forms of exploitation.

One of these is the direct use of coercive power for expropriation. Something akin to what Marx describes as primitive accumulation is taking place all over Africa: the direct use of coercion to appropriate economic surplus or the means of production. Sometimes this is done under the cover of political conflict; some people are denounced for some political crime and then murdered or imprisoned and their property seized. Sometimes it is done gangster style. Sometimes it is done under the cover of religious or ethnic conflict; a religious or ethnic group is denounced for being unpatriotic and subversive, or for economic exploitation of other groups, and popular hatred is built up against them. Then, under cover of this popular antipathy, the unfortunate group is abused, sometimes to a point amounting to genocide, and their property taken from them. Quite often it takes the form of direct class action. For instance many of the land registration and consolidation policies were a cover for depriving peasants of their land and for capitalizing agriculture.

The above is hardly a manner of accumulation conducive to the development of the forces of production. When primitive accumulation is carried out at the expense of peasants and workers it merely dramatizes the class contradictions of contemporary Africa and increases the mutual alienation of leaders and followers. This correspondingly reduces the ability of the leaders to mobilize the people and liberate their energy. When this process of primitive accumulation is directed against specific factions of the bourgeoisie or petty bourgeoisie, it is equally counter-productive. To begin with, those elements of the petty bourgeoisie or the bourgeoisie who are expropriated and/or liquidated by the politically hegemonic faction are likely to be the ones that have some entrepreneurial skill. To the extent that this assumption is correct, coercive accumulation depletes the small stock of people capable of making capitalism creative. More importantly, using violence to expropriate other members of the ruling class increases the level of insecurity within this class for everyone, including the hegemonic faction. This sets in motion a vicious circle of extremism and political violence. Insecurity makes political actors struggle even more grimly and tenaciously for political power and the high premium on political power inclines political actors to use any method which will produce desired results rather than confine themselves to methods of competition which are moral or legal. The further implication of all this is that everyone gets totally involved in the struggle for survival to the detriment of development. Under these conditions, neither culture nor industry can flourish. There is another sense in which development suffers. As the hegemonic faction of the ruling class successfully uses force to expropriate other factions of the ruling class as well as peasants and workers, the concentration of energy on politics is reinforced. In other words, this faction comes to feel even more strongly that what really counts is political power, that once one has political power one can have everything else, including economic wealth. It reinforces the belief already current in Africa that wealth comes not by engaging in productive activity but by acquiring political power.

We have an interesting paradox. Coercive exploitation arises mainly out of the ruling class's insecure hold on political power, and the need to support it with a sound material base. But the use of state power to engage in coercive expropriation leads to an exaggerated importance of political power with consequences that actually retard the development of the material base. Of course the objective reality of the importance of economic power asserts itself. Indeed, the passion for political power underlines the importance of the material base, for, as we have seen, it is precisely the material base which is partly responsible for generating this passion. This reality asserts itself in an even more forceful way, namely the continued insecurity of the African ruling class. Despite its attempts at accumulation by coercive and other means, the contradictions of this situation have not permitted the African bourgeoisie much success in consolidating its material base. Its hold on power remains tenuous and its insecurity persists and may even increase. The high incidence of political violence in both intra-class and inter-class competition underlines this insecurity and the importance of the material base.

The third type of policy which the African bourgeoisie uses to bolster its material base is to apply political pressure on the imperialist agents operating in Africa for a greater share of the surplus. These pressures take many forms. The major form is to mobilize nationalist feelings against foreign capital and then insist on partnership with it. With few exceptions, this is really what the drive for indigenization in Africa amounts to. The case studies in the previous chapter have already shown how indigenization is not so much a dislodging of imperialism as accommodation and partnership with it.

Let us now look at how indigenization and the other policies used by the African bourgeoisie to put foreign capital under pressure affect the prospects of development. To begin with, the general tendency of these policies is to prevent the development of an indigenous bourgeoisie with entrepreneurial skills, and to reinforce the divorce of the African bourgeoisie from production. In effect what these policies mean is that the African bourgeoisie interposes itself as a political middleman between international capital and the masses. What they offer in return for a greater share of surplus is political protection – the use of political power to curb labour unrest and control wages. They also promise to refrain from 'vindictive' restrictions on licences for foreign concerns, capital movements, etc. In short, even as they penetrate the economic sphere to reinforce their material base, they specialize in the political aspects of this sphere, that is, in the political management of the conditions of production.

However, we have seen that in some cases indigenization and related policies have been directed not simply at extracting more surplus from international capital by offering political protection in return, but by compelling international capital to take elements of the African bourgeoisie into partnership. The partnership usually takes two forms. One is the acquisition of shares by Africans in foreign-controlled enterprises.

The acquisition of shares is often completed by increasing indigenous participation on the Board of Directors. The other type of partnership is the acquisition of shares by the government, often to the point where the government or 'the public' becomes the majority shareholder. These forms of partnership do not usually amount to very much as far as developing indigenous entrepreneurial skill or involving the indigenous bourgeoisie in production is concerned. In the case of private ownership of shares the indigenous shareholders are usually 'sleeping partners' content to let foreign management get on with production and profit-making, and interested mainly in a good return on their investment. This is all the more so because those who buy into foreign business are people already employed in some other capacity.

The case of public ownership is not much different. To begin with, those who act for the government in the new enterprise will generally be bureaucrats who do not normally possess entrepreneurial skills or attempt to develop such skills. The actual management of production is generally left to the representatives of foreign capital. This trend is reinforced by the prevailing capitalist ethos, particularly commitment to profitability. Insofar as the government is anxious to make the enterprise profitable it tends to leave it to the management of the specialists in profit-making, the representatives of foreign capital. Foreign capital favours this arrangement and tries to ensure its perpetuation. Obviously its interest depends heavily on making itself indispensable. And it makes itself indispensable by jealously guarding its control of technology, by manipulating its entrepreneurial skills and its links with the international market. Because of such monopoly, foreign capital can effectively control an enterprise and sustain its exploitative operations even when public ownership of equity exceeds 80%. It is not at all peculiar for multinational corporations with immense investment in Africa, such as Lonrho, to be quite happy with the new trend of public participation.

So the new partnership promises little indigenous control of production. It promises even less involvement of the African bourgeoisie in production and virtually no enhancement of their entrepreneurial skill. Most importantly, the new partnership and the other policies used by the African bourgeoisie to get a greater share of the surplus vis-à-vis international capital are not reducing dependence, or eliminating the exploitative links of dependence. Far from eliminating it, the partnership makes the situation safer for foreign capital by supporting it with political power. All this cannot help the battle against underdevelopment or the liberation of the forces of production in Africa.

I now turn to the fourth method which the African bourgeoisie is using to strengthen its material base, namely state capitalism. By state capitalism I mean the accumulation of capital by the state. The state can be used by African bourgeoisies to accomplish this in various ways. One way which started in the colonial era involves state organs themselves using coercion to exact tribute from the population. In particular, the state extracts taxes from the people even when –notably in the rural areas – they get virtually nothing in return for the taxes they pay. A second common device and perhaps the most significant form of coercive exploitation by the state in terms of the quantity of the surplus involved, is government monopoly control over the marketing of primary commodities. Apart from the oil-producing countries and a few other minor exceptions, African countries on average get about 70% of their export revenues from primary products. The state uses parastatal organizations such as marketing boards to control the export of these commodities. Peasants and farmers are obliged to sell to these boards or to approved intermediary institutions or individuals who in turn sell to these boards. The boards then sell to the overseas market. The exploitation in this procedure lies in the enormous difference between what the state pays to the producers and what it gets from the overseas buyers.

State capitalism today – and this is one of the most interesting developments of the post-colonial state – takes yet another form: the state itself acting as entrepreneur. While the colonial state was statist, its statism consisted in ubiquitous and heavy-handed control of economy and polity. The post-colonial state has extended statism to the entrepreneurial role. Why this change is taking place is quite easy to understand. The colonial government could afford to concentrate on exploitation to the exclusion of development. But the African government which replaced it could not afford to do so; for reasons that are too obvious to detain us. Once a commitment to economic development was made, the state had to assume an entrepreneurial role because it controlled such a large proportion of the society's surplus and because there was very little capital to mobilize for entrepreneurial activities in the private sector, except that part of it associated with international capitalism. Another important stimulus to the development of the state's entrepreneurial role was the weak material base of the African bourgeoisie. To strengthen this base, they had to go beyond the obvious option of using political power to appropriate a greater share of the surplus. They also had to create wealth, and state power was their major access to substantial capital, as well as the easiest.

Insofar as the state is acting as an entrepreneur, the actual mechanism of exploitation is, in many respects, the same as in the case of the individual capitalist. The state employee gives up the use value of his labour to the state in return for wages, and the state appropriates the value of the product of this labour in excess of its wages or cost of reproduction. Why not then assimilate state capitalism into the first type of exploitation? Because that would obscure the singular importance of this capitalist role of the state. The fact that it is the state rather than individual capitalists which is exploiting workers, has notable consequences for the visibility of exploitation, the development of capitalism, the distribution of surplus, not to mention the character of the class struggle.

In Africa state capitalism has been associated both with the state founding new enterprises and with the extension of the state's control over the economy in other ways. This extension usually takes the form of nationalization. The resources which thus come under state control are mobilized and used as capital by the state acting as entrepreneur. What was said about the new partnership between the African bourgeoisie and international capital applies to the policy of nationalization. With few exceptions nationalization amounts merely to one concrete manifestation of the new partnership. Here again the African bourgeoisie largely confines itself to a political role, the role of providing political protection – partly because it lacks entrepreneurial skills and partly because it has no interest in provoking a breach with international capital. Generally, nationalization does very little to reduce the influence of the agents of foreign capital, influence which they are able to exercise by their control of technology, by skills in management and marketing, etc.

More importantly, state capitalism is a regressive form of capitalism. This point should not be difficult to grasp if one is careful not to confuse state capitalism with statism or with state control of the economy or state involvement in enterprises. When one talks of state capitalism, one presupposes the class cleavage of bourgeoisie and proletariat and the antagonism between capital and labour. Further, one presupposes that while production may be more or less social, appropriation will be largely private. What distinguishes state capitalism from the orthodox capitalism of the *Wealth of Nations* is its monopoly character. It is a peculiarly coercive monopoly. For instance, state capitalism entails coercive monopolization of capital, of markets etc.

The regressive character of state capitalism is inherent in the distortions brought about by its monopoly character. State capitalism is scarcely dynamic since it usually fails to make the contributions which competition for the market via a better and better input–output ratio can make to efficiency, expansion and technological innovation. It is also regressive in the sense that it is a form of capitalism which involves no risks, demands no imagination and sets no performance standards. It involves no risks because the bourgeoisie is not using its own capital but the resources of the public, and because state capitalism is typically directed at those forms of economic activity which are by their very nature highly profitable. And it is because it involves no risk that it demands no imagination and sets no standards. This is why state capitalism is not conducive to the rapid development of productive forces.

I will conclude this section by raising one objection to the case that the African bourgeoisie's attempts to reinforce its material base are not conducive to the development of productive forces and the overcoming of underdevelopment. The objection is as follows: irrespective of the immediate effect of these measures on the development of the productive forces, they are nevertheless the essential preliminary for such development. Capital has to be concentrated before capitalist development can take place. The measures in question help us to concentrate capital, to create a real capitalist class which will eventually engineer capitalist development

This argument is unsound. The measures under consideration have not done very much to expand the capitalist class or even strengthen substantially the material base of the bourgeoisie as a class. Even though members of the African bourgeoisie are aware of the weakness of their material base and the necessity of strengthening it, it cannot be presumed that they will rationally go about rectifying this weakness. Quite the contrary. The result of this objective will be mediated and distorted by the contradictions within the bourgeoisie, possibly to an extent that will largely defeat the original purpose. Individuals and factions within the class will think primarily of their particular interests, not of the collective interest of the class, and will act accordingly. Thus, opportunities for strengthening the material base of the class inevitably become occasions for inter-personal and inter-faction competition and to some extent defeat the collective interest.

But these are generalities. The question is whether circumstances in the African situation are such that this self-defeat might be said to be occurring. All the measures which the African bourgeoisie is taking to strengthen its material base tend to increase the level of political competition within this class. Coercive appropriation and accumulation undertaken primarily by the hegemonic faction of the bourgeoisie worries the other factions some of whose members inevitably become victims of the process. The attempt to pressure international capital into giving up a greater share of the surplus is made in the context of contradictions such as those between the comprador elements as against more national elements within the bourgeoisie. Inevitably it has a differential impact on the fortunes of the various factions and generates anxieties. Finally, nationalization of resources and state capitalism have enormous potential for increasing the power of the hegemonic faction of the bourgeoisie as well as for weakening non-hegemonic factions. In short, these measures reveal, deepen and politicize the contradictions within the bourgeoisie and increase the premium on winning the intra-class competition. Under these circumstances even the hegemonic faction of the bourgeoisie will not be thinking primarily of the collective good of the class. This is how it comes about that the purpose of strengthening the material base of the bourgeoisie is largely defeated. More specifically, it is defeated because in the heat of competition the hegemonic faction tries to restrict the access of the other factions to the accumulation of capital. Expanded opportunity for accumulation and stringent restrictions of access to accumulation combine to produce monopoly – monopoly of economic and political power by the hegemonic faction. In the meantime, the grim anxiety and struggle within the bourgeoisie reinforce its regressive tendencies. People look for quick wealth, and corruption grows. Everyone goes for mobile assets, capital is salted away overseas, and so on. I will now turn to the third and final aspect of the relationship between underdevelopment and the dynamics of class relations in Africa.

Depoliticisation: The African Bourgeoisie's Response to Revolutionary Pressures

There are strong revolutionary pressures in Africa: pressures against the maintenance of the existing exploitative class relations and hence pressures against the very survival of the African bourgeoisie. These pressures arise from: (a) the desperate poverty of the African masses; (b) the sharp and highly visible differences between the rich and the poor; (c) rising expectations associated with 'modernization'; (d) the example of developed countries made even more effective by their penetration of the periphery; (e) the politicization of the popular consciousness by the nationalist movement and by the dynamics of contradictions between the metropolitan bourgeoisie and the African bourgeoisie.

I will not elaborate on these pressures here. What interests me is not an account of these pressures but how the African bourgeoisie is reacting to them. Their options are limited to two broad strategies. One is to meet the demands inherent in these pressures. There are two kinds of demands involved here. One is the demand for equality which, carried to its logical conclusion is a demand for the abolition of the bourgeoisie and its privileges. The African bourgeoisie obviously cannot meet this demand. What it can do and what it is doing is to make some token gestures such as introducing slightly more egalitarian taxation and having government officials use more modest cars, etc. The African bourgeoisie will make marginal changes in the area of distribution without touching the core of the problem of inequality, which lies in the realm of production relations and which can be dealt with ultimately only by revolutionizing production relations. So equality is ruled out because the demand for equality cannot be met without a socialist revolution, which the ruling class will not sponsor. The second kind of demand made by the masses is only a little less difficult for the bourgeoisie to meet; it is the demand for social wellbeing, for easing the agony of extreme want. Even this demand cannot be met except in some marginal ways, since the very conditions of underdevelopment very drastically limit the expansion of the economic surplus. Even if the existing surplus were distributed more fairly, it would not make much difference. But the existing surplus will not be fairly distributed in the context of existing class contradictions.

That leaves the African bourgeoisie with the other broad strategy of discouraging these demands, and preventing their political manifestation and radicalization. That is what the African bourgeoisie is doing. Its strategy is depoliticization. Depoliticization entails reducing the effective participation of the masses and of non-hegemonic factions of the ruling class and preventing some interests and points of view from finding political expression. The point of reducing the effective political participation of the masses is to render them impotent, to prevent the political system from being overloaded with demands which are not conducive to its survival and to render the masses less available for socialization into radical political or oppositional behaviour by non-hegemonic factions of the ruling class. By preventing certain interests and opinions from finding political expression, the ruling class expects to obtain a level of political unity out of proportion to existing contradictions in the material base, and to reduce the possibility of harnessing the antipathies towards the political and economic system into a strong revolutionary force.

The process of depoliticization has made African countries political monoliths. Every African country is in effect a one-party state in the sense that every regime in Africa assumes its exclusive right to rule and prohibits organized opposition. Military regimes are in this respect similar to one-party systems. Most .importantly, the process of depoliticization has made African politics particularly brutal. Given the contradictions in contemporary African society, depoliticization cannot be carried out without brutal repression.

The one-party system is as much a tool for asserting the exclusive claims of the hegemonic faction within the new bourgeoisie as it is an instrument for disenfranchising the masses. Ironically insofar as depoliticization is necessary for maintaining the existing exploitative production relations, the hegemonic faction of the bourgeoisie which depoliticizes opposing factions is expressing the objective interests of these factions as a class even when it represses them. Even those factions of the exploiting class (such as those associated with the cultural apparatus of the state) who seem to have the least to gain by depoliticization will be obliged to engage in depoliticization if they become hegemonic. Two conclusions which follow from this are noteworthy. First, depoliticization within the exploiting class is only partially an effect of the struggle for power within this class; it is primarily a necessary condition for the maintenance of the class as a whole vis-à-vis the exploited class. Second, the popular assumption that return to civilian rule will significantly affect the incidence of political repression is altogether mistaken.

The effects of the process of depoliticizing the exploiting class are very complex. Insofar as this process helps to maintain the existing class structure, it might be said to promote political stability. Political stability is used here to refer to the persistence of the political structure, particularly the relationship of the dominant and subordinate systems of roles which express the class situation politically. While enhancing political stability in this way, depoliticization of the exploiting class tendentially accentuates governmental instability. Governmental instability describes a state of affairs in which the control of governmental institutions changes hands often and in an erratic manner. There is a sense, however, in which this process of depoliticization of the exploiting class promotes governmental stability. It does so insofar as it leads to the homogenization of the exploiting class. Depoliticization increases homogenization by imposing ideological unity, by building alliances between factions, by co-opting dangerous opponents into the hegemonic faction and by liquidating certain other factions altogether. Nevertheless, it would seem that, on balance, this intra-class depoliticization is more conducive to governmental instability than to stability. This is so mainly because it greatly reinforces the destabilizing effect which statism produces, by focusing the ambitions of all the factions of the exploiting class primarily on the capture of state power, by making the outcome of the struggle for hegemony among the factions of the bourgeoisie too important. The process of depoliticization intensifies these tendencies, because in effect it constitutes an attack by the hegemonic faction on the particularism of others, and even on their survival. This attack on particularism is all the more threatening because it seeks to abolish political particularism without abolishing (at least in the short term) the objective conditions of this particularism. Even when this attack succeeds, and something like a one-party system emerges, governmental instability remains, and perhaps increases. For the major effect of the one-party system is to compress the arena of struggle without reducing the objective basis of the differences between the factions. Thus pressure mounts, and explosions occur periodically. When major differences in this political monolith appear, a crisis invariably occurs. The options for resolving these differences are drastically limited. It usually comes down to suppressing either the leaders or those challenging them. Since in the one-party system it is rarely possible to remove the leaders by following the rules, they are removed in spite of the rules, just as the opposition is brutalized in spite of the rules.

Depoliticization and the Perpetuation of Underdevelopment

I now want to consider the consequences of depoliticization for the prospects of development. First, depoliticization reduces the prospect of overcoming underdevelopment by facilitating the ascendancy of the elements of the ruling class associated with the coercive machinery of the state. As we have seen, depoliticization entails massive repression which in turn leads to the enlargement of the role of the coercive institutions, especially the army and the police. Thus the bulk of African countries are governed by military governments or by civilian regimes so heavily dependent on the army that they are for all practical purposes merely agents of the men in uniform. The ascendancy of the specialists of coercion reinforces an unfortunate tendency which already exists in Africa, the tendency towards booty capitalism, which is not conducive to development – not even capitalist development. The point is easy enough to see. The weapon available to the new rulers for both political and economic competition is force. There is therefore a tendency to apply force ubiquitously in political and economic competition and also to appropriate surplus by force. Admittedly the dialectics of the situation will tend to mitigate this booty capitalism and transform it to something more like orthodox capitalism in the very long run. For the men in uniform soon accumulate and to some extent become exploiters by class situation. If indeed this were to happen, and quickly, it would be fortunate for Africa because orthodox capitalism is clearly far more conducive to economic growth than booty capitalism.

Unfortunately, we cannot posit a quick end to this phase of booty capitalism despite the tendency for the military to use instruments of violence to become capitalists proper (i.e. exploiters by class situation). The military itself is riddled with class contradictions. When the military comes to power, only the top leadership of its structure is able to accumulate substantially. Of course the demands of survival will encourage the upper strata to ensure that some rewards are passed down to the lower strata. Despite such prudent gestures, distribution will reflect differential effective control of the means of production. The lower military strata will strive to get to the top and when they do so others will strive to remove them. Insofar as the top military leadership accumulate and become capitalists proper, they intensify the desire of the lower strata to seize power and to increase their share of the booty. When the new coup occurs, movement away from booty capitalism is interrupted and the system regresses to booty capitalism. Thus the movement away from booty capitalism tends to negate itself.

The depoliticization of society expresses and brings into clear relief the alienation of the masses from their rulers. Having rendered the masses irrelevant except as payers of tribute, the process thereby excludes the possibility of mobilizing them and releasing their energies for development. This is perhaps the greatest setback to development; circumstances do not permit the tapping of the most valuable resource of a country, the energy of its people. All the talk about mobilization of the peasantry and primary emphasis on the development of the rural areas 'where most of our people live' leads nowhere. Not because the leaders have no interest in rural development, nor because of shortage of capital, lack of technology or the conservatism of peasants, but because, given the class situation, rural development policies will necessarily have an exploitative thrust and such policies will elicit a grudging performance at best.

To sum up, we have seen how the class structure of Africa constitutes an obstacle to development, even capitalist development, in Africa. By impeding development the class structure generates its own dialectical negation, for as we have seen, the persistence of underdevelopment, especially extreme poverty, in Africa is a source of strong revolutionary pressures.